FOOD IN THE CIVIL WAR ERA

Books in the American Food in History Series

FOOD
IN THE CIVIL WAR ERA

THE SOUTH

Edited by Helen Zoe Veit

Michigan State University Press

EAST LANSING

♾ The paper used in this publication meets the minimum requirements
of ANSI/NISO Z39.48-1992 (R 1997) (Permanence of Paper).

Michigan State University Press
East Lansing, Michigan 48823-5245

Printed and bound in the United States of America.

21 20 19 18 17 16 15   1 2 3 4 5 6 7 8 9 10

Library of Congress Control Number: 2014951528
ISBN: 978-1-61186-164-8 (cloth)
ISBN: 978-1-60917-451-4 (ebook: PDF)

Cover and book design by Erin Kirk New
Cover illustration is from Isaac Pim Trimble, *A Treatise on the Insect Enemies of Fruit and Fruit Trees*
(New York: W. Wood and Co., 1865), frontispiece, Michigan State University Special Collections.

Michigan State University Press is a member of the Green Press Initiative and
is committed to developing and encouraging ecologically responsible publishing practices.
For more information about the Green Press Initiative and the use of recycled paper
in book publishing, please visit www.greenpressinitiative.org.

Visit Michigan State University Press at www.msupress.org.

CONTENTS

ACKNOWLEDGMENTS

Many people helped make this project a reality, and I'm delighted to have the chance to thank them in print. The historian Jason Phillips provided extremely helpful comments on a draft of this manuscript, and his many good suggestions made this a much stronger book than it would have been otherwise. Christopher Farrish, the author of this book's introduction, was wonderful to work with, and I'm grateful for his generosity and patience during an extremely busy period in his career. I'm enduringly grateful to Gabriel Dotto, the head of Michigan State University Press, whose boundless enthusiasm for this series on historical cooking is truly infectious. Thank you, also, to the many other good people at the press, especially Kristine M. Blakeslee, Elise Jajuga, Travis Kimbel, and Annette Tanner.

Compiling these sources entailed a hunt for an elusive letter by Maria Barringer describing an 1865 dinner her household provided to Jefferson Davis as he fled Union troops after the war. Tom Fagart provided extensive help that finally led me to a copy of the original letter. Thank you, too, to Vern Brewer, Samantha Crisp, and Patricia Curl, who all aided the search.

I am extraordinarily lucky to have daily access to a world-class collection of historical cookbooks at Michigan State University's Special Collections. And I feel even luckier because the staff of Special Collections is so uniquely warm and welcoming, no one more so than Peter Berg. I also owe a large debt of gratitude to Leslie Behm, whose help in digitizing dozens of images from the historical cookbooks was indispensable.

FOOD IN THE CIVIL WAR ERA

Food in the Antebellum South and the Confederacy

CHRISTOPHER FARRISH

Mary Randolph did not write *The Virginia Housewife* in order to speak both back across Southern history and forward to what would become, broadly speaking, "Southern cuisine." But in many respects, that is exactly what she did. Published in 1824, Randolph's *Virginia Housewife* is considered by some to be the first truly American cookbook as well as the first regional cookery book. It reflects ingredients indigenous to the Americas as well as the peculiar nature of plantation cooking.[1] Before the publication of Randolph's text, American cookbooks had relied largely on English traditions. In fact many "American" cookbooks published in the late eighteenth and early nineteenth centuries were simply reprinted or plagiarized English cookbooks. Randolph's text departed from tradition by embracing local ingredients and reflecting realities unique to Virginia and the South in general: the spaces of the plantation home, the social role of the white mistress, and the institution of slavery.[2] *The Virginia Housewife* recorded a moment in the history of Southern food, but it doesn't tell the whole story. In fact, it doesn't even start the story. Randolph's text may have been the first American cookbook, but it was also distinctly local. *The Virginia Housewife* did not intend to reach across region, race, or class, but these categories weave their way through the text as much as they do all of Southern foodways.

This introduction looks at the long, twisting history of Southern food as it emerged across the region through the end of the Civil War. I begin by exploring the indigenous features of Southern foods, which increasingly clashed with and were adopted by white settlers. As whites pushed Native peoples out of the interior of the Lower South, corn—in the form of meal, whiskey, and hog flesh—increasingly dominated the diet of the region's settlers. This antagonism between Native people and white settlers played out in cultural conflict and culinary adaptation, and it underwrote much of what would become Southern food culture. This introduction also explores another culinary conflict. Like the clash between indigenous peoples and white settlers that defined the food of the interior South, the refined foods of plantation homes and many cities were also produced through conflict. The presence of enslaved laborers in plantation kitchens helped ensure that African ingredients would infiltrate the refined meals of plantation homes and influence the food culture and cookbooks of the region. Finally, this essay explores a third conflict that came to define what Southern food meant for many people past and present: the Civil War itself.

Southern food migrated with Native cultures, clashed with and was adopted by white settlers, moved along inland waterways in boats, and crossed the Atlantic in slave ships. It was prepared in plantation kitchens and sent to the tables of the Big House. The Civil War shook the foundations of Southern food culture, destroying fields and crops, dining rooms and larders and railroads. The war also destabilized a hierarchy—at least temporarily—that had defined some as food producers and others as its consumers. Southern cookbooks give instructions on how to cook, but they also expose this more complicated history of conflict and culinary adaptation.

From Native Roots to King Corn

Before white settlement in the Americas, Native Americans employed a fluid and mobile form of agriculture, which permeated surrounding fields, woods, and waters. Far from "wild," these territories were carefully managed in order to encourage plant growth or attract game.[3] Native diets were made up largely of meat, hunted or trapped, and various grains, beans, vegetables, and fruits, including corn, squashes, and pumpkins. While North America lacked large animals that could be domesticated or used as beasts of burden, indigenous people ate a range of animals including deer, turkey, rabbits, birds, turtles, opossum, and fish. In the Mississippi River and its tributaries, catfish were plentiful and easy to catch, with some fish weighing upwards of 100 pounds.

Despite the diverse and ecologically sound practices of Native hunting and farming, indigenous customs had been under attack since first contact. By the antebellum period, Native people were increasingly isolated or marginalized within the South. As a general in the U.S. Army and later as president, Andrew Jackson supervised the ethnic cleansing and removal of Native peoples across the region. Jackson's Indian Removal Act in 1830 was the final push in what had been for decades a slow-moving genocide. By then, the physical presence of the "Five Tribes"—the Choctaw, Creek, Chickasaw, Cherokee, and Seminole—had been marginalized to areas of the upland South and central Florida. The forced removal of the Choctaw, Creek, Chickasaw, and Cherokee to Indian Territory (in present-day

Oklahoma) stands as a defining moment of Jackson's presidency.[4]

The history of Indian removal is too frequently excluded from simplistic accounts of the culinary "contributions" of Native peoples to Southern eating habits. The culinary journey of items such as corn, native squash, and game speaks to a history of cultural oppression as well as culinary adaptation. Indigenous elements in Southern cuisine should be seen—much like African contributions—not as an addition to a new food culture, but as a culinary insurgent, a stubborn reminder of another people. Early on, in fact, most white settlers wanted nothing more than to escape Native foodways.[5] Many whites saw indigenous foods, and those who consumed them, as impediments to progress. Early settlers, or those in remote areas, were obliged to eat from the native larder. But once supply lines were established with major cities or routes of trade, settlers did not hesitate to bring familiar foods to the "new" region. When white settlers adopted native ingredients they usually did so out of necessity, because isolation or environmental factors made it impossible to adhere exclusively to European customs. As time went on, however, many native foods became familiar and even beloved staples among white settlers. And nowhere is this more obvious than with corn.[6]

As the region developed through the antebellum years, corn, perhaps more than any other indigenous food, would come to define cuisine and culture across the South. Corn was transformed into hominy, hoecakes, biscuits, bread, meal, and mush. It was a major component in the diets meted out to enslaved workers as well as a favorite of whites both rich and poor. Corn was used to fatten hogs, which were butchered, salted, smoked, or roasted.[7] Corn was also transformed into alcohol, which, like pork, was consumed in large quantities, and often. If in previous centuries indigenous

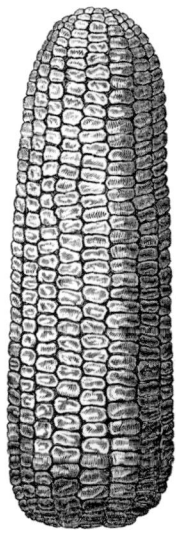

Corn was a staple of nineteenth-century Southern diets. Southerners sometimes ate corn as a vegetable in dishes like succotash or corn pudding. But most often they consumed it as a grain in the form of cornmeal, as a drink in the form of whiskey, or indirectly through the meat of hogs that had been raised on corn. Corn illustration in Fearing Burr, *The Field and Garden Vegetables of America: Containing Full Descriptions of Nearly Eleven Hundred Species and Varieties* (Boston: J. E. Tilton, 1865), 583, Michigan State University Special Collections.

people had seen corn as central to both their dietary and spiritual lives, faith in corn took on new meaning as antebellum planters increasingly devoted themselves to agricultural management, flows of capital, and the power of the market.[8]

The Lower South, stretching from western South Carolina to Texas, was known as the Cotton Belt, but corn also played a role in the culture and development of the region. Most obviously, corn was the staple that fed the workers who produced commodity crops. As the historian Walter Johnson writes, "Southern slaves metabolized Midwestern corn into cotton to be sold in the Atlantic market."[9] And just as cheap corn moved into the Mississippi Valley from the Midwest, the bodies of enslaved people were moved to the region from parts east. From 1820 to 1860 as many as one million enslaved people were moved through the South via the internal slave trade. These bodies needed to be fed, and to market-minded planters, the act of feeding could transform corn into cotton, and provender into profit.

Corn was a hardy crop with a fairly flexible cultivation schedule, which made it popular across the region. Wealthy planters were not necessarily interested in corn as a commodity with market value, because unlike cotton, corn could be eaten, fed to animals or enslaved people, and turned into grain alcohol. Despite the South's agricultural productivity, by the mid-nineteenth century the majority of the corn and pork that Southerners ate—as well as most of their wheat and beef—were imported from the Midwest and Ohio Valley. The famous journalist and landscape architect Fredrick Law Olmsted called this agricultural irony "bad management by intelligent planters."[10]

Corn also infiltrated white food culture, even if this indigenous product sometimes figured as a poor country cousin to the supposedly more refined wheat. For example, mid-nineteenth-century travelers through the Lower South frequently emphasized a connection between rustic foods like corn and the rough customs that produced them.[11] While traveling through the Southeast in 1853, Fredrick Law Olmsted annotated a passage on corn bread with the remark that "the best corn-bread that I have eaten was made simply by wetting coarse meal with pure water, adding only a little salt, and baking in the form of a breakfast-roll." He emphasized that the "addition of milk, butter, or eggs, damages" the final product.[12] Olmsted's recipe apparently used no leavening agent, yet he insisted that he was speaking from experience; this was his second journey through the region, and he said he always cooked his own meals. Wheat bread may have been a mark of refinement at established plantations, in port cities, or on the pages of published cookbooks, but in the frontier South, corn was king.[13]

Foods of the Rustic and Rural South

While onboard the steamboat *Fashion*, traveling from Montgomery to Mobile in 1856, Fredrick Law Olmsted witnessed a scene rivaling anything painted by the frontier landscape artist George Caleb Bingham. The ship's poor Irish and enslaved black laborers, although separated while working and at most meals, came together on this particular Sunday to dine as a group. Ten men sat on cotton bales and shared a "various and abundant" meal of "bean-porridge, bacon, corn bread, ship's biscuits, potatoes, duff (pudding), and gravy." The laborers had only one knife and used splintered bone and wood as forks. As they ate, they passed the porridge between them and drank from a communal tub.[14] To Olmsted's eyes, the men were "dirty and beast-like" but otherwise "good-natured"—a communal spirit forged in poverty and shared work.

The communal meals of the crew aboard the *Fashion* contrasted sharply with the fine dining generally associated with steamships. Away from coastal cities, the most elegant steamships were known as "Floating Palaces," where passengers paying full fare enjoyed luxurious accommodations and cosmopolitan meals. On these ships, three abundant meals a day, often produced by male African American cooks, were served in elegant dining rooms. The steward of a steamship, who was usually white, would have assistants, pastry cooks, bread makers, kitchen staff, and waiters.[15] On land, meanwhile, similarly decadent meals appeared on dining room tables—though only in a small minority of elite households. White settlement in Virginia, the Carolina coast, and lower Louisiana occurred relatively early.[16] By the mid-nineteenth century, the wealthiest people in those areas had access to an abundance of products grown in established and well-cultivated fields. Proximity to major ports opened an even larger world of foodstuffs. New Orleans, for example, had an ongoing culinary relationship not only with the larger Caribbean but also with France. French chefs began migrating to New Orleans in the early 1800s, and by midcentury that city had developed its own unique Creole cuisine.[17]

But the elegant meals of steamships or wealthy plantation homes were exceptional in the largely rural region. One didn't have to travel far from major waterways or settled areas to encounter a very different culinary world. As late as 1840, large areas of Georgia, Alabama, and Mississippi had few or no white settlers. As white settlers pushed inland from the eastern seaboard and Lower South, they brought their foodways with them when they could, and they often only grudgingly adopted the foods and customs that had for centuries sustained the Native inhabitants they were displacing.[18] Corn, hardy vegetables, and native game were central elements in the diets of white settlers by virtue of habitat if not taste.[19]

Travelers through what was then known as the Southwest (present-day Alabama, Mississippi, Louisiana, and Arkansas) frequently remarked on what they were served, meals of little variety and ample proportion. On an overland trip from New Orleans to Charleston in the 1830s the traveler Thomas Hamilton described Alabama's interior as "beyond the region of bread," by which he meant bread made with wheat. In much of the remote inland South, breads not made from cornmeal were a luxury enjoyed by few. Hamilton's fare consisted of "eggs, broiled venison, and cakes of Indian corn fried in some kind of oleaginous matter."[20] While traveling through Mississippi in 1837, James Creecy's meals were even worse. They included "rusty salt pork, boiled or fried . . . musty cornmeal dodgers, rarely a vegetable . . . no milk, butter, or eggs."[21] Even further east, conditions were quite rustic. Outside of Columbus, Georgia, in 1832, Swedish traveler Carl David Arfwedson was amazed to see that the centerpiece of his hosts' table was a bottle of whiskey, "of which both host and hostess partook in no measured quantity, before they tasted any of the dishes." Arfwedson's dinner was a three-course meal, but there all resemblance to a refined dinner ended. He recalled, "Pigs' feet pickled in vinegar formed the first course; then followed bacon with molasses; and repast concluded with a super-abundance of milk and bread, which the landlord, to use his own expression, washed down with a half a tumbler of whiskey."[22] The inland South of the 1830s was not lacking in hospitality. Those traveling through the region were treated to the goods on hand. But travelers found these meals, while plentiful, remarkable for their unusual character.

Some visitors to the Southwest saw frontier meals not simply as rustic but as downright crude. The region reflected a strange paradox of abundance and lack; meat, whiskey, and cornmeal were represented in force, but inland tables were not *refined*. For travelers like Olmsted, a superabundance of meat and free-flowing whiskey did not make up for poor decorum or culinary monotony. Native peoples in isolated areas ate well by their own standards; the same went for whites living in established cities or on large plantations; but the white settlers were too white to eat like Natives and too far inland to be refined. Settlers needed to produce food in response, not resistance, to the conditions of the land. Subsequently, corn, salted and smoked pork, and quick-growing vegetables such as turnip greens became staples in the frontier diet.[23]

The frontier may have lacked the refined cuisine of port cities such as New Orleans, Charleston, or Richmond, but it did not lack whiskey and meat. Pork and alcohol—both products made with corn—were mainstays of the rural table, something travelers often commented upon. For example, while traveling through Jefferson City, Missouri, in 1832, the explorer and naturalist Prince Maximilian of Wied (in present-day Germany) complained that he could not "obtain any provisions except salt pork, biscuits, and whiskey." Similarly, a Swedish man in nineteenth-century Alabama was served a three-course meal consisting of pigs' feet, bacon, and "a course of milk and black bread soaked in whiskey." To emphasize his point, he claimed he "had never undergone such gastronomic privations."[24]

Once distilled, whiskey was more portable and resistant to spoilage than corn. Alcohol's intoxicating effects obviously bolstered its popularity. But whiskey had yet another virtue: its relative purity as compared to other beverages. In fact, many saw whiskey as the most logical substitute for potable drinking water, which could be hard to find in remote regions of the inland South. Even along the Mississippi River, water was far too muddy to drink without letting it rest in a container for a period of time. The resulting sediment would often fill a quarter of the vessel. Deep wells were costly and time consuming to drill, and water from streams had to be lugged over rough, and frequently dangerous, terrain. In what was perhaps already an unfair fight, these impediments established whiskey as a clear favorite over water.[25]

Improved distilling techniques, introduced in 1825 by the Scottish doctor James Crow allowed for more yields and higher alcohol contents.[26] Some chose to double- or triple-distill their alcohol, producing whiskeys that could be as high as 190 proof. While traveling through the Lower South in 1836, another Scot, Alexander Mackay remarked that "from morning till night the barrooms of the hotels are full; the bar, indeed, being the chief source of the hotelkeepers' revenue."[27]

Dried corn kernels were not only ground into meal and eaten as bread or distilled into whiskey. Corn was also transformed into pork, ham, and bacon, the other staples of Southern tables both rich and poor. Introduced to the American South by early Spanish explorers, by the eighteenth century hogs were common domesticated animals for white, black, and Native people alike.[28]

A guide to pig butchery, from Annabella Hill, *Mrs. Hill's Southern Practical Cookery and Receipt Book*, facsimile of 1872 edition, ed. Damon L. Fowler (Columbia, SC: University of South Carolina Press, 1995), 156, Michigan State University Special Collections

As early as 1705, Robert Beverly remarked that in Virginia hogs were so plentiful they "swarm like Vermin upon the Earth, and are often accounted as such." Beverly saw hogs that "run where they list, and find their own Support in the Woods, without any Care of the Owner."[29] Self-sufficiency was a key factor in the hog's proliferation in the region. Well into the nineteenth century, hogs were turned loose into the forests and fields that separated plantation holdings; when rounded up, the animals were identified by branding or notching their ears. In the late autumn, they would be selected for slaughter and curing. By the mid-nineteenth century, hogs had become a key component in Southern culture and agriculture.

Bacon and other forms of cured pork were central to foodways across the region because of the relative ease with which they were produced. Small-scale canning was virtually unknown before midcentury, but salt curing and smoking meats were ancient and fairly simple forms of preservation.[30] By 1840, pork packing in the Ohio Valley had become fairly uniform and well organized due to the dominance of larger packinghouses. Throughout the South, curing meat was still performed on homesteads or in plantation smokehouses, and techniques varied across the region and from person to person. How

an animal was butchered, the length of time in salt or smoke, and the type of wood used were all factors in the final product. Smoke curing was not the only method of preservation. Warmer weather made the lengthy process of hanging and smoking impossible, so Southerners also pickled their pork during summer months. Flexibility, ease of preparation, and lack of a large industrial alternative made cured pork a major component in antebellum Southern foodways.[31]

From African Crops to Southern Tables

In the hands of wealthy planters and poor settlers, corn was transformed from a simple grain into products for personal consumption or trade on the market. Just as economic imperatives incentivized transforming corn into pork or whiskey, the brutal logics of slavery demanded that enslaved people were also best sustained with corn. Across the South, plantation owners and overseers made corn a central part of the foods rationed out to enslaved workers.

The diet and food culture of slavery cannot be understood outside the context of plantation rationing. On plantations across the region, provisions were meted out to enslaved people, usually centering around bacon, cornmeal, and molasses. Olmsted observed that "the general allowance of food was thought to be a peck and a half of meal, and three pounds of bacon a week."[32] Historical research bears out similar findings, and historians have estimated the rations for an

enslaved adult at a "peck (eight quarts) of cornmeal and two and a half to four pounds of pork or bacon per week."[33] Quantities may have fluctuated between regions and individual farms, but they were meager by any measure. The very nature of provisioning was restrictive and disciplinary. It reduced the act of eating to a calculus of inputs and outputs and alienated enslaved workers from the bounty their labor produced.[34] Plantation masters and mistresses carefully recorded in their account books the foods given out to the enslaved in an effort to minimize costs.[35] This calculated practice took food and eating out of a space of life and community and moved it into what the historian Orlando Patterson has called a zone of "social death."[36] Plantation ledger books often recorded both the expenses of food and eating and the values of the enslaved people whose work transformed rations into a planter's profit.

The outspoken abolitionist and former slave Frederick Douglass speculated that planters had a somewhat different motivation to provide an adequate diet. For Douglass, it was not so much economics or alienation as social pressure from other elite whites. "Every slaveholder," Douglass wrote, "is anxious to have it known of him, that he feeds his slaves well." In spite of this pressure, Douglass also recalled two enslaved women, Henrietta and Mary, whose diet left them looking like "mangled and emaciated creatures." To Douglass's eyes, the judgment of peers had varying effects within a moral economy corrupted by slavery.[37]

By the 1850s, planters actively debated what constituted a proper diet for enslaved workers. Writing to the periodical *The Southern Planter* in 1856, John A. Barksdale outlined the contours of the discussion. The Virginian thought "fat meat [was] injurious as an article of diet" for the enslaved. But others argued that "the abundant fatty matter which pork affords, [made it] better calculated than any other for the healthful sustenance of the negro race." Barksdale went on to speculate about the benefits of pork fat, suggesting that it was "a source of animal heat, the generation of which is more tardy in the black than the white man." While these claims were rooted in prevailing currents of racial supremacy, not science, the author hit the mark elsewhere. He noted that Virginians were fortunate that "hog and hominy are produced in such abundance in the South Country," and scolded planters who did not take full advantage of the region's climate, insisting that planters ought to balance their pork rations by encouraging enslaved people to grow and consume vegetables from their own gardens.[38]

Wrong as Barksdale was about race, he stumbled upon a truth when it came to the importance of produce.[39] For many enslaved African Americans, meager rations were supplemented by game hunted and trapped in the surrounding areas along with a variety of vegetables grown in gardens or "patches." Barksdale was right to suggest a monotonous diet needed vegetables, but his comments about the enslaved tending gardens and eating vegetables were more description than prescription. Bondspeople did not need the planter class to encourage their use of gardens or approve of their consumption of vegetables. In their gardens, enslaved people often employed African agricultural techniques and cultivated various plants native to Africa, many of which would become closely associated with Southern foodways.

Just as some indigenous foods remained part of Southern diets, elements of African American food culture also infiltrated white foodways. For example, the okra and cowpeas in Mary Randolph's cookbook can be traced back to West Africa via the transatlantic slave trade. Her recipe for "Gumbo—a West India Dish" is even linguistically tied to the word *kinggombo*, the Kimbundu word for okra. Yams, watermelon, sesame (benne), and black-eyed peas all have strong ties to the Yoruba, Akan, and Kimbundu cultures. Yams continue to have a central place in Ghanaian festivals; and Brazilian Condomblé ceremonies call for specific preparation of okra pods. The chile, tomato, and sweet potato are native to South

America and were brought by the Portuguese to West Africa as early as the sixteenth century and on to North America via the slave trade.[40]

The migration of African foods to the Americas is recorded in various registers. The logs of slave ships that brought black bodies to the New World record in their manifests the purchase of rice as well as vegetables, fava beans, and manioc (cassava) meal. African goods and customs were also recorded in the ground on which those black bodies would labor and die. Archaeological findings in the Chesapeake and elsewhere have uncovered small articles of jewelry indigenous to West Africa. It is a matter of debate whether abducted Africans brought the seeds of these various plants in lockets and jewelry, or if the crew used the produce as durable mess aboard slave ships.[41] Ships' manifests and faunal remains do not tell us much about the history of slavery from the perspective of those most affected by its brutality. Whatever the case, the crops themselves also speak to this migration. By the middle of the nineteenth century, many of these plants of African origin were thriving in small gardens around the South. These plots were often as large as an acre per family, and were frequently tended by older enslaved people, or during moments free from plantation labor. The foods grown in these "slave patches" were central to the enslaved diet.[42]

The gardens tended by enslaved people were successful enough for planters to take an interest in them beyond simple dietary concerns for their human chattel. In the late eighteenth century, Thomas Jefferson had hoped to transplant olive trees from the Mediterranean to Albemarle County, Virginia. Jefferson was interested in olive oil's potential as a substitute for pork fat, the cooking fat most commonly used by enslaved people. These olive tree experiments proved to be failures in both Virginia and the more hospitable climate of the Carolina low country, but ironically, a good oil substitute was already *in* Virginia, growing in enslaved gardens: sesame seed, or benne, was already a part of African and enslaved foodways. In 1808, the governor of Georgia, John Milledge, sent Jefferson a bottle of benne oil, and the president discovered what had been there all along, an oil with high fat yields and fine flavor, which grew readily in the U.S. South.[43]

Like corn, benne was not grown in large enough quantities to justify trade on the market, but planters frequently cultivated sesame for local use, or in rotation with other crops such as rice, cowpeas, or sweet potatoes. Since planters did not record the crops grown in slave gardens, we cannot estimate the true quantity of benne planted. However, by midcentury the seed had evolved from a fat substitute for the enslaved to a component in elegant dishes served in planter dining rooms.[44]

Enslaved people also used gardens as a source of drinking, eating, and storage vessels. The gourds of creeping vines were frequently hollowed out, dried, and used in various ways.[45] As an old man in the late 1930s, Baily Cunningham, who had been born into slavery almost a hundred years earlier, remembered how "all the work hands ate in the cabin and all the children took their *cymblin* [squash] *soup bowl* to the big kitchen and got it full of cabbage soup, then we were allowed to

Sesame, also called benne or bene, was one of many foods of African origin that became part of Southern diets. Some enslaved Southerners tended sesame plants in gardens, and by the mid-nineteenth century, sesame seeds and sesame oil appeared in dishes eaten by enslaved workers as well as by white elites. William Nathaniel White, *Gardening for the South: or, How to Grow Vegetables and Fruits*, p. 324, Michigan State University Special Collections.

go [to] the table where the white folks ate and get the crumbs from the table. We sat on the ground around the quarters to eat with wooden spoons."[46] Cunningham's recollection showed that, despite the degrading conditions and sadistic rituals of the chattel system, African customs sometimes survived in the most basic elements of daily life. A simple gourd, grown in a garden and fash-

ioned into a bowl, had both utility and the persistence of a tradition generations removed from the men and women forced onto slave ships in West Africa.

The food culture of enslaved people had roots in African traditions, it adapted to the abundance of the region, and it flourished in small garden plots. From the Chesapeake to the Mississippi and from the hills of Appalachia to the Gulf Coast, the region's native fish, fowl, plants, and game supplemented bondspeople's diets. Enslaved people ate local meats like opossum, raccoon, squirrel, turtles, fish, and shellfish. And by the nineteenth century, enslaved people also raised and consumed a variety of domesticated animals. For example, archeological studies of Mulberry Row, the slave quarter at Monticello, Thomas Jefferson's Virginia plantation, show that cow and pig bones are equally represented in the faunal remains, while pig bones predominate at other plantations. At Monticello, enslaved people reared animals in their gardens or in other spaces near the quarter or yard, and the meat from those animals could both supplement their diet and be sold at market.[47]

Monticello and other wealthy plantations were exceptional in the diversity of foods grown and consumed by free and enslaved. In the Upland South, for example, the farms of smallholding planters functioned for subsistence and needed to be self-sustaining year after year. They had fewer enslaved workers, limited access to markets, and less capital than larger plantations of the Lower South. And while pork was central to the diets of both black and white, diets were frequently supplemented by game hunted from the surrounding environment. Enslaved workers, in particular, consumed larger amounts of game. Domesticated animals such as cows or chickens were far less likely to appear as meals in the upland regions.[48]

Chicken has become closely associated with Southern cooking, and it is easy to forget that, in an era before refrigeration, chickens were valued more for eggs than meat. In the nineteenth century, poultry husbandry and trade were a small market, practiced locally at the margins of the larger economy, often by enslaved women. Trafficking in poultry could provide enslaved women financial benefit, relative autonomy, and access to the local market economy and public sphere. The trade also empowered enslaved women in areas separate from the structures of the plantation home.[49]

Power and Food in Plantation Domestic Space

Mistresses on large plantations are frequently associated with the elegant tables of the nineteenth-century dining room, but it was the cook who labored in the kitchen that created such meals. The white women of large plantations were also most likely to record and publish the culinary feats of their homes, which further silenced both enslaved cooks and white women of lower classes who cooked in their own kitchens. Women like Mary Randolph and Maria Barringer, wealthy white women whose cookbooks are excerpted later in this volume, had control over enslaved workers and the resources to record the dishes that labor produced. These women were exceptional in this regard. The recipes contained in these texts speak more to the particular circumstances of their authors than they do the region as a whole. It was not until Abbey Fisher's 1881 cookbook, also excepted here, that a formerly enslaved woman would testify to her own skill in a published text. However, historians have remarked on the tension behind the scenes of plantation food labor.

On large plantations across the nineteenth-century South, food labor was atomized into discrete outbuildings: smokehouses, dovecotes, dairies, and of course, kitchens. Enslaved cooks had a tremendous amount of power within this space. The historian Elizabeth Fox-Genovese notes that enslaved cooks were often "older, as well as more experienced, than the mistress they 'served.'" And in most cases, both cook and mistress knew that the lady of the house could not "run a proper household" without the cook's compliance.[50] The kitchen was a central point within the space of the nineteenth-century plantation yard, a space of both food production and the power associated with food labor. The South's heat and dampness made the kitchen particularly susceptible to odors, germs, and other intrusions from the natural world. These environmental factors and planters' increasing aversion to laboring black bodies helped to push the kitchen and other spaces of food labor outside of the home beginning in the seventeenth century.[51] Separating cooking from dining, and black labor from white consumption, allowed meals, as one scholar has put it, to "arrive at the dining table as if by magic."[52] Enslaved cooks had significant power in the kitchen, but the mistresses still policed the space.

White mistresses demonstrated their status in the dining room, showing domestic prowess through courtly behavior, not cooking.[53] The etiquette of the dining room was defined by elaborate social customs, which effectively separated the elite planter class from both the enslaved who waited on them and from the lower and middling classes of the region. The material of the dining room—its linens, silver, carved wood, and fine china—lent further distinction to the space.[54] Beginning in the mid-eighteenth century, the dining room became an important focal point for planter hospitality.[55] In the kitchen, enslaved cooks transformed agricultural raw materials into food, but the elegant tables of the Southeast hid this labor. In the dining room, food was transformed into a symbol of elegance, distinction, and performance.

While traveling in Virginia in the early 1850s, Frederick Law Olmsted recorded a meal typical of an elite planter home. His account contrasts starkly with his eating experiences in the inland Southwest. At a plantation outside of Petersburg, Virginia, Olmsted reported that his meal was attended by "two negro girls [who]

waited at the table, and a negro boy . . . who when . . . asked for a glass of water, was sent to get it." Olmsted may have also observed the cook, "an old negro woman [who] frequently came in from the kitchen, with hot biscuits and corn-cake." The meal also included "fried-fowl, and fried bacon and eggs, and cold ham; there were preserved peaches, and preserved quinces and grapes; there was hot wheaten biscuit and hot short-cake, and hot corn-cake, and hot griddle cakes, soaked in butter; there was coffee, and there was milk, sour or sweet, whichever I preferred to drink." The abundance of dishes at the meal Olmsted described speaks to a tremendous amount of skill in the kitchen. But when Olmsted praised the corn cake and preserved peaches and asked how they were made, his white hostess very pointedly evaded his question, only proclaiming that she feared "there wasn't anything on the table" her guest could eat. Evidently, the guest had asked the wrong question, or more to the point, asked it of the wrong person.[56] When Olmsted asked about the food's preparation, the mistress of the house fell back on a domestic performance enacted in the dining room, not labor in or knowledge of the kitchen. The hostess took credit for the superabundant meal, not by preparing it, but by feigning an apology for its shortcomings.[57]

Travelers across the South frequently remarked on the groaning tables of elite plantation dining rooms, but others saw the sinister side of these elaborate meals. Fredrick Douglass described them as haunted by "invisible spirits of evil, ready to feed the self-deluded gormandizers with aches, pains, fierce tempers, uncontrolled passions."[58] The prominent abolitionist and former slave Harriet Jacobs also experienced the obscene underside of dining room etiquette. In her 1861 autobiography, she recalled that if Sunday dinner was not served on time in the North Carolina home where she had been enslaved, her mistress would go into the kitchen and "spit in all the kettles and pans that had been used for cooking," to ensure that the cook and her family would not get to eat any of the leftover food.[59]

Because enslaved cooks were essential to elaborate plantation meals and the social distinction they lent elite whites, coaxing, coercing, and generally overseeing enslaved cooks was a central preoccupation of plantation management. The genteel education many young Southern planter-class women received did little to prepare them for their roles as domestic overseers.[60] For example, writing to *The Lady's Annual Register and Housewife's Memorandum-book* in 1838, Carole Gilman told readers to "let the first walk of the housewife after breakfast be—not to her boudoir or to her library, but—to the kitchen." Gilman insisted that frequent visits to the kitchen would "stimulate" the cook to perform more efficiently.[61] Elite Southern women understood that controlling enslaved labor was a central element in their role within plantation patriarchy.

Food in the Wartime Confederacy

On December 22, 1859, in anticipation of the coming conflict, Governor Henry A. Wise urged Virginia to "call home her children." He echoed a refrain that had been building over the course of the decade: that his state, and the South in general, had become too economically dependent on the North. He challenged his audience to "dress in the wool raised on our own pastures [and] eat the flour from our own mills, and if we can't get that, why let us go back to our old accustomed corn bread." Wise's injunctions were tragically prescient. In a few short years the South's agricultural production would be largely focused on growing corn to feed Confederate troops. Further complicating the picture was the fact that young white men—disproportionately those from poorer backgrounds—were going off to fight and die instead of working on their family farms. With crops increasingly dedicated to corn, and local officials increasingly impressing most of that crop to feed Confederate troops, many throughout the region suffered food shortages.[62]

Disruptions in domestic food supply were severely compounded by the federal blockade of Southern ports. By September 1862, the Union general Benjamin Butler reported from New Orleans, "The condition of the people here is a very alarming one. They have literally come down to starvation." By the end of that month Butler was issuing $50,000 worth of food aid to white families of that city. The diet and health of the thousands of black refugees in New Orleans was even worse; many were hungry, inadequately clothed, aged, or infirm.[63]

By the summer of 1863, the sieges of Vicksburg and Port Hudson along the Mississippi River disrupted supply lines in the western theater of war. At Vicksburg, Confederate troops were surrounded by Union soldiers, but they had the company of plenty of cattle and sheep, at least at first. Union sharpshooters made sure that entrapped Confederates couldn't allow animals to graze outside, and so besieged troops were forced to slaughter the animals before they starved, eating what they could of them before rot set in. After the last cows and sheep were killed, troops turned to mules, horses, and eventually rats. Many commented on the qualities of these novel proteins. One soldier wrote that mule flesh was "of a darker color than beef, of a finer grain, quite tender and juicy." A Confederate doctor recalled that rats were "superior, in the opinion of those who eat them, to spring chickens." The troops' lack of culinary scruples spoke volumes to the worsening conditions at the fort.[64]

While Confederate troops were penned in along the western front, Union troops in the East were looting other Southern larders. A year before the fall of Vicksburg and Port Hudson, in July 1862, Major General John Pope,

When Confederates at Vicksburg finally surrendered after a six-week siege on the Fourth of July, 1863, the Union army gained control of the Mississippi River, a crucial conduit for food and other materiel. Engraving of Vicksburg in Thomas Prentice Kettell, *History of the Great Rebellion from Its Commencement to Its Close* (Hartford, CT: L. Stebbins; Cincinnati: F. A. Howe, 1866), 646, Michigan State University Special Collections.

commander of a Union army in Virginia, had declared, "Hereafter, as far as practicable, the troops of this command will subsist upon the country in which their operations are carried on." By January of the following year, subsisting off the local larder had become standard in the Shenandoah and throughout Virginia. It bears repeating that the Civil War was largely waged on the farms and fields that had formerly sustained the region. Violence also pushed into domestic spaces, damaging plantation kitchens, larders, smokehouses, and dining rooms.[65] Plantation mistresses recorded the effects of Pope's "General Order #5" in their diaries. Sigismunda Stribling Kimball, of Clarke County, Virginia, described the sense of helplessness that overcame many plantation mistresses in her community. She recalled an incident in February 1863, in which Union troops forced their way into a neighbor's home. She recalled that the men "broke Mrs. Kounslar's front door open, and ordered her to get them a hot supper, she said her servants were in bed and she never made them get up, that time of night—they replied if she did not get it pretty soon, they would put their own cook in the kitchen . . . every thing was placed before them, and after satisfying their appetites left."[66] Kimball's neighbor faced a situation in which she was dispossessed of valuable foodstuffs and disempowered in her role as mistress. Union troops were not the only ones coming and going on the plantation in February 1863. As troops approached, the newly freed men and women fled plantations throughout Shenandoah County. And in many cases, elite women lost control of their place in the plantation home: food was stolen, space invaded,

and authority usurped. Confederate troops added to the disorder and loss on plantation homes. In July 1862, Orange County, Virginia, was the site of heavy fighting between Union and Confederate troops. "Selma," the home of Fannie Page Hume, had been overrun by Northern soldiers who stole whiskey and meat from the plantation smokehouse. Three days later, Southern forces were moving through the area. While happy to see friendly forces, Hume was not pleased to have troops occupying her space or interacting with the enslaved. She complained that "the yard is filled with [Confederate] solders, lounging about in every direction, impossible to escape them—the servants have done nothing but cook for them."[67] As if the constraints of impressments and federal raids were not enough, Hume's home was now hosting and feeding Confederate troops. Victory or loss, advance or retreat, either way Hume was dispossessed of food, space, and power.

Even under wartime conditions, rations, and scarcity, Southerners still shared and celebrated with food, when they could. In December 1862, Louisa Minor recorded a Christmas dinner at the Delevan Hospital in Charlottesville, which included contributions "sent by almost everyone in the county." The meal was large enough to feed more than 1,200 solders. After the troops finished, Minor noted, "The darkies of the establishment were treated." That Friday, the surgeons of the hospital provided a supper for the women who had assisted in nursing and cooking at Delevan over the previous year. Minor was pleased with the meal and the event, which included "plenty of beaux." She nonetheless felt the

In this postwar illustration, two Union soldiers steal milk directly from a Southern woman's cow. "Milking the Cow" illustration from Frazar Kirkland, *The Pictorial Book of Anecdotes of the Rebellion* (Hillsdale, MI: W. E. Allen, 1888), 451, Michigan State University Special Collections.

all enslaved people in Confederate states, marked a touchstone in the history of slavery and freedom. But freedom was much more complicated than a presidential proclamation—and much longer than a single day. In practice, many enslaved people didn't hear about the proclamation for weeks or months, and even then, many weren't able to pack up and leave. Moreover, Lincoln's Emancipation Proclamation did not simply *grant* freedom to those enslaved in the Confederacy.[69] Many people had already begun *taking* their freedom, claiming it in small acts of resistance, work stoppages, and flight. These experiments in freedom deeply affected the South's food culture.

In the war's final months, white Southerners began to realize they could no longer rely on a system of slave labor to provide for their well-being and define their senses of self. In the postwar home, cooking, cleaning, and even answering the door increasingly fell under the purview of white women.[70] Some whites negotiated with the formerly enslaved, taking on some tasks themselves, hiring out others, and jettisoning those deemed superfluous in a system that paid wages for work. Describing her enslaved childhood decades later, Minnie Folks recalled that her mother was hired to cook in the same house in which she had been enslaved, when her former mistress promised she would provide food and clothes if she stayed. Folks recalled that her mother took the deal, but she added that they had nothing and nowhere to go. Under these conditions, negotiations were clearly not in the favor of freed people.[71]

season "seemed so little like Xmas" and that she could not "wish for a merry one."[68] Free and enslaved, rich and poor, Southerners had to adapt to wartime conditions. From the start, Southerners fought to adapt to shortages in food production and supply. But as the war progressed they were also forced to reckon with sudden fluctuations in the labor market.

January 1, 1863, the date Abraham Lincoln issued the Emancipation Proclamation officially freeing

Transitions to freedom did not always go so easily. In February 1863, Sigismunda Stribling Kimball recounted a violent meeting with troops at her home. A freedman named William had returned to collect his brother's wife, Fairinda. The elite white mistress and the captain overseeing the affair exchanged heated words, with the captain mocking Kimball's claim that the woman "belonged" to her. He exclaimed, "O! they do not belong to anyone, the government has lifted that." He supplied the plantation mistress with his name and rank and noted that he was "what *you* would call *poor white trash*." He then asked Fairinda if she wanted "meat or flour, for if it is on the place you shall have it." To which the formerly enslaved cook replied "she did not want any thing but herself."[72] The exchange tapped into the swirling fears, hopes, and desires that would define the late 1860s, as well as the long decades that followed: the fear and anger of elite whites, the three-cornered battle between poor white, elite white, and free black Americans, and the legal recognition that one could possess one's own self.[73] The heated debate over ownership and class on Kimball's plantation in February 1863 was only one of many skirmishes in a decades-long struggle over American systems of racial and class hierarchy.

Conclusion

History clashed with memory as the South descended into the period known as the racial nadir—the gruesome decades that separated the Civil War and civil rights. During this period, the culinary contributions of African Americans went the way of the indigenous influences: ingredients, techniques, and dishes were celebrated as uniquely Southern, but the labor, traditions, and cultures from which these meals emerged were often left out of the discussion. Nostalgic white Southerners misremembered—or wholly invented—faithful mammies as family members whose labor was rooted in love rather than the conditions of slavery. Caricatures replaced real historical actors as fictions were projected onto the past. The proliferation of postwar cookbooks helped to rewrite this history, erasing as they did the pain and conflict that shaped antebellum Southern cooking.[74] Lost Cause nostalgia tried to rewrite history as Southern recipes hid the much more complicated stories behind their formation.

However, like a culinary cold case, the truth was in the evidence, especially in the ingredients themselves. Like corn and native game, items like okra, benne, and chiles pointed to a history of conflict and the culinary centrality of those on the margin, the enslaved, the indigenous, the poor, and women. Southern food was built in part by the labor and resistance of these groups, developing organically in the hands of a multitude of different people across the region, and across time. The recipes in Southern cookbooks are more than instructions on how to produce a dish or a meal. They are themselves the products of a long and complicated history, and reading those recipes today helps bring this past into the present.

Seeing the Civil War South through Its Recipes

The antebellum South was nothing if not agricultural. In fact, thanks to its vast farmlands, mild weather, and massive, enslaved workforce, the antebellum South was one of the most productive agricultural regions in history. The cotton gin, invented in 1792, had made it fast and easy to comb out seeds from cotton, just as early factories in the North were starting to spin cotton and weave it into cloth at high speed. Between the advent of the cotton gin and the eve of the Civil War, cotton boomed. It exploded through the Deep South and into the West, remaking the region as it multiplied across it. Cotton not only pushed the boundaries of the "South" farther and farther west, but it created an ever-growing market for enslaved workers to plant and harvest it. In the North, slavery had withered since the American Revolution, state by state. But in the South, slavery was flourishing like never before. By 1860, cotton had made slavery seem indispensable to Southern culture and the Southern economy alike.

On the eve of the Civil War, as white Southerners contemplated their prospects in the conflict, few imagined their agricultural system would be anything but an asset. After all, Southern cotton was the fuel driving the Industrial Revolution: mills in the Northern United States and in Northern England were ravenous for it. Many Southerners figured that if pressure from Northern industrialists to renew their regular cotton supply didn't make Abraham Lincoln concede swiftly to Confederate demands, European pressure would. High-priced cotton had also made the South—or at least an elite sliver of it—fabulously wealthy, and that wealth seemed like a major advantage in its own right.

But Southerners had overestimated the power of cotton and underestimated the power of food. Before the war, the South had imported a significant portion of food from outside the region, including much of its pork, beef, wheat, potatoes, cheese, and butter. Southerners knew that Union strategists hoped to exploit this weakness, but it seemed laughable to many that the North might actually be able to force a region as large and productive as the South to go *hungry*. After all, the South wasn't hopelessly monocultural. Southern farms already produced a decent amount of wheat and corn and meat, and they had a corner on rice and sugar.[1] Many Southerners believed that even without imports, their region's farms could produce enough food to make them self-sufficient for the duration of the war, especially since they expected it to be a short one.[2]

Those beliefs didn't last long, as the inadequacy of Southern food production became more and more obvious. The Union blockade of Southern ports reduced imports of food and other materials to a trickle, and the blockade only tightened as time went by. Periodicals aimed at cotton planters, like the long-running *Southern Cultivator*, pleaded with readers to give up cotton and start growing food: "Let it be understood at once, that the planter who cultivated cotton when there is such an urgent demand for food, is in effect giving aid and comfort to the enemy."[3] But too many Southern farmers were yoked to the infrastructure of cotton production and distracted by an increasingly all-consuming war. Many of them, in fact, had already left their farms to fight. And even when some farmers were able to grow surplus food, they often had no way to send it to market. The South's system of roads and railroads had never been nearly as comprehensive as the North's, and the war made transportation much worse as the military commandeered horses and wagons and took over what rails existed.[4] Southerners' inability to produce adequate food or to move the food they had where it was needed contributed directly to their defeat.

And then there were the armies themselves, as destructive to Southern food supply as the blockade and lack of transportation. Both armies lived and traveled and fought overwhelmingly on Southern soil, which meant that the South, in practice, often had to feed both massive armies.[5] On paper, both Confederate and Union soldiers were supposed to receive similar, ample rations of about a pound of meat and three-quarters of a pound of bread per day, supplemented with coffee and sugar and other items.[6] But plans on paper were a far cry from reality. Union troops occasionally went hungry, and for Confederates soldiers, deprivation and want became absolutely routine.[7] Southern soldiers started getting diminished rations only a few months after the start of the war, and their rations shrank steadily as time went on.[8] By 1864, the average Confederate ration had shrunk to a measly eight ounces of flour and four ounces of pork—and sometimes soldiers didn't even get that.[9] Hunger was worse when Confederates were fighting or on the move, and soldiers sometimes reported marching for two days on little more than a couple of crackers.[10]

Hunger defined the war experience of Confederate soldiers, and finding food became the central preoccupation of soldiers' daily lives.[11] Soldiers supplemented inadequate rations in a variety of ways: by foraging for nuts and berries, by seizing enemy provisions after a victory, or—very occasionally—with care packages from home.[12] But most often they got food by taking it from civilians.[13] For Confederates, of course, that usually meant they were taking food from their own people, which made the stealing and grubbing more complicated, morally.[14] Yet soldiers were desperate enough for

Finding food became the central preoccupation of soldiers' daily lives. According to a postwar anecdote, one rebel soldier crossed enemy lines because he caught the scent of real coffee brewing. When he saw how well equipped the enemy camp was, he decided to join the Union army. "Courtesies of Picket Life" illustration from Kirkland, *Pictorial Book of Anecdotes*, 273.

food that they generally did forage and steal when they could.[15]

Conditions were much worse for prisoners. Southern soldiers sometimes encountered awful conditions in Northern prisons, such as in New York's Elmira Prison, nicknamed "Hellmira," where nearly a quarter of the inmates died.[16] But imprisoned Northern soldiers fared much worse on average than their Southern counterparts. Southern prison food was scanty and monotonous at best, and inedible or nonexistent at worst.[17] In many cases, prisoners ate anything they could get their hands on, setting traps for rats, snaring songbirds.[18] Prisons like Andersonville in Georgia and Libby Prison

in Richmond became infamous for overcrowding, filth, lack of food and water, and astounding mortality rates.[19] Northern civilians were enraged to hear of thousands of Union soldiers locked up to die slowly from hunger or exposure. Emaciated and sick, one Northern solider kept a diary while imprisoned in Libby in 1864, which he later edited and published: "It seems to be the policy of our captors to give us as little food as possible themselves and allow none from our friends in the North, who are willing and anxious to relieve us. . . . The rations at present are really horrible. They consist of only a *little half-baked corn-bread, and a gill or two of rice.* . . . What a contrast between the ration given to the rebel prisoners, in the North, and the miserable, half-cooked stuff, eked out to Northern prisoners, here in the South."[20]

Wartime food shortages affected home life as well as military strategy, and food conditions became dire for many Southern civilians. Already by early 1862 Southerners were starting to go hungry, and things only got worse as the war dragged on.[21] The recipes in this book give a sense of how the war changed what Southerners ate, but if anything they don't show fully enough how desperate the food situation became, precisely because the written sources that survived were created overwhelmingly by the wealthiest Southerners, who were least exposed to privations. Even as commodities like coffee and salt dwindled, the wealthiest people on the home front usually had an adequate amount of total calories.[22] Put simply, the war did not affect all Southerners equally.

Poorer Southerners suffered more, and sometimes they suffered terribly indeed. Huge numbers of South-

As food conditions worsened during the war, Northern soldiers in Southern prisons fared worse than almost anybody. Libby Prison in Richmond, Virginia, was one of the most notorious prisons in the Confederacy, and Northern soldiers imprisoned there reported horrifying conditions and starvation rations. Image of Libby Prison in Kirkland, *Pictorial Book of Anecdotes*, 551.

erners went hungry at times, and small numbers of people actually starved.[23] For example, one 1864 article reported that some were starving in the Georgia mountains, an already poor area made desperate by the departure of able-bodied men, raids by soldiers in both armies, and bad weather. With the crops failed and the livestock dead, the article's author reported that people were "subsisting upon roots and weeds!"[24] Across the South, in fact, hunger drove people to eat all sorts of foods they had considered inedible before the war,

including rats, cats, dogs, mules, and insects.[25] These were pariah meats—that is, meat from animals that were *socially* inedible under normal circumstances. You won't find any recipes for them in published cookbooks, but it's important to remember that some people were eating them.

Poor white women whose husbands and other male family members left to fight for the Confederacy often became so desperate for food that they demanded help from city or state governments. For instance, in the fall of 1863, an author in the planter periodical *Southern Watchman* reported scornfully that a group of women near Columbus, Georgia, "claiming to be the wives of soldiers," wrote to the state governor demanding food and threatening to take it by force if their demands were not met.[26] In fact, Southern women by the thousands *did* take to the streets to demand food—or to seize it. Especially after 1863, as circumstances for many poor families went from bad to unbearable, thousands of poor women across the South rioted for food.[27] As the historian Joan Cashin writes, women taking to the streets in public protest was "a radical departure from antebellum gender roles," suggesting just "how desperate these women must have been."[28] Even when women didn't riot, they very often wrote to their husbands at war, begging them to return and help them farm—and men by the thousands deserted the Confederate army to do just that.[29] As conditions worsened across the South, women's inability to keep their families afloat gnawed away at the Confederate war effort.

The Southerners who were by far the poorest and who suffered the most were the four million people—a third of the Southern population—who had been enslaved. The war took a devastating toll on Southern African Americans, with hunger, exposure, and displacement contributing to staggering rates of sickness and death.[30] Money and race created gross differences in the ways Southerners experienced the war, insulating some from true want while exposing many others to the harshest deprivations and suffering. But no Southerners were unaffected by the war, and wartime experiences—and in particular the increasingly romanticized memories of those experiences—profoundly shaped Southern cuisine.

The Southern cuisine most people think of today bears a striking—if highly selective—resemblance to the foods in these nineteenth-century cookbooks. They teem with the kinds of recipes we expect to find when we go looking for Southern food: grits and gumbo, succotash and Hopping John, catfish, coleslaw, watermelon pickles, chitterlings, sweet potato pie, and many, many more. It's not a coincidence that Southern cuisine has a strong identity or that that identity is roped to the Civil War era.

When you look closely at the recipes here you'll see that many nineteenth-century cooking techniques were really forms of preservation. Jams, vinegars, alcohols, pickles, smoked meats—these were all ways to extend the life of perishable foods. Before reliable refrigeration, preserving food was crucial to survival.[31] But here's what's interesting about the prevalence of preserved foods in cookbooks from the Civil War era: many of the flavors we associate with Southern cuisine today are really the flavors of preservation, from the bite of vinegary peppers or homemade liquors to the sticky sweetness of fruit syrups and the saltiness of sausage.

What's even more interesting is that, at the time, the flavors on Northern tables wouldn't have been much different. Preservation techniques were ubiquitous in kitchens across the country by necessity. Meanwhile, other cooking techniques we associate with Southern

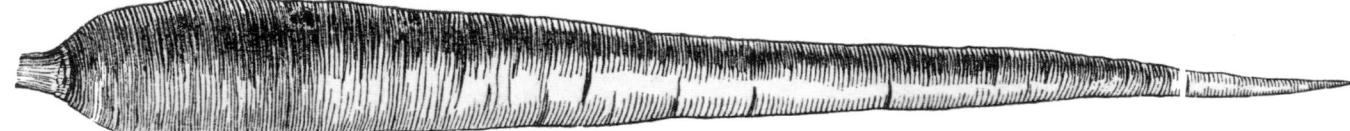

Nineteenth-century Americans worried much more than people do today about food's digestibility. As a result, people were careful to boil their vegetables for long periods of time, reasoning that prolonged cooking made them softer and easier to digest. This was especially true of carrots, which many pointed to as uniquely tough, fibrous, and indigestible without proper cooking. The carrot recipes in this volume reflect this fear, with authors calling for cooking times of up to two and a half hours. Carrot illustration in Burr, *Field and Garden Vegetables*, 25.

cuisine weren't at all exclusively Southern. For example, when we think of a mess of limp collards or green beans boiled down to a savory heap with salt pork, we think of them as uniquely Southern dishes. But people were boiling vegetables to death all over the United States in the mid-nineteenth century, mainly because many people believed they had to cook vegetables for hours to make them digestible.

Some of the flavors we associate with Southern cuisine today come from the ingredients themselves, foods of African or North American or European origins that flourished in the South's climate and were prized for their unique tastes. But many other flavors we associate with Southern cuisine are really the flavors of the nineteenth century, *not* necessarily flavors that were distinctive to the South. Why is that? A big reason is that people have been nostalgically celebrating the cuisine of the "Old South" ever since the end of the war, and as a result, Southern cuisine hung on to many nineteenth-century cooking techniques—and the tastes

and textures that resulted—in a way Northern cuisine did not. And for that matter, "Northern cuisine"? It hardly seems to exist. If somehow the war hadn't happened—if there'd never been an "Old South" versus a "New South"—Southern cuisine might not exist either. It certainly would have been very different because there would have been no reason to canonize the tastes and techniques of this particular time period.

As it was, nostalgia for antebellum eating began before the war was even over. Already by the early 1860s, Southern women like Maria Barringer and Annabella Hill were at work on cookbooks memorializing prewar cooking styles. And when those cookbooks were finally published in the late 1860s, both of them would fondly re-create "war" recipes, too.[32] Other cookbooks soon appeared devoted explicitly to the cuisine of "Old South." One of the best and most accurate of these is the 1881 *What Mrs. Fisher Knows about Old Southern Cooking*. Unlike many of the racist books that would be published in later decades by white authors claiming to re-create plantation cookery, the author of this book, Abby Fisher, was a formerly enslaved woman and an experienced cook.

After the Civil War, enthusiasm for Southern foods was deeply linked to romantic nostalgia for supposedly faithful slaves.[33] Especially between the 1880s and the 1940s, white Americans across the country built racist fantasies around the lavish plantation meals enslaved African American women had supposedly cooked lovingly for white masters. These fantasies were immortalized in industrial food products that started appearing in the 1880s like "Old South Brand Baked Beans" and in commercial figures like Aunt Jemima, invented in the 1890s to market pancake mixes.[34] By the early twentieth century, nostalgia for the Old South was inextricable from nostalgia for the institution of slavery itself, and both were a regular part of American popular culture, rehearsed in songs, minstrel shows, and dozens of cookbooks celebrating plantation cooking. For example, one of these books was the 1913 *Dishes & Beverages of the Old South*, written by a white woman named Martha McCulloch-Williams whose family had owned slaves when she was a child. McCulloch-Williams claimed that "Our Mammys"—the enslaved women who had cooked in elite households—"not only knew their business but loved it." She nostalgically recalled her own "mammy" as a short, obese woman who served her white masters "fondly" and "faithfully."[35]

In truth, enslaved African Americans had been central to the development of Southern food, but not in the ways imagined in racist fantasies. The origins of

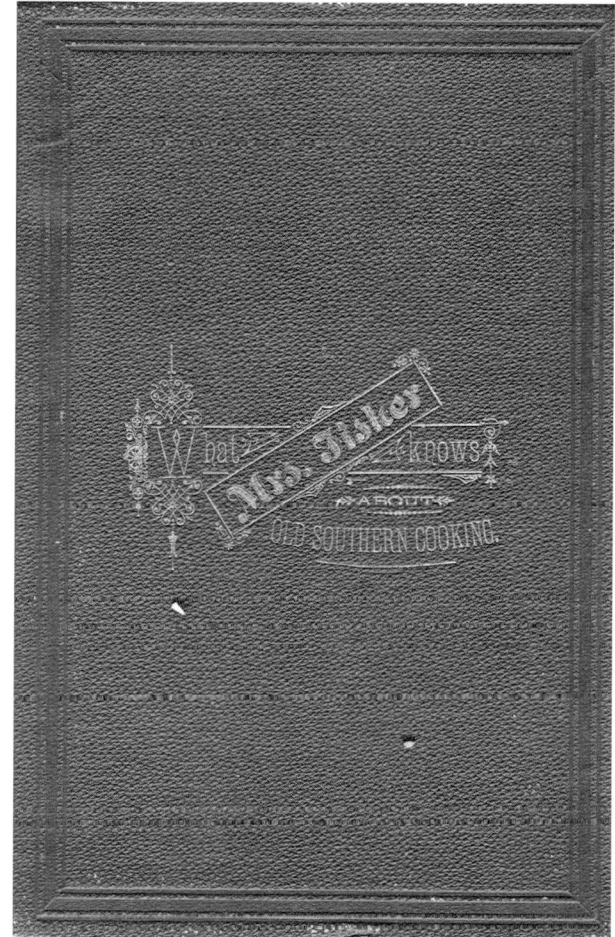

Abby Fisher's 1881 *What Mrs. Fisher Knows about Old Southern Cooking* was the first full-length cookbook published by a formerly enslaved cook. Cover, *What Mrs. Fisher Knows about Old Southern Cooking: Soups, Pickles, Preserves, Etc.* (San Francisco: Women's Co-operative Printing Office, 1881), Michigan State University Special Collections.

Dishes & Beverages of the Old South, published in 1913, was one of many cookbooks that appeared in the early twentieth century claiming to describe the cuisine of the antebellum South. Its author, Martha McCulloch-Williams, was an elite white woman who had been a child in a slaveholding household before the Civil War. In typical fashion, McCulloch-Williams sketched a racist caricature of the enslaved woman who had cooked for her own family, describing her as faithful and content. Cover, *Dishes & Beverages of the Old South* (New York: McBride, Nast, 1913), Michigan State University Special Collections.

the Southern cuisine canonized in the decades after the Civil War are complex, including a "cross-pollination" of European, Native American, and African ingredients and cooking techniques.[36] In fact, for all the resemblance between Southern and Northern cooking styles in the mid-nineteenth century, especially in their mutual reliance on preservation and prolonged cooking times, Southern cuisine *was* distinct in important ways. That was especially so in its deep ties to African cuisines. The slave trade diffused African crops around the Atlantic world; in the Americas, as the historian Judith Carney writes, "slaves Africanized the food systems of plantation societies."[37] Many enslaved Africans arrived in the American South with knowledge of farming, herding, and cooking techniques, valuable skills that shaped what people in the South grew and how they ate it.[38] West African foods like rice, okra, yams, and black-eyed peas became staples in Southern kitchens and dining rooms, along with indigenous North American ingredients like corn, tomatoes, sweet potatoes, peanuts, squash, and beans.

As with all cuisines, the borders of Southern cuisine get messy when you look closely because ingredients and recipes moved around all the time. By the mid-nineteenth century, Northerners frequently cooked and ate things we think of as Southern foods, like gumbo and chow chow and watermelon pickles, just as Southerners regularly cooked from Northern cookbooks and used wheat flour whenever they could get their hands on it. Look closely at the recipes in this book, and you might be surprised to find that in between recipes for corn

Although pork figures heavily in stereotypes about antebellum Southern cuisine, beef was also an important part of Southern diets. A guide to cow butchery, from Hill, *Mrs. Hill's Southern Practical Cookery*, facsimile of 1872 edition, 148.

bread and pigs' feet are many other dishes that don't sound "Southern" in the slightest. There are foods you might think of as New England specialties, like brown bread and clam chowder. There are seemingly English foods like Yorkshire pudding and roast beef. And there are a variety of continental European dishes, from fricassee to gazpacho. At the same time that Southerners were cooking a wide range of recipes, they were also shipping in much of their food from outside the region, either from other parts of the United States or from abroad, with imported ingredients like coffee, salt, pepper, cinnamon, chocolate, tapioca, vanilla, and wine all appearing regularly. And like all cuisines, Southern cuisine changed over time, according to the shifting availability of ingredients, the development of new cooking tools, and changes in fashion or taste.

Still, the cookbooks excerpted here were all clearly Southern books, with authors who conceived of them as such. In fact, unlike Northern authors, who often made little or no reference to region, all of these cookbook authors wore their Southern identities on their sleeves. Southern place-names figure heavily in recipe titles, like Wilmington Ice-Cream, Augusta Pudding, and Virginia Chicken Pudding. During and after the war, this inclination was more pronounced than ever, especially when authors were naming new recipes designed to get around wartime shortages, like Confederate Cakes or Rebel Pudding. Other Southern recipe titles served as a way for authors to honor people they admired, like Jackson Jumbles, a cookie probably named in honor of the Confederate general Stonewall Jackson. Especially in later books like *Mrs. Hill's New Cookbook* and *What Mrs. Fisher Knows about Old Southern Cooking*, it's obvious their authors realized that Southern cuisine was becoming an object of curiosity. Even as Hill claimed that she wrote her book to help "young and inexperienced Southern housekeepers," she clearly imagined Northern readers might also read her book and need explanations about Southern ways of doing things. For example, in her recipe for Scraffle (a variation on scrapple, a combination of pork scraps and spices and cornmeal), she explained it was made "during what we at the South call 'hog-killing.'" Likewise, when she mentioned gumbo in passing, she felt the need to define what gumbo was—"a thick soup."

Another way these books were different from the kinds of cookbooks written by Northern authors was in

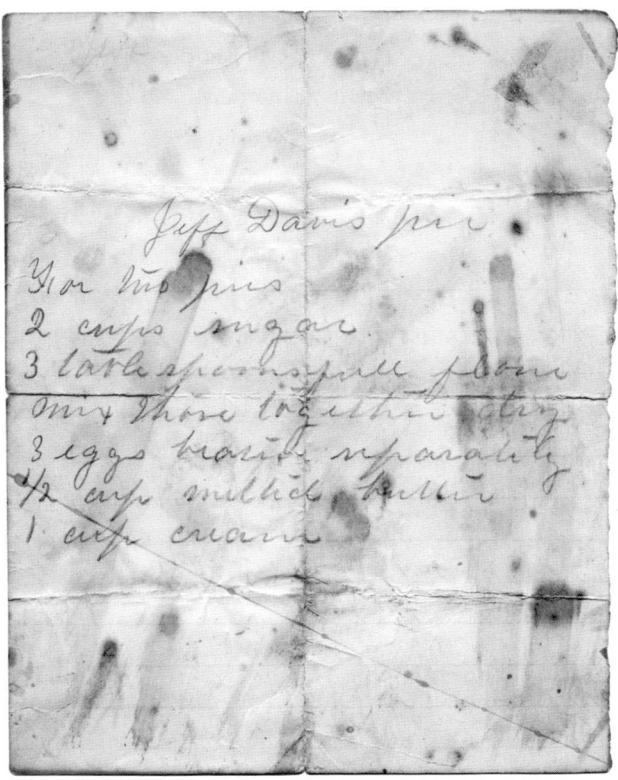

This anonymous, handwritten recipe for "Jeff Davis Pie," discovered tucked inside an 1870s cookbook, is an example of how Southerners used recipe titles to honor people they admired, including the Confederate president, Jefferson Davis. The recipe reads: "For two pies / 2 cups sugar / 3 table spoonsfull flour / Mix those together dry / 3 eggs beaten separately / ½ cup melted butter / 1 cup cream." It's also noteworthy that whoever jotted down this recipe knew enough about pie-making that she didn't feel the need to include more than the barest of instructions. Handwritten recipe on loose paper, tucked into *Housekeeping in the Blue Grass: A New and Practical Cook Book* (Cincinnati, OH: Robert Clarke, 1879), Michigan State University Special Collections.

their use of alcohol. In the North, the anti-alcohol movement had been gaining ground since the 1830s, and by the Civil War era, Northern cookbook authors realized that many of their readers wanted nothing to do with alcohol. When a Northern author called for wine in a recipe she very often included an alcohol-free alternative along with it, such as giving recipes for Mince Pie and Temperance Mince Pie back to back. In the South, the anti-alcohol movement was much less powerful, and Southern recipes reflect this. Recipe authors barely mentioned the existence of a temperance movement, and they were unapologetic about calling for alcohol in meat dishes, sauces, and desserts. They also happily walked readers through the steps of producing alcoholic drinks at home, giving recipes for an impressive array of beverages from Corn Beer to Cherry Cordial to Dewberry Bounce to Tomato Wine to Imperial Pop—a mildly alcoholic ginger beer. Southerners clearly relished these drinks. For example, the author of the Blackberry Wine recipe, in the *Confederate Receipt Book*, promised it would "make lips smack as they never smacked under similar influence before."

Another difference between Northern and Southern cookbooks in this period was their authors' attitudes about cooking. In truth, most middle-class American women were a little ambivalent about it. In the North, writers often alluded to the fact that their middle-class readers might have a servant doing most of the family's cooking, and they talked about the housewife as a manager as much as a manual laborer. But most Northern writers also assumed that many of their readers would be doing a lot of the cooking themselves. In contrast, Southern women who were wealthy enough to buy books before emancipation almost always would have had an enslaved woman to cook for them. That meant that prewar Southern cookbooks were targeted almost exclusively at women who didn't cook.

But even though elite white women rarely got their hands in the biscuit dough, that didn't mean they knew nothing about cooking. Maria Barringer, who wrote *Dixie Cookery* in the 1860s, was adamant on that point. Precisely because the cooks in elite Southern households were African Americans with no formal education or culinary training, Barringer argued, a white mistress had to know all about cooking because her cooks "must be of her own training, in the minutest particulars of every department." In reality, however, there was no substitute for experience. Elite white women didn't know *nothing* about cooking, but most of them probably didn't know a whole lot.[39] The war changed that, at least in some homes. When African Americans fled households where they had been enslaved, they often left behind white women who had to prepare much of their family's food for the first time. At a time when many elites associated cooking not just with poverty but with race, deteriorating conditions during the war gave some white women more contact with food production than they'd ever had before.[40] But that contact was often temporary. The war didn't demolish Southern hierarchies: white Southerners who had been wealthy before the war often kept a tenacious hold on money and privilege through Reconstruction and beyond.

The wealthiest Southerners usually maintained the privilege of ignorance about cooking, especially once the war was over. But as time went on, cookbooks both North and South were increasingly aimed at women who needed hands-on advice about cooking. Cooking in a nineteenth-century kitchen was hard even in the best of conditions. Just the physical tasks involved in a simple task like boiling carrots required time and muscle and judgment: a cook working by herself would have to pull carrots from a garden, haul water in order to wash them, scrape them and cut them up, chop wood or shovel coal, light and manage a fire, and haul more water to put in the pot. Executing multiple complicated recipes at once required high levels of skill. For those without experience, getting started must have felt overwhelming. Looking back from an age saturated in data, it can be hard to imagine how difficult it was for nineteenth-century Americans to get basic information about cooking, especially for the many uprooted Americans who had moved far from family or friends. For many Americans at the time, a detailed recipe would have been invaluable—although, of course, just having the resources to buy a book and the ability to read it were signs of privilege.[41]

Cookbooks were changing by the mid-nineteenth century, as authors gave more explicit instructions and made fewer assumptions about what a reader would know when she first opened the book. Annabella Hill apologized to "experienced housekeepers" that her directions might seem *"tediously minute."* She herself had married at age seventeen, she explained, and she said she was writing her cookbook to help newly married young women keeping house for the first time. Hill's book was part of a growing trend to include more precise ingredient quantities and more detailed descriptions about what to do with them, and sometimes she did just that. For instance, a beginner would have been grateful to read Hill's concrete instructions about frying fish: "It is important to know when the lard is hot enough. If not hot enough, the fish will be pale and sodden. A good and easy way to ascertain this is to throw a small piece of bread into the vessel. If it fries crisp, the lard is ready; if the bread burns, it is too hot."

Still, most of Hill's instructions will hardly look "tediously minute" to modern eyes. Most nineteenth-century cookbooks can seem incredibly vague, even those supposedly aimed at novices. Recipes often included no quantities at all for the ingredients they called for. And even when recipes did include quantities, they were often impressionistic, like butter "the size of a goose-egg" or "the weight of six eggs in sugar." To make matters worse, there weren't yet standardized measurements, so even seemingly precise descriptions like "a saltspoonful," "a wineglass of," or "a tumblerful" were approximations since everybody had different-sized spoons and glasses and tumblers.[42] Other recipes included *only* ingredients with no instructions about how to put them together, like the recipe for Molasses Custard in the Maryland recipe manuscript, which read in its entirety: "1 qt milk, 3 eggs well beaten, pinch salt, sweeten to your taste with molasses—nutmeg." Once a cook had estimated how much of each ingredient she needed and how to put them together, actually cooking was another exercise in guesswork because there was no reliable way to know how hot an oven was and no sure way to keep it at the same temperature. Cookbook authors tried to provide some guidance with phrases like "a moderate oven" or a "slow oven" or "a quick but not too hot oven." But it all really came down to guesswork and experience. For people with no experience, it must have seemed impossible.

Besides their brevity and vagueness, old recipes may surprise modern readers in other ways, too. One surprise might be the huge variety of animals people ate in the nineteenth century. There is plenty of pork and beef and chicken, but there are also recipes for frogs and squirrels, sheep and goats, partridges and pigeons, and turtles and eels, among other species. Nineteenth-century Southerners also ate much more of each animal's body, with recipes routinely calling for brain and heart and liver and lungs, ears and feet and skin. But even though the varieties of species and body parts called for in Southern cookbooks sound kaleidoscopic by our limited modern standards, it's worth reiterating that cookbooks still didn't capture the true breadth of what Southerners ate, especially during the upheavals of the war when some people became so desperate for food that they ate almost anything they could get their hands on.

Southern cookbooks also offer up other surprises, especially when they instruct readers to use ingredients in ways we might find strange or even disgusting today. Nineteenth-century Americans deep-fried cucumbers or dipped toasted bread in water before slathering it with sauce. They ate dishes like Tomato Pie and Irish Potato Pudding as sweet desserts, while they would have eaten recipes like Mary Randolph's oyster ice cream earlier in the meal. And when they gave a recipe for ketchup, they were just as likely to mean walnut or cucumber or oyster or mushroom ketchup as they were to mean tomato.

Another surprise is what a different meal breakfast was in the nineteenth century. Maria Barringer often noted when she thought a dish would be especially good for breakfast, but instead of pointing out pancakes or omelets, she suggested dishes like French Steak, pickled beef's liver, and eggplant. Annabella Hill suggested things like corned beef hash and fried sweet potatoes for breakfast. Nineteenth-century Americans often needed big breakfasts to fuel physically active workdays. But the middle- and upper-class practice of eating huge, hot breakfasts points to more than just calorie needs. Being able to eat costly meats, fresh breads, and cooked vegetables first thing in the morning was usually a sign the eater commanded the labor of a servant or a slave who could start cooking early in the morning. One reason modern American breakfasts took the form they did starting in the early twentieth century is that domestic servants were becoming less common and foods like eggs, boxed cereal, and toast made from bakery bread were all fast and easy to prepare.

This volume includes excerpts from seven sources: five formally published cookbooks, Confederate periodicals published during the war, and a never-before-published handwritten culinary manuscript from the Upper South. Some of the sources are already famous, like Mary Randolph's 1824 *Virginia Housewife*, widely considered the first Southern cookbook, and Abby Fisher's 1881 *What Mrs. Fisher Knows about Old Southern Cooking*, the first cookbook written by a formerly enslaved African American. Other sources here are more obscure, and the recipes from the handwritten Maryland manuscript have never before appeared in print. The sources are geographically diverse, with authors from Virginia, North Carolina, Georgia, Maryland, South Carolina, Alabama, and elsewhere across the South. And they span a relatively long period of time. Mary Randolph's book is by far the earliest, but it was enormously popular and was still influencing cooking throughout the region during the Civil War era; all the other sources excerpted here include some of the dishes and cooking styles Randolph described. Recipes from Confederate periodicals published over the course of the war gave Southerners a crash course in downward mobility as food conditions steadily worsened, and they give us a valuable sense of how concretely the war changed what people ate. The 1863 *Confederate Receipt Book*, the only cookbook published in the South during the war, offers a vivid snapshot of deteriorating conditions in the South and of the daily scramble for basic supplies. Although Maria Barringer's and Annabella Hill's books were both published after the war, they encapsulate prewar cooking styles in North Carolina and Georgia. The Maryland recipe manuscript, the only source from the Upper South, is a handwritten collection of recipes that span the 1850s to 1870. And Abby Fisher's book provides the perspective of a woman who had actually labored in the antebellum South as an enslaved cook.

Together, these sources provide an unusually rich picture of Southern cooking and eating in the Civil War era. But the nature of the sources that survived makes it a profoundly incomplete picture, with a disproportionate focus on the foods eaten by Southerners who were wealthy and white, precisely because poorer people left behind drastically fewer written sources. Very few Southerners would have had the luxury of free time in which to write a book. Even getting supplies of paper and ink would have been an insurmountable barrier to most potential authors, and that's for those lucky enough to be literate if the first place. The poorer you were, the less likely you were to know how to read and write, and that was particularly true if you were enslaved, since slave codes in many states had made it illegal to teach an enslaved person to read. It's no coincidence that Abby Fisher, the one formerly enslaved author included here, was illiterate and had to rely on others to transcribe the recipes she knew by heart. It's also no coincidence that while all the other postwar sources here included recipes with celebratory titles like "Secession Biscuits" or "Rebel Wine," only Fisher's book doesn't celebrate the Confederacy in any way.

A Note on Spelling, Punctuation, and Unfamiliar Terms

Nineteenth-century Americans sometimes spelled words differently. In these recipes you'll see words like *sallad, cullender, woffles, toffie, tumerick, ochra, brocoli, potatos, egg yelks*, and many other nonstandard spellings. Occasionally authors (or maybe editors) were inconsistent, and different spellings of one word appear in the same text. In general, I haven't changed nineteenth-century spelling or grammar to conform to modern rules unless I thought the text contained a typo that the authors themselves would have corrected if they had noticed it. In those cases, I either used brackets to insert a missing word or punctuation mark, or I corrected a typo and indicated that change in a note. I have inserted "[*sic*]" only very occasionally, when I thought there might be confusion over whether an error was original to the text.

At the end of the book is a glossary of terms that appeared multiple times in the cookbooks, which the editor judged likely to be unfamiliar to modern readers.

Mary Randolph,
The Virginia Housewife: or, Methodical Cook

First published in 1824, *The Virginia Housewife* is the earliest formally published Southern cookbook. And it is very Southern, with recipes for barbecued hog and gumbo, lima beans and hominy, corn bread and bacon, field peas and sweet potatoes. But look closer and you'll see the book plays against type, too, revealing how incredibly varied the food was that elite Southerners were eating in the nineteenth century. For every recipe for fried chicken, there are a half dozen more like baked mutton or pork with pease pudding or calf's feet fricassee. For every recipe for drop biscuits there are pages of recipes for polenta or broccoli or plum pudding or flummery. Look closer still, and you'll see that some ingredients that sound stereotypically Southern are full of surprises. A catfish recipe, for example, wasn't for fried fillets but for stewed fish covered with a curry sauce made with imported spices. One of Randolph's recipes for oysters instructs readers to make a thick oyster soup and then to freeze it and eat it like ice cream.

Mary Randolph subtitled her book *Methodical Cook*, and she laid heavy stress throughout on the importance of method. In her introduction, she argued that it was crucial to apply a rigorous system to home management. With proper organization and an hour's worth of planning from the mistress each morning, she promised, the household would run smoothly. But without a good system in place, "the mistress must then be called out, and thus have the horrible drudgery of keeping house all day." Imposing order was the task of the white mistress, in other words—not "drudgery." Drudgery was for slaves, a word Mary Randolph used openly, in contrast to later generations of Southerners who increasingly used only the misleading euphemism "servants" instead.

Randolph was writing to elite women in slaveholding households like hers, and she urged them to give their enslaved cooks *exactly* the amount of ingredients needed to cook each dish, one meal at a time. In this way, Randolph said, the cooks wouldn't be tempted to steal, as they surely would if barrels of white flour and crocks of butter and sides of ham were simply out for the taking. Randolph justified this parsimony by invoking the Lord's Prayer, saying it would be immoral to lead her enslaved workers into temptation. But she surely knew that enslaved people might be tempted to steal precisely because the rations parceled out to them were killingly monotonous in content—usually a variation on corn, molasses, and bacon—and sometimes miserly in quantity.

Randolph also urged her readers to adopt the habit of setting the table for the midday meal—and setting it grandly—right after breakfast, ensuring there was no unseemly rush before dinner. The table should be laid in the same way every day, she wrote, with "scrupulous regard to exact neatness and method, as if a grand company was expected." This sort of domestic order had all sorts of benefits, especially because a wife in constant readiness for unexpected visitors was a social boon to her husband, who could then feel free to invite friends at any time. Randolph also promised that a well-run home would be an inviting refuge for husbands themselves, making them less likely to flee to "haunts of dissipation," like a saloon. Sons and daughters raised in such a home, Randolph predicted, would turn out well. Grown sons would crave the atmosphere or morality and order in which they had grown up, and daughters would model themselves on their mother.

Randolph stressed the housewife's managerial role in the kitchen, rather than her involvement in the actual physical labor needed to cook food. Still, like many nineteenth-century cookbook writers, she assumed that her readers would know a lot about where their food came from. For example, she sometimes called for "new laid eggs" or instructed that lettuce should be gathered early in the morning. In some recipes she indicated that vegetables like okra, scallions, or beets, or animals like hogs and chickens, should be young. She also assumed her readers would be involved in butchery, or would at least be able to give instructions regarding it. In her recipe for rennet, for example, she told readers to remove "the stomach from the calf as soon as it is killed." Randolph's cookbook did not call for exclusively local food by any means; like all elite Southerners, much of her food would have been shipped from other places in the United States and even from other countries. But it's still telling that Mary Randolph assumed her readers would know things about their food's age and provenance and freshness that very few Americans do today.

Before reliable refrigeration, nineteenth-century Americans couldn't always get their hands on lettuce. But when they did eat it, it was often extremely fresh. Mary Randolph, for example, instructed readers to gather lettuce from the garden on the morning they planned to serve it. Illustration of white Silesian lettuce in Burr, *Field and Garden Vegetables*, 361.

Introduction

Management is an art that may be acquired by every woman of good sense and tolerable memory. If, unfortunately, she has been bred in a family where domestic business is the work of chance, she will have many difficulties to encounter; but a determined resolution to obtain this valuable knowledge, will enable her to surmount all obstacles. She must begin the day with an early breakfast, requiring each person to be in readiness to take their seats when the muffins, buckwheat cakes, &c. are placed on the table. This looks social and comfortable. When the family [members] breakfast by detachments, the table remains a tedious time; the servants are kept from their morning's meal, and a complete derangement takes place in the whole business of the day. No work can be done till breakfast is finished. The Virginia ladies, who are proverbially good managers, employ themselves, while their servants are eating, in washing the cups, glasses, &c.; arranging the cruets, the mustard, salt-sellers, pickle vases, and all the apparatus for the dinner table. This occupies but a short time, and the lady has the satisfaction of knowing that they are in much better order than they would be if left to the servants. It also relieves her from the trouble of seeing the dinner table prepared, which should be done every day with the same scrupulous regard to exact neatness and method, as if a grand company was expected. When the servant is required to do this daily, he soon gets into the habit of doing it well; and his mistress having made arrangements for him in the morning, there is no fear of bustle and confusion in running after things that may be called for during the hour of dinner. When the kitchen breakfast is over, and the cook has put all things in their proper places, the mistress should go in to give her orders. Let all the articles intended for the dinner, pass in review before her: have the butter, sugar, flour, meal, lard, given out in proper quantities; the catsup, spice, wine, whatever may be wanted for each dish, measured to the cook. The mistress must tax her own memory for with all this: we have no right to expect slaves or hired servants to be more attentive to our interest than we ourselves are: they will never recollect these little articles until they are going to use them; the mistress must then be called out, and thus have the horrible drudgery of keeping house all day, when one hour devoted to it in the morning, would release her from trouble until the next day. There is economy as well as comfort in a regular mode of doing business. When the mistress gives out every thing, there is no waste; but if temptation be thrown in the way of subordinates, not many will have power to resist it; besides, it is an immoral act to place them in a situation which we pray to be exempt from ourselves. The prosperity and happiness of a family depend greatly on the order and regularity established in it. The husband, who can ask a friend to partake of his dinner in full confidence of finding his wife unruffled by the petty vexations attendant on the neglect of household duties who can usher his guest into the dining-room assured of seeing that methodical nicety which is the essence of true elegance, will feel pride and exultation in the possession of a companion, who gives to his home charms that gratify every wish of his soul, and render the haunts of dissipation hateful to him. The sons bred in such a family will be moral men, of steady habits; and the daughters, if the mother shall have performed the duties of a parent in the superintendence of their education, as faithfully as she has done those of a wife, will each be a treasure to her husband; and being formed on the model of an exemplary mother, will use the same means for securing the happiness of her own family, which she has seen successfully practised under the paternal roof.

Asparagus Soup

Take four large bunches of asparagus, scrape it nicely, cut off one inch of the tops, and lay them in water, chop the stalks and put them on the fire with a piece of bacon, a large onion cut up, and pepper and salt; add two quarts of water, boil them till the stalks are quite soft, then pulp them through a sieve, and strain the water to it, which must be put back in the pot; put into it a chicken cut up, with the tops of asparagus which had been laid by, boil it until these last articles are sufficiently done, thicken with flour, butter and milk, and serve it up.

Oyster Soup

Wash and drain two quarts of oysters, put them on with three quarts of water, three onions chopped up, two or three slices of lean ham, pepper and salt; boil it till reduced one-half, strain it through a sieve, return the liquid into the pot, put in one quart of fresh oysters, boil it till they are sufficiently done, and thicken the soup with four spoonsful of flour, two gills of rich cream, and the yelks of six new laid eggs beaten well; boil it a few minutes after the thickening is put in. Take care that it does not curdle, and that the flour is not in lumps; serve it up with the last oysters that were put in. If the flavour of thyme be agreeable, you may put in a little, but take care that it does not boil in it long enough to discolour the soup.

Ochra Soup

Get two double handsful of young ochra, wash and slice it thin, add two onions chopped fine, put it into a gallon of water at a very early hour in an earthen pipkin, or very nice iron pot; it must be kept steadily simmering, but not boiling: put in pepper and salt. At 12 o'clock, put in a handful of Lima beans; at half-past one o'clock, add three young cimlins cleaned and cut in small pieces, a fowl, or knuckle of veal, a bit of bacon or pork that has been boiled, and six tomatos, with the skin taken off; when nearly done, thicken with a spoonful of butter, mixed with one of flour. Have rice boiled to eat with it.

Hare or Rabbit Soup

Cut up two hares, put them into a pot with a piece of bacon, two onions chopped, a bundle of thyme and parsley, which must be taken out before the soup is thickened, add pepper, salt, pounded cloves, and mace, put in a sufficient quantity of water, stew it gently three hours, thicken with a large spoonful of butter, and one of brown flour, with a glass of red wine; boil it a few minutes longer, and serve it up with the nicest parts of the hares. Squirrels make soup equally good, done the same way.

Catfish Soup

An excellent dish for those who have not imbibed a
needless prejudice against those delicious fish.

Take two large or four small white catfish that have been caught in deep water, cut off the heads, and skin and clean the bodies; cut each in three parts, put them in a pot, with a pound of lean bacon, a large onion cut up, a handful of parsley chopped small, some pepper and salt, pour in a sufficient quantity of water, and stew them till the fish are quite tender but not broken; beat the yelks of four fresh eggs, add to them a large spoonful of butter, two of flour, and half a pint of rich milk; make all these warm and thicken the soup, take out the bacon, and put some of the fish in your tureen, pour in the soup, and serve it up.

Brisket of Beef Baked

Bone a brisket of beef, and make holes in it with a sharp knife about an inch apart, fill them alternately with fat bacon, parsley and oysters, all chopped small and seasoned with pounded cloves and nutmeg, pepper and salt, dredge it well with flour, lay it in a pan with a pint of red wine and a large spoonful of lemon pickle; bake it three hours, take the fat from the gravy and strain it; serve it up garnished with green pickles.

Beef Olives

Cut slices from a fat rump of beef six inches long and half an inch thick, beat them well with a pestle; make a forcemeat of bread crumbs, fat bacon chopped, parsley, a little onion, some shred suet, pounded mace, pepper and salt; mix it up with the yelks of eggs, and spread a thin layer over each slice of beef, roll it up tight, and secure the rolls with skewers, set them before the fire, and turn them till they are a nice brown; have ready a pint of good gravy, thickened with brown flour and a spoonful of butter, a gill of red wine, with two spoonsful of mushroom catsup, lay the rolls in it, and stew them till tender; garnish with forcemeat balls.

A Fricando of Beef

Cut a few slices of beef six inches long, two or three wide, and one thick, lard them with bacon, dredge them well, and make them a nice brown before a brisk fire; stew them half an hour in a well seasoned gravy, put some stewed sorrel or spinage in the dish, lay on the beef, and pour over a sufficient quantity of gravy; garnish with fried balls.

A Nice Little Dish of Beef

Mince cold roast beef, fat and lean, very fine, add chopped onion, pepper, salt, and a little good gravy, fill scollop shell two parts full, and fill them up with potatos mashed smooth with cream, put a bit of butter on the top, and set them in an oven to brown.

Beef Steak Pie

Cut nice steaks, and stew them till half done, put a puff paste in the dish, lay in the steaks with a few slices of boiled ham, season the gravy very high, pour it in the dish, put on a lid of paste and bake it.

To Make a Pie of Sweetbreads and Oysters

Boil the sweetbreads tender, stew the oysters, season them with pepper and salt, and thicken with cream, butter, the yelks of eggs and flour, put a puff paste at the bottom and around the sides of a deep dish, take the oysters up with an egg spoon, lay them in the bottom, and cover them with the sweetbreads, fill the dish with gravy, put a paste on the top, and bake it. This is the most delicate pie that can be made. The sweetbread of veal is the most delicious part, and may be broiled, fried, or dressed in any way, and is always good.

Calf's Feet Fricassee

Boil the feet till very tender, cut them in two and pull out the large bones, have half a pint of good white gravy, add to it a spoonful of white wine, one of lemon pickle, and some salt, with a tea-spoonful of curry powder, stew the feet in it fifteen minutes, and thicken it with the yelks of two eggs, a gill of milk, a large spoonful of butter, and two of white flour, let the thickening be very smooth, shake the stew pan over the fire a few minutes, but do not let it boil lest the eggs and milk should curdle.

To Prepare Rennet

Take the stomach from the calf as soon as it is killed—do not wash it, but hang it in a dry cool place for four or five days; then turn it inside out, slip off all the curd nicely with the hand, fill it with a little saltpetre mixed with the quantity of salt necessary, and lay it in a small stone pot, pour over it a small tea-spoonful of vinegar, and sprinkle a handful of salt over it, cover it closely and keep it for use. You must not wash it—that would weaken the gastric juice, and injure the rennet. After it has been salted six or eight weeks, cut off a piece four or five inches long, put it in a large mustard bottle, or any vessel that will hold about a pint and a half; put on it five gills of cold water, and two gills of rose brandy—stop it very close, and shake it when you are going to use it: a table-spoonful of this is sufficient for a quart of milk. It must be prepared in very cool weather, and if well done, will keep more than a year.

Baked Leg of Mutton

Take the flank off, but leave all the fat, cut out the bone, stuff the place with a rich forcemeat, lard the top and sides with bacon, put it in a pan with a pint of water, some chopped onion and cellery cut small, a gill of red wine, one of mushroom catsup and a tea-spoonful of carry powder, bake it and serve it up with the gravy, garnish with forcemeat balls fried.

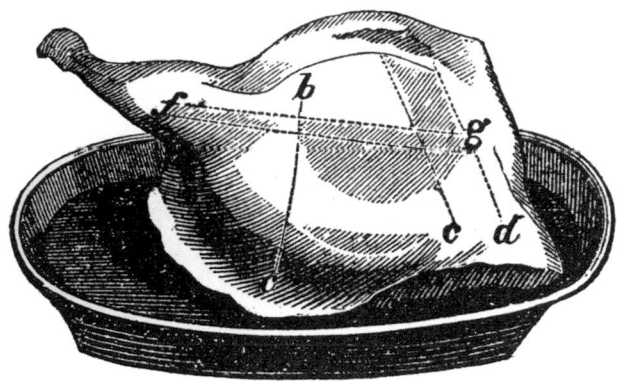

A diagram showing how to carve mutton. Hill, *Mrs. Hill's Southern Practical Cookery*, facsimile of 1872 edition, 87.

To Cure Bacon

Hogs are in the highest perfection, from two and a half to four years old, and make the best bacon, when they do not weigh more than one hundred and fifty or sixty at farthest; they should be fed with corn, six weeks at least, before they are killed, and the shorter distance they are driven to market, the better will their flesh be. To secure them against the possibility of spoiling, salt them before they get cold; take out the chine or back-bone from the neck to the tail, cut the hams, shoulders and middlings; take the ribs from the shoulders and the leaf fat from the hams: have such tubs as are directed for beef, rub a large table spoonful of saltpetre on the inside of each ham, for some minutes, then rub both sides well with salt, sprinkle the bottom of the tub with salt, lay the hams with the skin downward, and put a good deal of salt between each layer; salt the shoulders and middlings

in the same manner, but less saltpetre is necessary; cut the jowl or chop from the head, and rub it with salt and saltpetre. You should cut off the feet just above the knee joint; take off the ears and nose, and lay them in a large tub of cold water for souse. When the jowls have been in salt two weeks, hang them up to smoke[;] do so with the shoulders and middlings at the end of three weeks, and the hams at the end of four. If they remain longer in salt they will be hard. Remember to hang the hams and shoulders with the hocks down, to preserve the juices. Make a good smoke every morning, and be careful not to have a blaze; the smoke-house should stand alone, for any additional heat will spoil the meat. During the hot weather, beginning the first of April, it should be occasionally taken down, examined[,] rubbed with hickory ashes, and hung up again.

The generally received opinion that saltpetre hardens meat, is entirely erroneous: it tends greatly to prevent putrefaction, but will not make it hard; neither will laying in brine five or six weeks in cold weather, have that effect, but remaining in salt too long, will certainly draw off the juices, and harden it. Bacon should be boiled in a large quantity of water, and a ham is not done sufficiently, till the bone on the under part comes off with ease. New bacon requires much longer boiling than that which is old.

To Make Souse

Let all the pieces you intend to souse, remain covered with cold water twelve hours; then wash them out, wipe off the blood, and put them again in fresh water; soak them in this manner, changing the water frequently, and keeping it in a cool place, till the blood is drawn away; scrape and clean each piece perfectly nice, mix some meal with water, add salt to it, and boil your souse gently, until you can run a straw into the skin with ease. Do not put too much in the pot, for it will boil to pieces and spoil the appearance. The best way is to boil the feet in one pot, the ears and nose in another, and the heads in a third; these should be boiled till you can take all the bones out; let them get cold, season the insides with pepper, salt, and a little nutmeg; make it in a tight roll, sew it up close in a cloth, and press it lightly. Mix some more meal and cold water, just enough to look white; add salt, and one-fourth of vinegar; put your souse in different pots, and keep it well covered with this mixture, and closely stopped. It will be necessary to renew this liquor every two or three weeks. Let your souse get quite cold after boiling, before you put it in the liquor, and be sure to use pale coloured vinegar, or the souse will be dark. Some cooks singe the hair from the feet, etcetera, but this destroys the colour: good souse will always be white.

To Roast a Pig

The pig must be very fat, nicely cleaned, and not too large to lie in the dish; chop the liver fine and mix it with crumbs of bread, chopped onion and parsley, with pepper and salt, make it into a paste with butter and an egg, stuff the body well with it, and sew it up, spit it, and have a clear fire to roast it; baste with salt and water at first, then rub it frequently with a lump of lard wrapped in a piece of clean linen; this will make it much more crisp than basting it from the dripping pan. When the pig is done, take off the head, separate the face from the chop, cut both in two and take off the ears, take out the stuffing, split the pig in two parts lengthways, lay it in the dish with the head, ears, and feet, which have been cut off, placed on each side, put the stuffing in a bowl with a glass of wine, and as much dripping as will make it sufficiently liquid, put some of it under the pig, and serve the rest in a boat.

To Barbecue Shote

This is the name given in the southern states to a fat young hog, which, when the head and feet are taken off, and it is cut into four quarters, will weigh six pounds per quarter. Take a fore-quarter, make several incisions between the ribs, and stuff it with rich forcemeat; put it in pan with a pint of water, two cloves of garlic, pepper, salt, two gills of red wine, and two of mushroom catsup, bake it, and thicken the gravy with butter and brown flour; it must be jointed, and the ribs cut across before it is cooked, or it cannot be carved well; lay it in the dish with the ribs uppermost; if it be not sufficiently brown, add a little burnt sugar to the gravy, garnish with balls.

Leg of Pork with Pease Pudding

Boil a small leg of pork that has been sufficiently salted, score the top and serve it up; the pudding must be in a separate dish; get small delicate pease, wash them well, and tie them in a cloth, allowing a little room for swelling, boil them with the pork, then mash and season them, tie them up again and finish boiling it; take care not to break the pudding in turning it out.

To Make Sausages

Take the tender pieces of fresh pork, chop them exceedingly fine—chop some of the leaf fat, and put them together in the proportion of three pounds of pork to one of fat, season it very high with pepper and salt, add a small quantity of dried sage rubbed to a powder, have the skins nicely prepared, fill them and hang them in a dry place. Sausages are excellent made into cakes and fried, but will not keep so well as in skins.

To Make Black Puddings

Catch the blood as it runs from the hog, stir it continually till cold to prevent its coagulating; when cold thicken it with boiled rice or oatmeal, add leaf fat chopped small, pepper, salt, and any herbs that are liked, fill the skins and smoke them two or three days; they must be boiled before they are hung up, and prick them with a fork to keep them from bursting.

A Sea Pie

Lay at the bottom of a small Dutch oven some slices of boiled pork or salt beef, then potatos and onions cut in slices, salt, pepper, thyme and parsley shred fine, some crackers soaked, and a layer of fowls cut up, or slices of veal; cover them with a paste not too rich, put another layer of each article, and cover them with paste until the oven is full; put a little butter between each layer, pour in water till it reaches the top crust, to which you must add wine, catsup of any kind you please, and some pounded cloves; let it stew until there is just gravy enough left; serve it in a deep dish and pour the gravy on.

To Make Paste for the Pie

Pour half a pound of butter or dripping, boiling hot, into a quart of flour, add as much water as will make it a paste, work it and roll it well before you use it. It is quite a savoury paste.

To Bake a Shad

The shad is a very indifferent fish unless it be large and fat; when you get a good one, prepare it nicely, put some forcemeat inside, and lay it at full length in a pan with a pint of water, a gill of red wine, one of mushroom catsup, a little pepper, vinegar, salt, a few cloves of garlic, and six cloves: stew it gently till the gravy is sufficiently reduced; there should always be a fish-slice with holes to lay the fish on, for the convenience of dishing without breaking it; when the fish is taken up, slip it carefully into the dish; thicken the gravy with butter and brown flour, and pour over it.

To Fry Perch

Clean the fish nicely, but do not take out the roes; dry them on a cloth, sprinkle some salt; and dredge them with flour, lay them separately on a board; when one side is dry, turn them, sprinkle salt and dredge the other side; be sure the lard boils when you put the fish in, and fry them with great care; they should be a yellowish brown when done. Send melted butter or anchovy sauce in a boat.

To Pickle Oysters

Select the largest oysters, drain off their liquor, and wash them in clean water; pick out the pieces of shells that may be left, put them in a stew pan with water proportioned to the number of oysters, some salt, blades of mace, and whole black pepper; stew them a few minutes, then put them in a pot, and when cold, add as much pale vinegar as will give the liquor an agreeable acid.

To Make a Curry of Catfish

Take the white channel catfish, cut off their heads, skin and clean them, cut them in pieces four inches long, put as many as will be sufficient for a dish into a stew pan with a quart of water, two onions, and chopped parsley; let them stew gently till the water is reduced to half a pint, take the fish out and lay them on a dish, cover them to keep them hot, rub a spoonful of butter into one of flour, add a large tea-spoonful of curry powder, thicken the gravy with it, shake it over the fire a few minutes, and pour it over the fish; be careful to have the gravy smooth.

Chowder, a Sea Dish

Take any kind of firm fish, cut it in pieces six inches long, sprinkle salt and pepper over each piece, cover the bottom of a small Dutch oven with slices of salt pork about half boiled, lay in the fish, strewing a little chopped onion between; cover with crackers that have been soaked soft in milk, pour over it two gills of white wine, and two of water; put on the top of the oven, and stew it gently about an hour; take it out carefully, and lay it in a deep dish; thicken the gravy with a little flour and a spoonful of butter, add some chopped parsley, boil it a few minutes, and pour it over the fish[;] serve it up hot.

To Dress Cod Fish

Boil the fish tender, pick it from the bones, take an equal quantity of Irish potatos, or parsnips boiled and chopped, and the same of onions well boiled; add a sufficiency of melted butter, some grated nutmeg, pepper, and salt, with a little brandy or wine; rub them in a mortar till well mixed; if too stiff, liquify it with cream or thickened milk, put paste in the bottom of a dish, pour in the fish, and bake it. For change, it may be baked in the form of patties.

Cod Fish Pie

Soak the fish, boil it and take off the skin, pick the meat from the bones, and mince it very fine; take double the quantity of your fish, of stale bread grated; pour over it as much new milk, boiling hot, as will wet it completely, add minced parsley, nutmeg, pepper, and made mustard, with as much melted butter as will make it sufficiently rich; the quantity must be determined by that of the other ingredients[;] beat these together very well, add the minced fish, mix it all, cover the bottom of the dish with good paste, pour the fish in, put on a lid and bake it.

Fish in Jelly

Fill a deep glass dish half full of jelly[;] have as many small fish-moulds as will lie conveniently in it, fill them with blanc mange; when they are cold, and the jelly set, lay them on it, as if going in different directions; put in a little more jelly, and let it get cold, to keep the fish in their places then fill the dish so as to cover them. The jelly should be made of hog's feet, very light coloured, and perfectly transparent.

To Pitchcock Eels

Skin and wash your eels, then dry them with a cloth, sprinkle them with pepper, salt, and a little dried sage, turn them backward and forward, and skewer them; rub a gridiron with beef suet, broil them a nice brown, put them on a dish with good melted butter, and lay around fried parsley.

To Scollop Oysters

When the oysters are opened, put them in a bowl, and wash them out of their own liquor; put some in the scollop shells, strew over them a few bread crumbs, and lay a slice of butter on them, then more oysters, bread crumbs, and a slice of butter on the top; put them into a Dutch oven to brown, and serve them up in the shells.

To Fry Oysters

Take a quarter of a hundred of large oysters, wash them and roll them in grated bread, with pepper and salt, and fry them a light brown; if you choose, you may add a little parsley, shred fine. They are a proper garnish for calves' head, or most made dishes.

To Make Oyster Loaves

Take little round loaves, cut off the tops, scrape out all the crumbs, then put the oysters into a stew pan with the crumbs that came out of the loaves, a little water, and a good lump of butter; stew them together ten or fifteen minutes, then put in a spoonful of good cream, fill your loaves, lay the bit of crust carefully on again, set them in the oven to crisp. Three are enough for a side dish.

To Roast a Goose

Chop a few sage leaves and two onions very fine, mix them with a good lump of butter, a tea-spoonful of pepper, and two of salt, put it in the goose, then spit it, lay it down, and dust it with flour; when it is thoroughly hot, baste it with nice lard; if it be a large one, it will require an hour and a half, before a good clear fire; when it is enough, dredge and baste it, pull out the spit, and pour in a little boiling water.

To Make Sauce for a Goose

Pare, core and slice some apples; put them in a sauce pan, with as much water as will keep them from burning, set them over a very slow fire, keep them closely covered till reduced to a pulp, then put in a lump of butter, and sugar to your taste, beat them well, and send them to the table in a china bowl.

To Boil a Turkey with Oyster Sauce

Grate a loaf of bread, chop a score or more of oysters fine, add nutmeg, pepper and salt to your taste, mix it up into a light forcemeat with a quarter of a pound of butter, a spoonful or two of cream, and three eggs; stuff the craw with it, and make the rest into balls and boil them; sew up the turkey, dredge it well with flour, put it in a kettle of cold water, cover it, and set it over the fire; as the scum begins to rise, take it off, let it boil very slowly for half an hour, then take off your kettle and keep it closely covered; if it be of a middle size, let it stand in the hot water half an hour, the steam being kept in, will stew it enough, make it rise, keep the skin whole, tender, and very white; when you dish it, pour on a little oyster sauce, lay the balls round, and serve it up with the rest of the sauce in a boat.

N.B. Set on the turkey in time, that it may stew as above; it is the best way to boil one to perfection. Put it over the fire to heat, just before you dish it up.

To Make Sauce for a Turkey

As you open the oysters, put a pint into a bowl, wash them out of their own liquor, and put them in another bowl; when the liquor has settled, pour it off into a sauce pan with a little white gravy, and a tea-spoonful of lemon pickle[;] thicken it with flour and a good lump of butter; boil it three or four minutes, put in a spoonful of good cream, add the oysters, keep shaking them over the fire till they are quite hot, but don't let them boil, for it will make them hard and appear small.

To Roast Young Chickens

When you kill young chickens, pluck them very carefully, truss and put them down to a good fire, dredge and baste them with lard; they will take a quarter of an hour in roasting; froth them up, lay them on the dish, pour butter and parsley on, and serve them up hot.

Fried Chickens

Cut them up as for the fricassee, dredge them well with flour, sprinkle them with salt, put them into a good quantity of boiling lard, and fry them a light brown; fry small pieces of mush and a quantity of parsley nicely picked, to be served in the dish with the chickens; take half a pint of rich milk, add to it a small bit of butter, with pepper, salt, and chopped parsley; stew it a little, and pour it over the chickens, and then garnish with the fried parsley.

To Roast Woodcocks or Snipes

Pluck, but do not draw them, put them on a small spit, dredge and baste them well with lard, toast a few slices of bread, put them on a clean plate, and set it under the birds while they are roasting; if the fire be good, they will take about ten minutes; when you take them from the spit, lay them upon the toasts on the dish, pour melted butter round them, and serve them up.

To Roast Wild Ducks or Teal

When the ducks are ready dressed, put in them a small onion, pepper, salt, and a spoonful of red wine; if the fire be good, they will roast in twenty minutes; make gravy of the necks and gizzards, a spoonful of red wine, half an anchovy, a blade or two of mace, one onion, and a little cayenne pepper; boil it till it is wasted to half a pint, strain it through a hair sieve, and pour it on the ducks[;] serve them up with onion sauce in a boat; garnish the dish with raspings of bread.

To Roast Partridges or Any Small Birds

Lard them with slips of bacon, put them on a skewer, tie it to the spit at both ends, dredge and baste them, let them roast ten minutes, take the grated crumb of half a loaf of bread, with a piece of butter, the size of a walnut, put it in a stew pan, and shake it over a gentle fire till it is of a light brown, lay it between your birds, and pour over them a little melted butter.

To Roast Rabbits

When you have cased the rabbits, skewer their heads with their mouths upon their backs, stick their fore-legs into their ribs, skewer the hind-legs doubled, then make a pudding for them of the crumb of half a loaf of bread, a little parsley, sweet marjoram and thyme, all shred fine, nutmeg, salt and pepper to your taste, mix them up into a light stuffing, with a quarter of a pound of butter, a little good cream, and two eggs; put it into the body, and sew them up; dredge and baste them well with lard, roast them near an hour, serve them up with parsley and butter for sauce, chop the livers, and lay them in lumps round the edge of the dish.

To Stew Wild Ducks

Having prepared the fowls, rub the insides with salt, pepper, and a little powdered cloves; put a shallot or two with a lump of butter in the body of each, then lay them in a pan that will just hold them, putting butter under and over them, with vinegar and water, and add pepper, salt, lemon peel, and a bunch of sweet herbs; then cover the pan close, and let them stew till done[;] pass the liquor through a sieve, pour it over the ducks, and serve them up hot, with a garnish of lemon sliced, and raspings of bread fried. The same way may teal, &c. be dressed.

To Make a Dish of Curry after the East Indian Manner

Cut two chickens as for fricassee, wash them clean, and put them in a stew pan with as much water as will cover them; sprinkle them with a large spoonful of salt, and let them boil till tender, covered close all the time, and skim them well; when boiled enough, take up the chickens, and put the liquor of them into a pan, then put half a pound of fresh butter in the pan, and brown it a little; put into it two cloves of garlic, and a large onion sliced, and let these all fry till brown, often shaking the pan; then put in the chickens, and sprinkle over them two or three spoons-ful of curry powder; then cover the pan close, and let the chickens do till brown, often shaking the pan; then put in the liquor the chickens were boiled in, and let all stew till tender; if acid is agreeable, squeeze the juice of a lemon or orange in it.

Ochra and Tomatos

Take an equal quantity of each, let the ochra be young, slice it, and skin the tomatos; put them into a pan without water, add a lump of butter, an onion chopped fine, some pepper and salt, and stew them one hour.

Gumbo—a West India Dish

Gather young pods of ochra, wash them clean, and put them in a pan with a little water, salt and pepper, stew them till tender, and serve them with melted butter. They are very nutritious, and easy of digestion.

Pepper Pot

Boil two or three pounds of tripe, cut it in pieces, and put it on the fire with a knuckle of veal, and a sufficient quantity of water; part of a pod of pepper, a little spice, sweet herbs according to your taste, salt, and some dumplins [sic]; stew it till tender, and thicken the gravy with butter and flour.

To Make an Ollo—a Spanish Dish

Take two pounds beef, one pound mutton, a chicken, or half a pullet, and a small piece of pork; put them into a pot with very little water, and set it on the fire at ten o'clock, to stew gently; you must sprinkle over it an onion chopped small, some pepper and salt, before you pour in the water; at half after twelve, put into the pot two or three apples or pears, peeled and cut in two, tomatos with the skin taken off, cimblins cut in pieces, a handful of mint chopped, lima beans, snaps, and any kind of vegetable you like; let them all stew together till three o'clock; some cellery tops cut small, and added at half after two, will improve it much.

Chicken Pudding, a Favourite Virginia Dish

Beat ten eggs very light, add to them a quart of rich milk, with a quarter of a pound of butter melted, and some pepper and salt; stir in as much flour as will make a thin good batter; take four young chickens, and after cleaning them nicely, cut off the legs, wings, &c. put them all in a sauce pan, with some salt and water, and a bundle of thyme and parsley, boil them till nearly done, then take the chicken from the water and put it in the batter, pour it in a deep dish, and bake it; send nice white gravy in a boat.

To Make Polenta

Put a large spoonful of butter in a quart of water, wet your corn meal with cold water in a bowl, add some salt, and make it quite smooth, then put it in the buttered water when it is hot, let it boil, stirring it continually till done; as soon as you can handle it, make it into a ball, and let it stand till quite cold then cut it in thin slices, lay them in the bottom of a deep dish so as to cover it, put on it slices of cheese, and on that a few bits of butter; then mush, cheese and butter, until the dish is full; put on the top thin slices of cheese and butter, put the dish in a quick oven; twenty or thirty minutes will bake it.

Macaroni

Boil as much macaroni as will fill your dish, in milk and water, till quite tender; drain it on a sieve, sprinkle a little salt over it, put a layer in your dish, then cheese and butter as in the polenta, and bake it in the same manner.

To Make Croquets

Take cold fowl or fresh meat of any kind, with slices of ham, fat and lean[;] chop them together very fine, add half as much stale bread grated, salt, pepper, grated nutmeg, a teaspoonful of made mustard, a table-spoonful of catsup, and a lump of butter; knead all well together till it resembles sausage meat, make them in cakes, dip them in the yelk of an egg beaten, cover them thickly with grated bread, and fry them a light brown.

To Make Vermecelli

Beat two or three fresh eggs quite light, make them into a stiff paste with flour, knead it well, and roll it out very thin, cut it in narrow strips, give them a twist, and dry them quickly on tin sheets. It is an excellent ingredient in most soups, particularly those that are thin. Noodles are made in the same manner, only instead of strips they should be cut in tiny squares and dried. They are also good in soups.

Fondus

Put a pint of water, and a lump of butter the size of an egg, into a sauce pan; stir in as much flour as will make a thick batter, put it on the fire, and stir it continually till it will not stick to the pan; put it in a bowl, add three quarters of a pound of grated cheese, mix it well, then break in two eggs, beat them well, then two more until you put in six; when it looks very light, drop it in small lumps on buttered paper, bake it in a quick oven till of a delicate brown; you may use corn meal instead of flour for a change.

A Nice Twelve O'Clock Luncheon

Cut some slices of bread tolerably thick, and toast them slightly; bone some anchovies, lay half of one on each toast, cover it well with grated cheese and chopped parsley mixed; pour a little melted butter on, and brown it with a salamander;[1] it must be done on the dish you send it to table in.

Cabbage a-la-Creme

Take two good heads of cabbage, cut out the stalks, boil it tender, with a little salt in the water have ready one large spoonful of butter, and a small one of flour rubbed into it, half a pint of milk, with pepper and salt; make it hot, put the cabbage in after pressing out the water, and stew it till quite tender.

Gaspacho—Spanish

Put some soft biscuit or toasted bread in the bottom of a sallad bowl, put in a layer of sliced tomatos with the skin taken off, and one of sliced cucumbers, sprinkled with pepper, salt, and chopped onion; do this until the bowl is full; stew some tomatos quite soft, strain the juice, mix in some mustard, oil, and water, and pour over it; make it two hours before it is eaten.

Fish Sauce, to Keep a Year

Chop twenty-four anchovies, bones and all, ten shallots, a handful of scraped horse radish, four blades of mace, one quart of white wine, one pint of anchovy liquor, one pint of claret, twelve cloves, and twelve pepper corns; boil them together till reduced to a quart, then strain it off into a bottle for use. Two spoonsful will be sufficient for a pound of butter.

Sauce for Wild Fowl

Take a gill of claret, with as much water, some grated bread, three heads of shallots, a little whole pepper, mace, grated nutmeg, and salt; let them stew over the fire, then beat it up with butter, and put it under the wild fowl, which being a little roasted, will afford gravy to mix with this sauce.

Gravy

Take a rasher or two of bacon, and lay it at the bottom of a stew pan, putting either veal, mutton, or beef, cut in slices, over it; then add some sliced onions, turnips, carrots, celery, a little thyme, and alspice. Put in a little water, and set it on the fire, stewing till it be brown at the bottom, which you will know from the pan's hissing; then pour boiling water over it, and stew it an hour and a half; but the time must be regulated by the quantity. Season it with salt and pepper.

Shrimp Sauce

Wash half a pint of shrimps very clean[;] mince and put them in a stew-pan, with a spoonful of anchovy liquor, and a pound of thick melted butter; boil it up for five minutes, and squeeze in half a lemon. Toss it up, and put in a sauce-boat.

Oyster Sauce for Fish

Scald a pint of oysters, and strain them through a sieve; then wash some more in cold water, and take off their beards; put them in a stew-pan, and pour the liquor over them; then add a large spoonful of anchovy liquor, half a lemon, two blades of mace, and thicken it with butter rolled in flour. Put in half a pound of butter, and boil it till it is melted[;] take out the mace and lemon, and squeeze the lemon juice into the sauce; boil it, and stir it all the time, and put it in a boat.

Celery Sauce

Wash and pare a large bunch of celery very clean, cut it into little bits, and boil it softly till it is tender; add half a pint of cream, some mace, nutmeg, and a small piece of butter rolled in flour; then boil it gently. This is a good sauce for roasted or boiled fowls, turkeys, partridges, or any other game.

Mushroom Sauce

Clean and wash one quart of fresh mushrooms, cut them in two, and put them into a stew-pan, with a little salt, a blade of mace, and a little butter; stew them gently for half an hour, and then add half a pint of cream, and the yelks of two eggs beat very well[;] keep stirring it till it boils up. Put it over the fowls or turkies or you may put it on a dish with a piece of fried bread first buttered then toasted brown, and just dipped into boiling water. This is very good sauce for white fowls of all kinds.

Caper Sauce

Is made by mixing a sufficient quantity of capers, and adding them to the melted butter, with a little of the liquor from the capers; where capers cannot be obtained, pickled nasturtiums make a very good substitute, or even green pickle minced and put with the butter.

Oyster Catsup

Get fine fresh oysters, wash them in their own liquor, put them in a marble mortar with salt, pounded mace, and cayenne pepper, in the proportions of one ounce salt, two drachms mace, and one of cayenne to each pint of oysters; pound them together, and add a pint of white wine to each pint; boil it some minutes, and rub it through a sieve; boil it again, skim it, and when cold, bottle, cork, and seal it. This composition gives a fine flavour to white sauces, and if a glass of brandy be added, it will keep good for a considerable time.

Celery Vinegar

Pound two gills of celery seed, put it into a bottle and fill it with strong vinegar; shake it every day for a fortnight, then strain it, and keep it for use. It will impart a pleasant flavour of celery to any thing with which it is used. A very delicious flavour of thyme may be obtained, by gathering it when in full perfection; it must be picked from the stalks, a large handful of it put into a jar, and a quart of vinegar or brandy poured on it; cover it very close next day, take all the thyme out, put in as much more; do this a third time; then strain it, bottle and seal it securely. This is greatly preferable to the dried thyme commonly used, during the season when it cannot be obtained in a fresh state. Mint may be prepared in the same way. The flavour of both these herbs must be preserved by care in the preparation: if permitted to stand more than twenty hours in the liquor they are infused in, a coarse and bitter taste will be extracted, particularly from mint.

To Dress Salad

To have this delicate dish in perfection, the lettuce, pepper grass, chervil, cress, &c. should be gathered early in the morning, nicely picked, washed, and laid in cold water, which will be improved by adding ice; just before dinner is ready to be served, drain the water from your salad, cut it into a bowl, giving the proper proportions of each plant; prepare the following mixture to pour over it: boil two fresh eggs ten minutes, put them in water to cool, then take the yelks in a soup plate, pour on them a table spoonful of cold water, rub them with a wooden spoon until they are perfectly dissolved; then add two spoonsful of oil: when well mixed, put in a teaspoonful of salt, one of powdered sugar, and one of made mustard;

when all these are united and quite smooth, stir in two table spoonsful of common [vinegar], and two of tarragon vinegar; put it over the salad, and garnish the top with the whites of the eggs cut into rings, and lay around the edge of the bowl young scallions, they being the most delicate of the onion tribe.

Potato Balls

Mix mashed potatos with the yelk of an egg, roll them into balls, flour them, or cover them with egg and bread crumbs, fry them in clean dripping, or brown them in a Dutch oven. They are an agreeable vegetable relish, and a supper dish.

Asparagus

Set a stew-pan with plenty of water on the fire, sprinkle a handful of salt in it, let it boil, and skim it; then put in the asparagus prepared thus: scrape all the stalks till they are perfectly clean; throw them into a pan of cold water as you scrape them; when they are all done, tie them in little bundles, of a quarter of a hundred each, with bass, if you can get it, or tape; cut off the stalks at the bottom, that they may be all of a length; when they are tender at the stalk, which will be in from twenty to thirty minutes, they are done enough. Great care must be taken to watch the exact time of their becoming tender; take them just at that instant, and they will have their true flavour and colour; a minute or two more boiling destroys both. While the asparagus is boiling, toast a slice of a loaf of bread, about a half an inch thick; brown it delicately on both sides; dip it lightly in the liquor the asparagus was boiled in, and lay it in the middle of a dish; pour some melted butter on the toast, and lay the asparagus upon it; let it project beyond the asparagus, that the company may see there is a toast. Do not pour butter over them, but send some in a boat.

Sea-Kale

Is tied up in bundles, and dressed in the same way as asparagus.

A cousin of cabbage, sea kale was a popular vegetable in early nineteenth-century America, and a favorite of Thomas Jefferson's. Its stems could be prepared like asparagus, as Randolph suggested here, while the large leaves could be prepared like collard greens. Sea kale illustration in White, *Gardening for the South*, 298.

Red Beet Roots

Are not so much used as they deserve to be; they are dressed in the same way as parsnips, only neither scraped nor cut till after they are boiled; they will take from an hour and a half to three hours in boiling, according to their size; to be sent to the table with salt fish, boiled beef, &c. When young, small and juicy, it is a very good variety, an excellent garnish, and easily converted into a very cheap and pleasant pickle.

Carrots

Let them be well washed and scraped—an hour is enough for young spring carrots; grown carrots will take from an hour and a half to two hours and a half. The best way to try if they are done enough, is to pierce them with a fork.

To Mush Turnips

When they are boiled quite tender, squeeze them as dry as possible[;] put them into a sauce pan, mash them with a wooden spoon, and rub them through a colander; add a little bit of butter, keep stirring them till the butter is melted and well mixed with them, and they are ready for table.

Brocoli

The kind which bears flowers around the joints of the stalks, must be cut into convenient lengths for the dish; scrape the skin from the stalk, and pick out any leaves or flowers that require to be removed; tie it up in bunches, and boil it as asparagus; serve it up hot, with melted butter poured over it. The brocoli that heads at the top like cauliflowers, must be dressed in the same manner as the cauliflower.

Peas

To have them in perfection, they must be quite young, gathered early in the morning, kept in a cool place, and not shelled until they are to be dressed; put salt in the water, and when it boils, put in the peas; boil them quick twenty or thirty minutes, according to their age; just before they are taken up, add a little mint chopped very fine; drain all the water from the peas, put in a bit of butter, and serve them up quite hot.

Ragout of French Beans, Snaps, String Beans

Let them be young and fresh gathered, string them, and cut them in long thin slices; throw them in boiling water for fifteen minutes; have ready some well seasoned brown gravy, drain the water from the beans, put them in the gravy, stew them a few minutes, and serve them garnished with forcemeat balls; there must not be gravy enough to float the beans.

Lima, or Sugar Beans

Like all other spring and summer vegetables, they must be young and freshly gathered: boil them till tender, drain them, add a little butter, and serve them up. These beans are easily preserved for winter use, and will be nearly as good as fresh ones. Gather them on a dry day, when full grown, but quite young: have a clean and dry keg, sprinkle some salt in the bottom, put in a layer of pods, containing the beans, then a little salt[;] do this till the keg is full; lay a board on with a weight, to press them down; cover the keg very close, and keep it in a dry, cool place[;] they should be put up as late in the season, as they can be with convenience. When used, the pods must be washed, and laid in fresh water all night; shell them next day, and keep them in water till you are going to boil them; when tender, serve them up with melted butter in a boat. French beans (snaps) may be preserved in the same manner.

Egg Plant

The purple ones are best; get them young and fresh; pull out the stem, and parboil them to take off the bitter taste; cut them in slices an inch thick, but do not peel them; dip them in the yelk of an egg, and cover them with grated bread, a little salt and pepper[;] when this has dried, cover the other side the same way[;] fry them a nice brown. They are very delicious, tasting much like soft crabs. The egg plant may be dressed in another manner: scrape the rind and parboil them; cut a slit from one end to the other, take out the seeds, fill the space with a rich force-meat, and stew them in well seasoned gravy, or bake them, and serve up with gravy in the dish.

Sweet Potatos Stewed

Wash and wipe them, and if they be large, cut them in two lengths; put them at the bottom of a stew pan, lay over some slices of boiled ham; and on that, one or two chickens cut up with pepper, salt, and a bundle of herbs; pour in some water, and stew them till done, then take out the herbs, serve the stew in a deep dish[;] thicken the gravy, and pour over it.

Sweet Potatos Broiled

Cut them across without peeling, in slices half an inch thick, broil them on a griddle, and serve them with butter in a boat.

Spinach

Great care must be used in washing and picking it clean; drain it, and throw it into boiling water[;] a few minutes will boil it sufficiently: press out all the water, put it in a stew pan with a piece of butter, some pepper and salt[;] chop it continually with a spoon till it is quite dry: serve it with poached eggs or without, as you please.

Cabbage Pudding

Get a fine head of cabbage, not too large; pour boiling water on, and cover it till you can turn the leaves back, which you must do carefully; take some of those in the middle of the head off, chop them fine, and mix them with rich forcemeat; put this in, and replace the leaves[;] to confine the stuffing tie it in a cloth, and boil it[;] serve it up whole, with a little melted butter in the dish.

Squash or Cimlin

Gather young squashes, peel, and cut them in two; take out the seeds, and boil them till tender; put them into a colander, drain off the water, and rub them with a wooden spoon through the colander; then put them into a stew pan, with a cup full of cream, a small piece of

In the nineteenth century, cimlin (sometimes spelled sim-lin, cymlin, cymling, or cimberline) was a common term for a summer squash. Illustration of a scalloped squash in Peter Henderson, *Gardening for Profit: A Guide to the Successful Cultivation of the Market and Family Garden* (New York: Orange Judd, 1874), 246, Michigan State University Special Collections.

butter, some pepper and salt[;] stew them, stirring very frequently until dry. This is the most delicate way of pre-paring squashes.

Field Peas

There are many varieties of these peas; the smaller kind are the most delicate. Have them young and newly gath-ered, shell and boil them tender; pour them in a colander to drain; put some lard in a frying pan; when it boils, mash the peas, and fry them in a cake of a light brown; put it in the dish with the crust uppermost[;] garnish with thin bits of fried bacon. They are very nice when fried whole, so that each pea is distinct from the other;

but they must be boiled less, and fried with great care. Plain boiling is a very common way of dressing them.

To Boil Rice

Put two cups full of rice in a bowl of water, rub it well with the hand, and pour off the water; do this until the water ceases to be discoloured; then put the rice into two and a half cups of cold water; add a tea-spoonful of salt, cover the pot close, and set it on a brisk fire; let it boil ten minutes, pour off the greater part of the water, and remove the pot to a bed of coals, where it must remain a quarter of an hour to soak and dry.

Rice Journey, or Johnny Cake

Boil a pint of rice quite soft, with a tea-spoonful of salt; mix with it while hot a large spoonful of butter, and spread it on a dish to cool; when perfectly cold, add a pint of rice flour and half a pint of milk[;] beat them all together till well mingled. Take the middle part of the head of a barrel, make it quite clean, wet it, and put on the mixture about an inch thick, smooth with a spoon, and baste it with a little milk; set the board aslant before clear coals; when sufficiently baked, slip a thread under the cake and turn it: baste and bake that side in a simi-lar manner, split it, and butter while hot. Small homony boiled and mixed with rice flour, is better than all rice; and if baked very thin, and afterwards toasted and but-tered, it is nearly as good as cassada bread.

To Make Puff Paste

Sift a quart of flour, leave out a little for rolling the paste, make up the remainder with cold water into a stiff paste, knead it well, and roll it out several times; wash the salt from a pound of butter, divide it into four parts, put one of them on the paste in little bits, fold it up, and continue to roll it till the butter is well mixed; then put another portion of butter, roll it in the same manner; do this till all the butter is mingled with the paste; touch it very lightly with the hands in making—bake it in a moderate oven, that will permit it to rise, but will not make it brown. Good paste must look white, and as light as a feather.

A Sweetmeat Pudding

Make a quart of flour into puff paste; when done, divide it into three parts of unequal size; roll the largest out square and moderately thin, spread over it a thin layer of marmalade, leaving a margin all round about an inch broad; roll the next largest in the same manner, lay it on, cover that with marmalade, leaving a margin; then roll the smallest, and put it on the other two, spreading marmalade; fold it up, one fold over the other, the width of your hand press the ends together, tie it in a cloth securely, and place it in a kettle of boiling water, where it can lie at length without doubling; boil it quickly, and when done, pour melted butter with sugar and wine in the dish.

Flummery

One measure of jelly, one of cream, and half a one of wine; boil it fifteen minutes over a slow fire, stirring all the time; sweeten it, and add a spoonful of orange flower or rose water; cool it in a mould, turn it in a dish, and pour around it cream, seasoned in any way you like.

Burnt Custard

Boil a quart of milk and when cold, mix with it the yelks of eight eggs; stir them together over the fire a few minutes; sweeten it to your taste, put some slices of savoy cake in the bottom of a deep dish, and pour on the custard; whip the whites of the eggs to a strong froth, lay it lightly on the top, sift some sugar over it, and hold a salamander over it until it is a light brown; garnish the top with raspberry marmalade, or any kind of preserved fruit.

An English Plum Pudding

Beat eight eggs very light, add to them a pound of flour sifted, and a pound of powdered sugar; when it looks quite light, put in a pound of suet finely shred, a pint of milk, a nutmeg grated, and a gill of brandy; mix with it a pound of currants, washed, picked, and dried, and a pound of raisins stoned and floured[;] tie it in a thick cloth, and boil it steadily eight hours.

Sweet Potato Pudding

Boil one pound of sweet potatos very tender, rub them while hot through a colander; add six eggs well beaten, three quarters of a pound of powdered sugar, three quarters of butter, and some grated nutmeg and lemon peel, with a glass of brandy; put a paste in the dish, and when the pudding is done, sprinkle the top with sugar, and cover it with bits of citron. Irish potato pudding is made in the same manner, but are not so good.

An Arrow Root Pudding

Boil a quart of milk, and make it into a thick batter, with arrow root; add six eggs, half a pound of butter, the same of pounded sugar, half a nutmeg, and a little grated lemon peel; put a paste in the dish, and bake it nicely; when done, sift sugar over it, and stick slips of citron all over the top.

Quire of Paper Pancakes

Beat sixteen eggs, add to them a quart of milk, a nutmeg, half a pound of flour, a pound of melted butter, a pound of sugar, and two gills of wine; take care the flour be not in lumps; butter the pan for the first pancake, run them as thin as possible, and when coloured, they are done; do not turn them, but lay them carefully in the dish, sprinkling powdered sugar between each layer[;] serve them up hot. This quantity will make four dozen pancakes.[2]

Bread Pudding

Grate the crumb of a stale loaf, and pour on it a pint of boiling milk[;] let it stand an hour, then beat it to a pulp; add six eggs, well beaten, half a pound of butter, the same of powdered sugar, half a nutmeg, a glass of brandy, and some grated lemon peel[;] put a paste in the dish, and bake it.

Apple Pie

Put a crust in the bottom of a dish, put on it a layer of ripe apples, pared and sliced thin[,] then a layer of powdered sugar; do this alternately till the dish is full; put in a few tea-spoonsful of rose water and some cloves[;] put on a crust and bake it.

An Excellent and Cheap Dessert Dish

Wash a pint of small homony very clean, and boil it tender; add an equal quantity of corn meal, make it into a batter with eggs, milk, and a piece of butter; bake it like batter cakes on a griddle, and eat it with butter and molasses.

Baked Indian Meal Pudding

Boil one quart of milk, mix in it two gills and a half of corn meal very smoothly, seven eggs well beaten, a gill of molasses, and a good piece of butter; bake it two hours.

Pumpkin Pudding

Stew a fine sweet pumpkin till soft and dry; rub it through a sieve, mix with the pulp six eggs quite light, a quarter of a pound of butter, half a pint of new milk, some pounded ginger and nutmeg, a wine glass of brandy, and sugar to your taste. Should it be too liquid, stew it a little drier, put a paste round the edges, and in the bottom of a shallow dish or plate pour in the mixture, cut some thin bits of paste, twist them, and lay them across the top, and bake it nicely.

Maccaroni Pudding

Simmer half a pound of maccaroni in a plenty of water, with a table-spoonful of salt, till tender, but not broke—strain it, beat five yelks, two whites of eggs, half a pint of cream—mince white meat and boiled ham very fine, add three spoonsful of grated cheese, pepper and salt; mix these with the maccaroni, butter the mould, put it in, and steam it in a pan of boiling water for an hour[;] serve with rich gravy.

Apple Fritters

Pare some apples, and cut them in thin slices[;] put them in a bowl, with a glass of brandy, some white wine, a quarter of a pound of pounded sugar, a little cinnamon finely powdered, and the rind of a lemon grated; let them stand some time, turning them over frequently; beat two eggs very light, add one quarter of a pound of flour, a table-spoonful of melted butter, and as much cold water as will make a thin batter; drip the apples on a sieve, mix them with the batter, take one slice with a spoonful of batter to each fritter, fry them quickly of a light brown, drain them well, put them in a dish, sprinkling sugar over each, and glaze them nicely.

To Make Mush

Put a lump of butter the size of an egg into a quart of water, make it sufficiently thick with corn meal and a little salt; it must be mixed perfectly smooth[;] stir it constantly till done enough.

To Make Drop Biscuit

Beat eight eggs very light, add to them twelve ounces of flour, and one pound of sugar; when perfectly light, drop them on tin sheets, and bake them in a quick oven.

Tavern Biscuit

To one pound of flour add half a pound of sugar, half a pound of butter, some mace and nutmeg powdered, and a glass of brandy or wine; wet it with milk, and when well kneaded, roll it thin, cut it in shapes, and bake it quickly.

Rusk

Rub half a pound of sugar into three pounds of flour[;] sift it, pour on half a pint of good yeast, beat six eggs, add half a pint of milk[;] mix all together, and knead it well: if not soft enough, add more milk[;] it should be softer than bread; make it at night in the morning, if well risen, work in six ounces of butter, and bake it in small rolls; when cold, slice it, lay it on tin sheets, and dry it in the oven.

Ginger Bread

Three quarts of flour, three quarters of a pound of brown sugar, a large spoonful of pounded ginger, one teaspoonful of powdered cloves[;] sift it, melt half a pound of butter in a quart of rich molasses, wet the flour with it, knead it well, and bake it in a slack oven.

Dough Nuts—a Yankee Cake

Dry half a pound of good brown sugar, pound it, and mix it with two pounds of flour, and sift it; add two spoonsful of yeast, and as much new milk as will make it like bread: when well risen, knead in half a pound of butter, make it in cakes the size of a half dollar, and fry them a light brown in boiling lard.

Pound Cake

Wash the salt from a pound of butter, and rub it till it is soft as cream[;] have ready a pound of flour sifted, one of powdered sugar, and twelve eggs well beaten; put alternately into the butter, sugar, flour, and the froth from the eggs[,] continuing to beat them together till all the ingredients are in, and the cake quite light: add some grated lemon peel, a nutmeg, and a gill of brandy; butter the pans, and bake them. This cake makes an excellent pudding, if baked in a large mould, and eaten with sugar and wine. It is also excellent when boiled, and served up with melted butter, sugar and wine.

To Make Nice Biscuit

Rub a large spoonful of butter into a quart of risen dough, knead it well, and make it into biscuit, either thick or thin: bake them quickly.

Rice Bread

Boil six ounces of rice in a quart of water, till it is dry and soft[;] put it into two pounds of flour, mix it in well; add two tea-spoonsful of salt, two large spoonsful of yeast, and as much water as will make it the consistence of bread: when well risen, bake it in moulds.

Soufle Biscuits

Rub four ounces of butter into a quart of flour, make it into paste with milk, knead it well, roll it as thin as paper, and bake it to look white.

Corn Meal Bread

Rub a piece of butter the size of an egg, into a pint of corn meal[,] make it a batter with two eggs, and some new milk[;] add a spoonful of yeast, set it by the fire an hour to rise, butter little pans, and bake it.

Sweet Potato Buns

Boil and mash a potato, rub into it as much flour as will make it like bread[;] add spice and sugar to your taste, with a spoonful of yeast; when it has risen well, work in a piece of butter, bake it in small rolls, to be eaten hot with butter, either for breakfast or tea.

Rice Woffles

Boil two gills of rice quite soft, mix with it three gills of flour, a little salt, two ounces melted butter, two eggs beaten well, and as much milk as will make it a thick batter[;] beat it till very light, and bake it in woffle irons.

Buckwheat Cakes

Put a large spoonful of yeast and a little salt, into a quart of buckwheat meal; make it into a batter with cold water; let it rise well, and bake it on a griddle—it turns sour very quickly, if it be allowed to stand any time after it has risen.

Observations on Ice Creams

It is the practice with some indolent cooks, to set the freezer containing the cream, in a tub with ice and salt, and put it in the ice house; it will certainly freeze there; but not until the watery particles have subsided, and by the separation destroyed the cream. A freezer should be twelve or fourteen inches deep, and eight or ten wide. This facilitates the operation very much, by giving a larger surface for the ice to form, which it always does on the sides of the vessel; a silver spoon with a long handle should be provided for scraping the ice from the sides as soon as formed; and when the whole is congealed, pack it in moulds (which must be placed with care, lest they should not be upright,) in ice and salt, till sufficiently hard to retain the shape—they should not be turned out till the moment they are to be served. The freezing tub must be wide enough to leave a margin of four or five inches all around the freezer, when placed in the middle—which must be filled up with small lumps of ice mixed with salt—a larger tub would waste the ice. The freezer must be kept constantly in motion during the process, and ought to be made of pewter, which is less liable than tin to be worn in holes, and spoil the cream by admitting the salt water.

Ice Creams

When ice creams are not put into shapes, they should always be served in glasses with handles.

Strawberry Cream

[Make a quart of rich boiled custard—when cold, pour it on a quart of ripe red strawberries; mash them in it, pass it through a sieve, sweeten, and freeze it.] [T]he strawberries must be very ripe, and the stems picked out. If rich cream can be procured, it will be infinitely better[;] the custard is intended as a substitute, when cream cannot be had.

Cocoa Nut Cream

Take the nut from its shell, pare it, and grate it very fine; mix it with a quart of cream, sweeten, and freeze it. If the nut be a small one, it will require one and a half to flavour a quart of cream.

Chocolate Cream

Scrape a quarter of a pound of chocolate very fine, put it in a quart of milk, boil it till the chocolate is dissolved, stirring it continually[;] thicken with six eggs. A Vanilla bean boiled with the milk, will improve the flavour greatly.

Oyster Cream

Make a rich soup, (see directions for oyster soup,) strain it from the oysters, and freeze it [like ice cream].

Coffee Cream

Toast two gills of raw coffee till it is a light brown, and not a grain burnt; put it hot from the toaster without grinding it, into a quart of rich, and perfectly sweet milk; boil it, and add the yelks of eight eggs; when done, strain it through a sieve, and sweeten it; if properly, done, it will not be discoloured. The coffee may be dried, and will answer for making in the usual way to drink, allowing more for the quantity of water, than if it had not gone through this process.

Lemonade Iced

Make a quart of rich lemonade, whip the whites of six fresh eggs to a strong froth[;] mix them well with the lemonade, and freeze it. The juice of morello cherries, or of currants mixed with water and sugar, and prepared in the same way, make very delicate ices.

Lemon Cream

Pare the rind very thin from four fresh lemons, squeeze the juice, and strain it[;] put them both into a quart of water, sweeten it to your taste, add the whites of six eggs, beat to a froth; set it over the fire, and keep stirring until it thickens, but do not let it boil[,] then pour it in a bowl; when cold, strain it through a sieve, put it on the fire, and add the yelks of the eggs—stir it till quite thick, and serve it in glasses.

Tea Cream

Put one ounce of the best tea in a pitcher, pour on it a table spoonful of water, and let it stand an hour to soften the leaves[,] then put to it a quart of boiling cream, cover it close, and in half an hour strain it; add four teaspoonsful of a strong infusion of rennet in water, stir it, and set it on some hot ashes, and cover it; when you find by cooling a little of it, that it will jelly, pour it into glasses, and garnish with thin bits of preserved fruit.

Curds and Cream

Turn one quart of milk as for the slip[;] let it stand until just before it is to be served: then take it up with a skimming dish, and lay it on a sieve when the whey has drained off, put the curds in a dish, and surround them with cream[;] use sugar and nutmeg. These are Arcadian dishes; very delicious, cheap, and easily prepared.

To Make Slip

Make a quart of rich milk moderately warm: then stir into it one large spoonful of the preparation of rennet, (see receipt to prepare rennet,) set it by, and when cold, it will be as stiff as jelly. It should be made only a few hours before it is used, or it will be tough and watery; in summer, set the dish in ice after it has jellied[;] it must be eaten with powdered sugar, cream, and nutmeg.

Lemon Pickle

Grate the yellow rind from two dozen fine fresh lemons, quarter them, but leave them whole at the bottom; sprinkle salt on them, and put them in the sun every day until dry; then brush off the suit, put them in a pot with one ounce of nutmegs, and one of mace pounded; a large handful of horse radish scraped and dried, two dozen cloves of garlic, and a pint of mustard seed; pour on one gallon of strong vinegar, tie the pot close, put a board on, and let it stand three months[;] strain it, and when perfectly clear, bottle it.

Salmagundi

Turn a bowl on the dish, and put on it in regular rings, beginning at the bottom, the following ingredients, all minced: anchovies with the bones taken out, the white meat of fowls without the skin, hard boiled eggs, the yelks and whites chopped separately, parsley, the lean of old ham scraped, the inner stalks of celery; put a row of capers round the bottom of the bowl, and dispose the others in a fanciful manner; put a little pyramid of butter on the top, and have a small glass with egg mixed as for sallad, to eat with the salmagundi.

Tomato Marmalade

Gather full grown tomatos while quite green; take out the stems, and stew them till soft; rub them through a sieve, put the pulp on the fire seasoned highly with pepper, salt, and pounded cloves; add some garlic, and stew all together till thick: it keeps well, and is excellent for seasoning gravies, &c. &c.

Tomato Sweet Marmalade

Prepare it in the same manner [as Tomato Marmalade], mix some loaf sugar with the pulp, and stew until it is a stiff jelly.

Pepper Vinegar

Get one dozen pods of pepper when ripe, take out the stems, and cut them in two; put them in a kettle with three pints of vinegar, boil it away to one quart, and strain it through a sieve. A little of this is excellent in gravy of every kind, and gives a flavour greatly superior to black pepper; it is also very fine when added to each of the various catsups for fish sauce.

Mushroom Catsup

Take the flaps of the proper mushrooms from the stems—wash them, add some salt, and crush them; then boil them some time, strain them through a cloth, put them on the fire again with salt to your

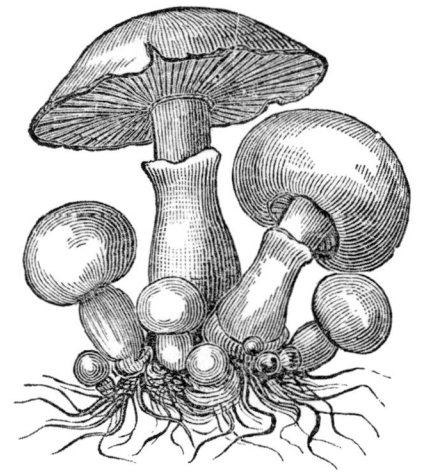

Recipes like Mary Randolph's Mushroom Catsup remind us that nineteenth-century condiments—especially ketchups—were much more various than the mass-produced versions that followed in later decades. An illustration of cultivated mushrooms, in Henderson, *Gardening for Profit*, 203.

taste, a few cloves of garlic, and a quarter of an ounce of cloves pounded, to a peck of mushrooms; boil it till reduced to less than half the original quantity—bottle and cork it well.

Curry Powder

One ounce turmeric, one [ounce] coriander seed, one [ounce] cummin seed, one [ounce] white ginger, one of nutmeg, one of mace, and one of Cayenne pepper; pound all together, and pass them through a fine sieve; bottle and cork it well[;] one tea-spoonful is sufficient to season any made dish.

To Pickle Cucumbers

Gather them full grown, but quite young—take off the green rind, and slice them tolerably thick; put a layer in a deep dish, strew over it some chopped onion and salt; do this until they are all in; sprinkle salt on the top, let them stand six hours, put them in a colander—when all the liquor has run off, put them in a pot, strew a little cayenne pepper over each layer, and cover them with strong cold vinegar; when the pot is full, pour on some sweet oil, and tie it up close; at the end of a fortnight, pour off the first vinegar, and put on fresh.

To Make Yellow Pickle

Put all the articles intended for the yellow pickle in a pot, and pour on them boiling salt and water[;] let them stand forty-eight hours, take advantage of a clear hot day, press the water from the articles, and lay them to dry in full sunshine, on a table covered with a thick soft cloth, with the corners pinned securely, that they may not blow up over the things[;] the cloth absorbs the moisture; and by turning them frequently on a dry place, they become white, and receive the colour of the turmeric more readily[;] one day of clear sunshine is enough to prepare them for the first vinegar; When dried, put them in a pot of plain cold vinegar, with a little turmeric in it let them remain in it two weeks to draw off the water from them, and to make them plump[,] then put them in a clean pot, and pour on the vinegar, prepared by the following directions[;] this is the most economical and best way of keeping them[;] mix the turmeric very smoothly, before you add it to your pickles.

To Pickle Onions

Get white onions that are not too large, cut the stem close to the root with a sharp knife, put them in a pot, pour on boiling salt and water to cover them, stop the pot closely, let them stand a fortnight, changing the salt and water every three days; they must be stirred daily, or those that float will become soft; at the end of this time, take off the skin and outer shell, put them in plain cold vinegar with a little turmeric. If the vinegar be not very pale, the onion will not be of a good colour.

To Pickle Nastertiums

Gather the berries when full grown but young, put them in a pot, pour boiling salt and water on, and let them stand three or four days; then drain off the water, and cover them with cold vinegar; add a few blades of mace, and whole grains of black pepper.

To Pickle Radish Pods

Cut them in nice bunches as soon as they are fully formed; they must be young and tender—pour boiling salt and water on them, cover with a thick cloth, and pewter plate, to keep in the steam; repeat this every day till they are a good green; then put them in cold vinegar, with mace and whole pepper; mix a little turmeric, with a small portion of oil, and stir it into the vinegar; it will make the pods of a more lively green. They are very pretty for garnishing meats.

Ginger Wine

To three gallons of water, put three pounds of sugar, and four ounces of race ginger, washed in many waters to cleanse it; boil them together for one hour, and strain it through a sieve; when lukewarm, put it in a cask with three lemons cut in slices, and two gills of beer yeast; shake it well, and stop the cask very tight; let it stand a week to ferment; and if not clear enough to bottle, it must remain until it becomes so; it will be fit to drink in ten days after bottling.

Orgeat

A Necessary Refreshment at all Parties.

Boil two quarts of milk with a stick of cinnamon and let it stand to be quite cold, first taking out the cinnamon; blanch four ounces of the best sweet almonds, pound them in a marble mortar with a little rose-water; mix them well with the milk, sweeten it to your taste, and let it boil a few minutes only, lest the almonds should be oily; strain it through a very fine sieve till quite smooth, and free from the almonds; serve it up either cold or lukewarm, in glasses with handles.

Cherry Shrub

Gather ripe morello cherries, pick them from the stalk, and put them in an earthen pot, which must be set into an iron pot of water; make the water boil, but take care that none of it gets into the cherries; when the juice is extracted, pour it into a bag made of tolerably thick cloth, which will permit the juice to pass, but not the pulp of your cherries; sweeten it to your taste, and when it becomes perfectly clear, bottle it[;] put a gill of brandy into each bottle, before you pour in the juice cover the corks with rosin. It will keep all summer, in a dry cool place, and is delicious mixed with water.

To Make Cherry Brandy

Get equal quantities of morello and common black cherries; fill your cask, and pour on (to a ten gallon cask) one gallon of boiling water; in two or three hours, fill it up with brandy[;] let it stand a week, then draw off all, and put another gallon of boiling water, and fill it again with brandy at the end of the week, draw the whole off, empty the cask of the cherries, and pour in your brandy with water, to reduce the strength; first dissolving one pound of brown sugar in each gallon of your mixture. If the brandy be very strong, it will bear water enough to make the cask full.

Rose Brandy

Gather leaves from fragrant roses without bruising, fill a pitcher with them, and cover them with French brandy; next day, pour off the brandy, take out the leaves, and fill the pitcher with fresh ones, and return the brandy; do this till it is strongly impregnated, then bottle it; keep the pitcher closely covered during the process. It is better than distilled rose water for cakes, &c.

Raspberry Cordial

To each quart of ripe red raspberries, put one quart of best French brandy; let it remain about a week, then strain it through a sieve or bag, pressing out all the liquid; when you have got as much as you want, reduce the strength to your taste with water, and put a pound of powdered loaf sugar to each gallon[;] let it stand till refined. Strawberry cordial is made the same way. It destroys the flavour of these fruits to put them on the fire.

Mint Cordial

Pick the mint early in the morning while the dew is on it, and be careful not to bruise it; pour some water over it, and drain it[;] put two handsful into a pitcher, with a quart of French brandy, cover it, and let it stand till next clay; take the mint carefully out, and put in as much more, which must be taken out next day[;] do this the third time: then put three quarts of water to the brandy, and one pound of loaf sugar powdered; mix it well together and when perfectly clear, bottle it.

Spruce Beer

Boil a handful of hops, and twice as much of the chippings of sassafras root, in ten gallons of water; strain it, and pour in, while hot, one gallon of molasses, two spoonsful of the essence of spruce, two spoonsful of powdered ginger, and one of pounded allspice; put it in a cask—when sufficiently cold, add half a pint of good yeast; stir it well, stop it close, and when fermented and clear, bottle and cork it tight.

Molasses Beer

Put five quarts of hops, and five of wheat bran, into fifteen gallons of water; boil it three or four hours, strain it, and pour it into a cask with one head taken out; put in five quarts of molasses, stir it till well mixed, throw a cloth over the barrel; when moderately warm, add a quart of good yeast, which must be stirred in; then stop it close with a cloth and board. When it has fermented and become quite clear, bottle it—the corks should be soaked in boiling water an hour or two, and the bottles perfectly clean, and well drained.

Vinegar of the Four Thieves

Take lavender, rosemary, sage, wormwood, rue, and mint, of each a large handful; put them in a pot of earthen ware, pour on them four quarts of very strong vinegar, cover the pot closely, and put a board on the top; keep it in the hottest sun two weeks, then strain and bottle it, putting in each bottle a clove of garlic. When it has settled in the bottle and become clear, pour it off gently; do this until you get it all free from sediment. The proper time to make it is when the herbs are in full vigour, in June. This vinegar is very refreshing in crowded rooms, in the apartments of the sick; and is peculiarly grateful when sprinkled about the house in damp weather.

To Dry Herbs

Gather them on a dry day, just before they begin to blossom; brush off the dust, cut them in small branches, and dry them quickly in a moderate oven; pick off the leaves when dry, pound and sift them—bottle them immediately, and cork them closely. They must be kept in a dry place.

Selections from Confederate Periodicals, 1861–1865

One of the most revealing glimpses into how eating and cooking changed during the Civil War comes from Southern periodicals. Aimed at planters and yeomen farmers, these periodicals had been an important source of information before the war on everything from farming to slave keeping to domestic management. Once the war started, they became an invaluable source of information on changing food conditions. In most of the periodicals, recipes and articles on food had never appeared in special sections aimed at women, but rather mixed in with everything else. But if categories of cultivating, preserving, and cooking food had always been somewhat porous, the war blew them wide open, as all sorts of people who had never cooked before—from plantation mistresses to soldiers to enslaved field hands—either learned rudimentary cooking skills or went hungry.

Few people needed help cooking more than men at war. Confederate soldiers were left to cook for themselves, for the most part, usually with little resembling pots or pans or cooking spoons, not to mention eating utensils.[1] Meat could be spit-roasted easily enough;

when they managed to find meat, Southern soldiers speared it on a stick and held it over a fire. Baking bread without an oven was harder, but soldiers developed a method, apparently widespread by the end of the war, of winding ropes of raw dough around their rifle barrels and holding them over a fire to cook, too.[2] Soldiers rarely used cookbooks since they usually wouldn't have had the ingredients or equipment called for.[3] But wartime periodicals were different because some of their cooking tips were aimed specifically at soldiers. Periodicals offered valuable ideas, like a description of "panola"—a dish made by pounding and seasoning dried corn, or a recipe for a nourishing drink that could be made by stirring up cornmeal and vinegar in water, or a description of preserved potatoes that were light, durable, and "could be carried readily in a soldier's haversack."

Some of the periodicals' recipes blurred the line between food and medicine, such as one article that praised pickles' health properties and suggested vinegar—thought to resemble gastric juices—as an antidote to dysentery. In fact, just as many men learned to cook for the first time during the war, some also learned to perform previously feminized tasks like preparing home remedies and nursing the sick. Epidemic diseases were a terrifying scourge in the nineteenth century, even in peacetime, and disease rates were astronomical in army camps. Sometimes the periodicals provided explicit instructions to soldiers on preparing the same kinds of homeopathic remedies that their wives or mothers might have prepared at home, like the 1862 article, "Every Soldier his own Physician," that included recipes promising to do everything from curing measles to relieving chills to reversing drunkenness. As soldiers faced daunting expectations about manly courage and masculine behavior, simultaneous expectations about cooking and nursing the sick could cause tensions. But some men clearly took pride in their new skills, like one soldier who boasted in a letter to his wife, "I will be able to learn you something in the art of cooking by the time I get home."[4]

At the same time that men by the tens of thousands were learning to cook, many women at home were cultivating food for the first time in the fields. Making sense of such gender role reversals without upsetting gender categories altogether took some mental maneuvering. For example, in a *Southern Cultivator* article published in early 1864, an observer reported that on small country farms in rural Tennessee, "Many a woman who never before held a plow is now seen in the corn-field—many a young girl who would have blushed at the thought before of handling a plow line, now naturally and unconsciously cries 'gee-up' to Dobbin, to the silvery tones of which the good brute readily responds, as if a pleasure

to comply with so gentle a command."[5] It was fitting that white women felt some initial shame in taking up farmwork, the author implied, but such work was ultimately not threatening because their femininity was so essential to their beings that field work couldn't affect it: even as they pushed a plow, their commands to the draft animals were "gentle" and "silvery," supposedly making the animals all the more eager to work. Of course, such descriptive acrobatics weren't just about maintaining gender categories but also about maintaining hierarchies of race and class; enslaved women and poor white women had worked in Southern fields for centuries, but it was only when white women from formerly comfortable circumstances took up plows that such work seemed noteworthy.

The recipes in this section aren't organized by category but by time, because seeing how advice on food changed over the course of the war gives a vivid sense of how the Southern food situation deteriorated. The first recipes come from early 1861, before the war had started but after some Southern states had seceded. In the first months and years of the war, these periodicals make clear, many Southerners—especially those literate white Southerners able to afford luxuries like a periodical subscription—still had access to relatively abundant food, and the blockade was sometimes permeable. As late as January 1863, for example, the *Southern Field and Fireside*'s recipe for Orange Jelly blithely called for twelve Havana oranges. Other recipes, like the one published a few months later for Tea Cake, demanded lavish amounts of sugar and eggs and butter. As time went on, however, recipes calling for large amounts of animal products or for any ingredients produced outside the region became rare.

One of the first commodities to disappear from Southern kitchens was salt. Before the war, Southerners had used more salt than anyone in the world, with ships arriving in Southern ports bulging with salt from Welsh mines.[6] Besides salting their food generously, Southerners had used salt as a preservative, crucial for keeping meat and fish and butter before refrigeration. Southern salt reserves began shrinking as the blockade choked off imports, and these periodicals reported on the scramble to find a new supply.[7] Some predicted the South might be able to produce all its own salt by boiling down ocean water. "Our immediate sea coast is said to be thronged with parties engaged in boiling salt," a South Carolina paper reported in early 1862, "and many have succeeded in making a good supply." But large-scale sea salt production turned out to be impossible, mainly because boiling vats of salt water down to crystals required a mammoth firewood supply. In 1862, Southerners also started mining a natural salt dome in Louisiana, but Union forces— fully aware of its value to the Confederacy—seized it the next year.[8] Although Confederates exploited a few other natural salt deposits around the South, southern salt production never came close to meeting demand. These periodicals show the desperation and inventiveness of people who tried to produce their old staple preservative in any way they could think of. Some people sifted through the dirt floors of old smokehouses, where decades worth of salt had dripped. One man reported he made a little salt by boiling old salt sacks. Other people just tried to get along without it, and at least one Louisiana sugar planter claimed you could cure meat with molasses.

Supplies of other commodities shrank, too, and many of the recipes in these periodicals were substitutes for other foods Southerners had consumed in peacetime. Pomegranate juice could stand in for imported lemons, one article informed readers. Potatoes could take the place of midwestern wheat flour; sunflower seed oil could substitute for milder imported oils; sassafras blossoms or dried blackberry leaves could make an adequate tea; whipped raw egg could pass as cream. One writer suggested optimistically that buckwheat bread might become just as beloved a staple as buckwheat pancakes. Even seemingly mundane Southern recipes, like the 1864 recipe for Corn Bread, would have served both as a substitute for wheat bread and, with a little more processing, as a coffee substitute, since its author pointed out that the "crust, if not burned, will make excellent coffee."

In fact, after salt, coffee was probably the import Southerners missed most, and recipes for imitation coffee appeared more commonly than anything else. In these periodicals, as well as in the other sources excerpted in this volume, you'll see recipes for "coffee" made with things like wheat, rye, corn, okra, and acorns—all of which must have been weak understudies for the real thing. But many Southerners described the willingness to eat wartime substitutes, no matter how vile, as a sign of their patriotism. For example, in

1863 one woman wrote proudly that her sixty-year-old mother was "drinking wheat coffee, without sugar—eating corn meal, instead of flour, and willing to do it the rest of her life (to use her own words), *'if we can only whip the Yankees.'*"

Southerners also increasingly looked for alternatives to meat. Although we might think of pork as a preeminently Southern food, by the eve of the Civil War the South was importing much of its pork, along with much of its beef, from the Midwest. Once the war started, formerly commonplace meats became hard to find, especially cured meats like bacon that required pork *and* salt. Since bacon had been a major part of slave diets, planters debated how little they could get away with including in rations while still expecting maximum productivity from enslaved workers. For example, one 1861 article in the *Southern Cultivator* argued, "With plenty of corn bread, and peas, and molasses, negroes will grow fat, and do good work, and be contented with one ration of meat per week."

As the war continued and the South's infrastructure buckled, some Confederate periodicals went under, not only because of paper shortages and transportation problems, but because their readers could no longer afford to pay subscription fees.[9] As early as August 1861, the editor of the *Southern Cultivator* announced that he would accept payment for subscription costs in grain as well as in cash. Southerners had never operated in a cash economy to nearly the same extent as Northerners, and even prosperous yeomen had often been cash poor. But the war made the economy drastically worse, and towards the end Confederate currency lost virtually all value. Those periodicals that survived became all the more valuable because of their tips on finding and preparing food amid worsening shortages. By the final winter of the war, the unrelenting theme of food advice had become the search for basic supplies, as pleas for staple ingredients replaced recipes in the remaining Confederate periodicals. You can hear the desperation as one writer pleaded from Athens, Georgia, in January 1865, "If our friends in the country ever expect to send any thing here—particularly corn, corn meal, syrup, potatoes, turnips, &c.—now is the time to do it!"

Light-Bread

Sift together 1 quart of Flour, 1 table-spoon full of Yeast Powder, 1 tea-spoon full of Salt; take Milk or Water and make a thick dough, mixing it with a spoon altogether. Smooth off the tops of the loaves with a spoon, dipped in water. Bake quick.

Southern Cultivator, p. 39, vol. 19, no. 1, January 1861, Atlanta

Broiled Beef Steak

It should be cut from a well-kept rump, and they are generally liked about three-quarters of an inch thick. Most cooks beat them with a rolling pin for ten minutes; but if the meat is of good quality, and the rump has been well kept, there will be no necessity for this. Just before finishing, rub a lump of butter over, and lightly dredge with pepper and salt. Pickles and scraped horse-radish make a good garnish, and for sauce, suit your taste.

Southern Cultivator, p. 71, vol. 19, no. 2, February 1861, Atlanta

Negroes inherit the tastes of their African progenitors. They rejoice in grease. They do not relish lean meat of any kind. Give them beef and mutton as fat as the Bacon they are accustomed to, and their objection to both will soon vanish.

Southern Cultivator, p. 73, vol. 19, no. 3, March 1861, Atlanta

Sweet Brown Bread

Take two quarts of corn meal, one quart of rye meal, (or rye flour) one pint of wheat meal, (all of which must be very fresh) half a teaspoonful of molasses or brown sugar, two tablespoonfuls of yeast; mix these ingredients into as thick a dough as can be stirred with a spoon, using warm water for wetting. It will require several hours to rise[;] when [risen] put it into a *deep* pan and bake five or six hours.

Southern Cultivator, p. 82, vol. 19, no. 3, March 1861, Atlanta

To carry out the culinary reforms which the health and comfort of our families demand, the close superintendence and, to some extent, the participation of the *mistress* in the preparation of our meals, will be requisite, at least till our cooks shall have become better instructed and more skillful than they are at present. But *our* fair readers are not among those who are ashamed to know how to make a loaf of bread, or to stir up a batch of biscuits, if need be, with their own hands. Even the kitchen is a place of dignity and honor in their presence, and love sanctifies the baking and the boiling.

Southern Cultivator, p. 83, vol. 19, no. 3, March 1861, Atlanta

The squash may be cooked and eaten when tender, as any other squash, but no perfection of taste until thoroughly ripe. When ripe, open and take out the seed; put in an oven with the covering attached, and cook until done. Then take it up, season with salt, pepper, and butter or cream, to taste; place back in the oven and cook a little while, so as the seasoning may be thoroughly mingled.

Southern Cultivator, p. 125, vol. 19, no. 4, April 1861, Atlanta

Parsnips are not properly appreciated among us [Southerners]. Boil half an hour, or till tender. They are good without any dressing, but are improved by [a sauce]. Cut in slices and browned on a griddle, they are very nice.

Southern Cultivator, p. 129, vol. 19, no. 4, April 1861, Atlanta

Guinea Squash, or Egg Plant, should be cut in slices a quarter of an inch thick, sprinkled with salt and piled on a plate, one side of which must be raised to allow the acrid juice to run off. In half an hour, wash them in fresh water, dip them in a batter of eggs and bread crumbs, and brown on a griddle.

Southern Cultivator, p. 129, vol. 19, no. 4, April 1861, Atlanta

A Cheap Dessert

The Southern *Literary Messenger* suggests the following as a cheap dessert for camp life. It might be if the cream were readily procurable, and *tin pan* were substituted for *tureen*.

Lay half a dozen crackers in a tureen; pour[10] enough boiling water over them to cover them. In a few minutes they will be swollen to three or four times their original size. Now grate loaf sugar and a little nutmeg over them, and dip on enough sweet cream to make a nice sauce; and you have a delicious and simple dessert that will rest lightly upon the stomach—and it is so easily prepared. Leave out the cream, and it is a valuable recipe for sick room cookery.

Edgefield Advertiser, p. 4, May 15, 1861, Edgefield, SC

Baked Batter Pudding

Beat well 3 eggs, add one teacup of sugar, two cups of sour cream, flour to make a batter, one teaspoonful saleratus, a little salt. Bake in a quick oven; eat with sugar and cream.

Farmer and Planter, p. 192, vol. 12, no. 6, June 1861, Columbia, SC

Ham Toast

Boil a quarter of a pound of lean ham; chop it small, with the yolk of 3 egg[s] well beaten, half an ounce of butter, two tablespoonfuls of cream, and a little cayenne. Stir it over the fire till it thickens, and spread it on hot toast with the crust cut off. Garnish with parsley.

Farmer and Planter, p. 192, vol. 12, no. 6, June 1861, Columbia, SC

Baked Corn Pudding

To one teacupful of corn add one quart of milk, three eggs, and a little ginger. Bake one hour.

Farmer and Planter, p. 192, vol. 12, no. 6, June 1861, Columbia, SC

To Make Hasty Pudding

Take ½ doz. eggs; 3 tablespoonfuls of sugar; 1 cup of flour; a lump of butter, large as an egg, and half a[11] nutmeg; you may add, if you like, ½ lb. raisins; mix well and bake quick.

Farmer and Planter, p. 192, vol. 12, no. 6, June 1861, Columbia, SC

Editor[']s Appeal

I gave a recipe last week which was published in the [*Memphis Daily Appeal*], to make biscuit that would keep sound a month or more in hot or cold weather, with the hope that mothers and sisters would avail themselves of the satisfaction of making and forwarding to their sons and brothers in the southern army.

Letter to the Editor, p. 2, *Memphis Daily Appeal*, July 4, 1861, Mecklenburg, NC

A lady correspondent writes us, requesting that we publish some recipe for the making of Blackberry Brandy. She thinks that it will be highly useful among the sick of the army, and that it will be proper and timely that a great deal of it shall be made the present season.

Blackberry Wine

To one gallon of clear blackberry juice add one quart of water and three pounds of white sugar. Mix well together and put the mixture into an earthen vessel, which should be kept almost full. Skim well every twenty-four hours until it is done fermenting, which will be in about a month; then bottle and cork tightly. Lay the bottles down on the sides in a cool, dry place. This is a recipe that can be fully relied on if the directions be properly attended to.

Daily Dispatch, p. 2, July 11, 1861, Richmond, VA

Grain

We are frequently asked if we will receive grain in payment of dues [subscription to newspaper]. We answer, yes. It may be delivered here at the market price of this place—or it will be received by our agents at the current rates of their respective counties.

Southern Watchman, p. 2, August 28, 1861, Athens, GA

Persimmon Beer

At this season of the year, all can make Persimmon Beer; so we re-publish from a former number of our paper:

The best persimmons ripen soft and sweet, having a clear, thin transparent skin, without any rough taste. A good ripe persimmon is a delicious morsel; most animals fatten on them; the chicken, duck, turkey, goose, dog, hog, sheep and cow all eat them greedily. The fruit when mashed and strained through a coarse wire sieve, makes delightful bread, pies, and pudding. When kneaded with wheat bran, and well baked in an oven, the bread may be put away for winter use in making beer, and used when wanted.

The following is one of the best recipes for making the beer.

Sweet ripe persimmons mashed and strained, 1 bushel; wheat bran ½ bushel.

Mix well together and bake in loaves of convenient size; break them in a clean barrel, and add 12 gallons of water, and two or three ounces of hops. Keep the barrel in a warm room. As soon as fermentation subsides, bottle off the beer, having good long corks, and place the bottles in a low temperature, and it will keep and improve for twelve months.

This beer, when properly made, in a warm room, is an exquisite delightful beverage, containing no alcohol, and is, to the connoisseur of temperate taste, not inferior to the fermented juice of the vine.

Edgefield Advertiser, p. 4, November 13, 1861, Edgefield, SC

Save Your Red Pepper

Red Pepper is essentially necessary for our troops in Virginia during the winter. It should be carefully preserved by all who wish to minister to the comfort and health of our forces in the field, ground up, and packed in bags, boxes or kegs.

Edgefield Advertiser, p. 4, November 13, 1861, Edgefield, SC

Colored Cooks and Servants

The fidelity and efficiency of colored cooks, bond and free, and of negro[12] servants in camp, have been thoroughly tested by Southern officers and volunteers. Dr. McFarlane, of New Orleans, strongly urges a preference for such cooks and servants for our army messes where they can be obtained.

He remarks: "Every negro is instinctively a cook, and is never more at home than when groping in the smoke around the camp fire, whether in the peaceful pursuits of the hunter or the more imposing circumstances of war. . . ."[13]

To those of us who remain at home and enjoy our regular and comfortable meals, the subject of this and my former article may appear a matter of little importance; but when, after the toils of military duty, the young soldier, perchance, cold, wet, hungry and exhausted, returns to camp with a certainty of finding a hot and well cooked meal, and a cheerful and garrulous negro with whom he has possibly been familiar from infancy, to welcome him, his comfort will be vastly enhanced, and his health infinitely more promoted than after the toils, and labors, and possibly combats of the day, he has to go to work to procure wood, and make fires, and cook a hurried and badly prepared meal.

Besides, this war differs from all others which have ever occurred.

Among its entanglements and combinations it is the destiny of the South to demonstrate to the deluded and infatuated fools and fanatics of the North that the negro serves his master from innate love and devotion, and not from constant dread of punishment. What could more effectually settle this Abolition heresy than to exhibit our confidence in them and their devotion to us on the field of battle!

Southern Cultivator, p. 296, vol. 19, no. 11, November 1861, Atlanta

Rye as a Substitute for Coffee

A correspondent of the Memphis Avalanche, gives two methods of preparing Rye in order to use as a substitute for coffee, and says that when properly prepared, not one in ten can distinguish between the beverage made of rye and the pure coffee grain. We have heard that by mixing half the usual amount of coffee with the same amount of rye, that the flavor is much improved. . . .

Take rye and parboil it over a slow fire, then wash it in two or three waters till thoroughly clean: dry in the sun, spreading it thin, when dry parch in small quantities over a slow fire, taking care to brown, but not to burn it. Grind and make as usual.

Southern Cultivator, p. 296, vol. 19, no. 11, November 1861, Atlanta

How to Dress Rice

A lady recommends the following recipe for dressing rice: Soak the rice in cold salted water for several hours; have ready a stew pan with boiling water; throw the rice in and boil briskly for ten minutes; drain it in a colander; cover it up hot by the fire for a few minutes and then serve. The grains will be found double the usual size and distinct from each other. In view of the fact that rice has become a very common article of diet now, and that so few persons know how to prepare it properly, it would be well to give this receipt a trial.

Daily Dispatch, p. 2, November 13, 1861, Richmond, VA

Blistered Feet

I had for several years two sons at school at Geneva, Switzerland. In their vacations they, in company with their tutor, made excursions through Switzerland, Italy, Germany, &c., on foot; bearing their knapsacks containing their necessary wants for a month.

They were provided with a small bar of common brown soap, and before putting on their stockings turned them inside out, and rubbed the soap well into the threads of them, consequently they never became foot sore, or had blistered feet. Let our volunteers try it, and my word for it, they won't complain of sore or blistered feet.

Southern Cultivator, p. 296, vol. 19, no. 11, November 1861, Atlanta

Pomegranates vs. Lemons

Editors Southern Cultivator:—The blockade has made Lemons a scarce article, and the want of acids is sensibly felt in the military hospitals. Our Pomegranates (the acid ones) furnish a juice, equal to the best Lemon acid. Leave the fruits on the bushes until thoroughly ripe, which is, when they are bursting. Take out the pulpy seeds and put them on the fire in a preserving kettle to heat. They will soon yield a beautiful clear acid, which may be put in bottles. . . . Pomegranates are raised so easily, that we never need be in want of the very best acid.

Robert Nelson

Montgomery, Ala. Oct. 1861

Southern Cultivator, p. 290, vol. 19, no. 11, November 1861, Atlanta

Sugar and Molasses for Negroes

Reprinted from suggestion from a sugar planter published in the New Orleans *Picayune*. "The cotton planters of our Confederacy are entirely cut off from any market for their cotton, and the great bread and meat question rises up before them in the most formidable proportions. Molasses and sugar, as food, approaches nearer to bread and meat than any other article.

With plenty of corn bread, and peas, and molasses, negroes will grow fat, and do good work, and be contented with one ration of meat per week.

With a little concert of action among our sugar planters, I am sure their patriotism will soon devise some plan by which our cotton planters could obtain all the molasses necessary to feed their negroes, to be paid for only when they shall be able to send their cotton to market.

Southern Cultivator, p. 301, vol. 19, no. 12, December 1861, Atlanta

Salt from Sea Water

It is amusing to see how numerous and urgent the appeals are in our country exchanges on the subject of making salt.

It is true that salt is a very necessary article, one that we cannot dispense with; and it is equally true that the chances for obtaining it from Liverpool are rather gloomy. But to persons who live here on the sea shore no uneasiness is felt whatever. The only thing to be wondered at here, is that people will be so simple as to let the merchants impose such enormous prices on them, for any man in this community can have all the salt he wants simply for the trouble of going to the sea or sound and barreling up a little water and bringing it and boiling it down . . . The idea of suffering for salt or submitting to extortionate prices when the whole end of our State is washed with it for hundreds of miles, that may be had for the packing up, is ridiculous.

Southern Cultivator, p. 301, reprinted from the *Newbern* (NC) *Progress*, vol. 19, no. 12, December 1861, Atlanta

How to Save your Salt

To 5 gallons water, add 7 lbs salt, 1 lb. sugar, 1 pint of molasses, 1 teaspoonful saltpetre—mix well, and after sprinkling the flesh side of the hams with salt, pack in a tight barrel—hams first, then shoulders, lastly middlings. Pour over the brine, and if not enough to cover, make another draft of the above and repeat till covered, leaving the meat in the brine from 4 to 7 weeks according to size.

Southern Cultivator, p. 301, vol. 19, no. 12, December 1861, Atlanta

Celebrated Indian Bread

. . . as prepared at the St-Charles Hotel, New Orleans

Beat two eggs very light, mix alternately with them one pint of sour milk, or buttermilk, and one pint of *fine* Indian meal, melt one table-spoonfull of butter and add to the mixture, dissolve one table-spoonfull of soda or saleratus,[14] &c., in a small portion of the milk and add to the mixture the last thing, beat very hard and bake in a pan in a quick oven.

Southern Cultivator, p. 313, vol. 19, no. 12, December 1861, Atlanta

The following recipe has been handed us by an extensive sugar planter:

Beef can be preserved with molasses, and is far more delicate than salted meats, in using the following process:

Sprinkle the meat with salt, put it in a barrel, and allow it to remain twelve hours. At the expiration of that time, throw out the water exuded from the meat, and fill up the barrel with molasses.

If intended to keep for several months, it will be necessary, two months after having packed it, to reboil the molasses.

Before cooking, wash it well, and your meat will not have the slightest taste of molasses, and will be equal to the finest fresh beef. The quantity of salt required is less than half a peck to the barrel.

Daily Picayune, p. 6, December 10, 1861, New Orleans

A Substitute for Milk and Cream

Beat up the whole of a fresh egg, in a basin, and then pour boiling tea over it gradually, to prevent its curdling. It is difficult from the taste to distinguish the composition from the richest cream.

Southern Cultivator, p. 32, vol. 20, no. 1, January 1862, Atlanta

Our Christmas table was graced by a splendid stalk of white, crisp, tender and finely-flavored Celery—the gift of our kind friend, Gen. GEO. W. EVANS of this city. It was from his "Idlewild Farm," where many other good things of a similar kind are produced. It is one of our favorite vegetables, and should be more abundantly raised everywhere in the South.

Southern Cultivator, p. 21, vol. 20, no. 1, January 1862, Atlanta

The Salt Boilers

Our immediate sea coast is said to be thronged with parties engaged in boiling salt, and many have succeeded in making a good supply. The quality of the salt thus made is excellent, and some which we have seen was as good as the best quality of ground salt.

Southern Cultivator, excerpted from *Horry* (SC) *Dispatch*, p. 45, vol. 20, no. 2, February 1862, Atlanta

Salt from Smoke Houses

A correspondent of the Columbus *Sun* says, that if those who have smoke houses, that have been used some time, will take the earth floor, put it in barrels and leech it as they do ashes, then boil down the lixivated[15] water, they will obtain more than enough Salt to pay for their

trouble. The writer knows of two instances in which the yield of one was ten sacks, and the other enough to supply a large family for a year.

Southern Cultivator, p. 71, vol. 20, nos. 3 and 4, March and April 1862, Atlanta

Make Sugar

"If the war lasts six months longer" (says the Raleigh *Standard*) "Virginia and North Carolina especially, will be without a pound of sugar." At present scarcely any sugar can be brought by railroad from Louisiana into these States; what there is, has been put up by the extortioners at such prices, that the poor will not be able to use it much longer. What is to be done? Let the farmers plant the Chinese Sugar Cane. And, perhaps it would pay, now while it can be done, to import the Sugar Cane from Louisiana for planting. Florida, South Alabama, and Georgia could make sugar, and we doubt not it could be done in portions of other States in the Confederacy.

Southern Cultivator, p. 76, vol. 20, nos. 3 and 4, March and April 1862, Atlanta

Let it be understood at once, that the planter who cultivated cotton when there is such an urgent demand for food, is in effect giving aid and comfort to the enemy by crippling the resources of the country.

Southern Cultivator, excerpt from the *Montgomery Advertiser*, p. 77, vol. 20, nos. 3 and 4, March and April 1862, Atlanta

The entire Press of the Confederacy is united in one voice of exhortation and warning to the tillers of the soil, to RAISE NO COTTON, this year—to plant CORN! and RICE and SUGAR, and WHEAT and GARDEN VEGETABLES!—to raise hogs and beeves[16] and sheep and poultry. . . . It is not now a matter of *choice* with us: it is a matter of *necessity*.

Southern Cultivator, p. 80, vol. 20, nos. 3 and 4, March and April 1862, Atlanta

Substitute for Soda

A lady sends the following to the Charleston *Courier*, and we publish it for the information of house keepers:

To the ashes of corn cobs, add a little boiling water. After allowing it to stand for a few minutes, pour off the lye, which can be used at once with an acid (sour milk, or vinegar.) It makes the bread as light almost as soda.

Southern Cultivator, p. 96, vol. 20, nos. 3 and 4, March and April 1862, Atlanta

Cooks in the Army

A resolution has been adopted in the House of Representatives of the Confederate Congress, to provide cooks for the army.

This is a judicious move. . . . Much of the sickness in camps arises from badly cooked food. The Volunteer has no experience in culinary matters, and is a perfect novice in the art of preparing his food, and especially his bread. . . . We have heard of biscuits in the company messes which, if hurled against the side of a house or tree, would stick there through a heavy rain storm. A man might as well take so much lead or leather into his stomach as such bread as this.

Southern Cultivator, p. 115, vol. 20, nos. 5 and 6, May and June 1862, Atlanta

The servants' crop of the South forms no inconsiderable proportion of the general amount. The Augusta *Constitutionalist* advises that the servants be encouraged and aided in devoting all their crop lands to provisions this year.

Southern Cultivator, p. 117, vol. 20, nos. 5 and 6, May and June 1862, Atlanta

Sunflower Seed Oil

As this is the season for planting, it may be well, in the general scarcity of oils, to inform farmers and planters that sunflower seed makes[17] an oil useful for many purposes, and is an admirable substitute for olive oil for table use. It is easy to cultivate and yields abundant seed.

Southern Cultivator, p. 117, vol. 20, nos. 5 and 6, May and June 1862, Atlanta

Every Soldier his own Physician

Editor Enquirer:—Horrified at the rabidity[18] with which our soldiers die in camp, we are tempted to give them the following recipes, the result of some experience, in hopes that some may be saved by using remedies simple, safe, and generally sure cures:

TO PREVENT SICKNESS

Have a jug of salted vinegar, seasoned with pepper, and take a mouthful just before going to bed. The salt and vinegar make a near approach to the digestive gastric juice of the stomach, and are besides antidotes to many of the vegetable and miasmatic poisons.

FOR CHILLS

Put a tablespoonful of salted pepper vinegar in a cup of warm water, go to bed and drink; in two hours drink a cup of strong water-willow bark tea; in two hours more another tablespoonful of the vinegar and warm water, and so on, alternating, until the fever is broken up. After sweating, and before going into the out-door air, the body ought always to be wiped off with a cloth dipped in cold water. Dogwood will do if water-willow cannot be obtained.

FOR MEASLES

Put a small piece yeast in a tumbler of warm sweetened water, let it draw, and drink a mouthful every 15 or 20 minutes, and drink plentifully of cold or hot catnip, balson, hoarhound, or alder tea; and use in place of oil or salts, one tablespoonful salted pepper vinegar, melted together and taken warm. Take once a day, if necessary—keep out of the wet and out-door air.

FOR DIARRHOEA

A teaspoonful of the salted pepper vinegar every one or two hours. Take [a] teaspoonful of the puffs that grow round oak twigs, powdered fine; take twice a day in one tablespoonful of brandy, wine or cordial. If these yellow puffs cannot be found, suck frequently on a piece of alum. The quantity of alum depends upon the severity of the attack; take slowly and little at a time.

FOR CAMP FEVERS

One tablespoonful of salted pepper vinegar, slightly seasoned, and put into a cup of warm water—drink and often, from 4 to 8 cupfuls a day, with fever or without fever. Pour a cupful more or less of the salted pepper vinegar into cold water, and keep the body, particularly the stomach and head, well bathed with a cloth dipped in it. Give enemas of cold water, and for oil use a tablespoonful molasses, a teaspoonful of lard, and a teaspoonful pepper vinegar, melted together and taken warm. If the pepper is too exciting for delicate patients, leave it out in drinks and bathings, and use simply the salt and vinegar in water, and very little salt.

ANTIDOTE FOR DRUNKENNESS: FOR THE BENEFIT OF OFFICERS

One cup of strong black coffee[19] without milk or sugar, and twenty drops of laudanum. Repeat the dose if necessary. Or take one teaspoonful of tincture lobelia in a tumbler of milk; if taken every ten or fifteen minutes it will act as an emetic; taken in longer intervals, say thirty minutes, it will act as an antidote. The Yankees declared that poisoned liquor was put on the counters to poison their soldiers. No body doubts liquor being poisoned, but it was made of poisons to sell to our own Southern boys; and it is horrifying to think of the liquors now being made down in cellars, of sulphuric acid, strychnine, buckeye, tobacco leaves, coloring matter and rainwater. For this poisoned liquor, the best antidote is an emetic, say lobelia and warm salt and water, and then drink freely of sugared vinegar water.

Southern Watchman, reprinted from the *Columbus Enquirer*, June 18, 1862, p. 1, Athens, GA

Panola

An officer of [the] army has shown us an article of food prepared by some ladies of an interior county and sent into camp. It is the same known on the Western plains and among the Mexicans as "panola." It is simply parched corn, well ground or beaten in a mortar, and seasoned to the taste with salt, or with sugar and cinnamon. It has great merits as a camp food, particularly on a march, being very nutritious, easily prepared, convenient to carry, always ready for use, very palatable, and keeping a long time without spoiling. It is an excellent corrective, too, of those conditions of body which camp life is apt to produce.

The officer who left the sample with us is of the opinion, and we agree with him, that Government could not provide a better food for the soldiers when a march is contemplated, or one which would be more agreeable as a change at all times. The friends of soldiers will also take the hint.

Southern Watchman, reprinted from the *Richmond Enquirer,* p. 4, July 2, 1862, Athens, GA

A correspondent of the Atlanta *Confederacy* says that the common blackberry leaves, dried in the shade and made into tea, make a better, stronger and sweeter flavored tea than the best quality of China green.

Southern Cultivator, p. 179, vol. 20, nos. 9 and 10, September and October 1862, Atlanta

Green Corn

Take roasting ears, husk them, and boil them not quite as done as for table use; cut the corn off the cob and dry it on pans or boards in the sun. It will dry in two days, so it can be put up in large quantities, when it can be[20] hung up in small bags and used all the year as green corn.

Southern Cultivator, p. 184, vol. 20, nos. 9 and 10, September and October 1862, Atlanta

Mr. Editor:—The following is a homely drink but it is invigorating and refreshing, and in the reach of every soldier:

One table spoonful of finely sifted corn meal; 1 tea spoonful of vinegar; 1 tea spoonful of sugar or molasses—stirred into a tumbler of water, and drank before it settles.

Signed C******

Southern Cultivator, p. 184, vol. 20, nos. 9 and 10, September and October 1862, Atlanta

Cabbage Salad

Chop enough cabbage fine to fill a vegetable dish. Heat a coffee cup of strong vinegar, with a lump of butter in it the size of a small egg. Pepper and salt. When hot, beat an egg very light and stir in; then pour all on to the chopped cabbage.

Southern Cultivator, p. 184, vol. 20, nos. 9 and 10, September and October 1862, Atlanta

Recipe for Making Tomato Wine

Take ripe tomatoes, press and strain them, then to one quart of the juice add one half pint of sugar, bottle and let it stand until it ferments, then it is ready for use.

Southern Cultivator, p. 184, reprinted from *Gainsville* (FL) *Cotton States*, August 9, vol. 20, nos. 9 and 10, September and October 1862, Atlanta

Recipes like Tomato Wine were essential tools for preserving highly perishable summer tomatoes. They also show the inventiveness of Southerners who produced alcohol at home using the ingredients they had at hand. Image illustrating hoop-training of garden tomatoes in Burr, *Field and Garden Vegetables*, 630.

A Receipt for the Times

Eds. Columbus Sun:—I have the opportunity of knowing that many persons are using flour who cannot procure lard; and as the times are hard, I will give a plan for making bread, which I all times regard as infinitely better than bread made of *hog grease* and *physic* (soda, salaratus, cream tartar, &c.).[21] Take the quantity of flour to be used with salt added to suit taste; pour upon it boiling water, stir with a spoon, and when sufficiently cool to handle place the dough upon a board covered with flour, and roll it to the thickness of half an inch, cut about the same width and roll it round with the hand as you would marbles; then bake it in a hot stove or oven (covering the vessel with flour) until brown. This bread will be light, nice and sweet. It rises upon the principle of expansion by heat.

Persons who imagine that they cannot eat bread which does not contain *fat* and *drugs*, may use butter and syrup, and the most cultivated taste scarcely observes the difference. This I have seen tried upon the most fastidious. VEGETARIAN.

Southern Watchman, p. 2, October 15, 1862, Athens, GA

To Save Pork

A correspondent gives, through the *Columbus Enquirer*, the following recipe for saving pork, in an economical manner. He says several gentlemen have successfully practiced it in the past year, in Harris County, Ga.:

To five gallons of water add seven pounds of salt, one pint of syrup, and one teaspoonful of pounded saltpetre.

After the pork is cooled in the usual way, pack in barrels, and cover with the above mixture. Let it remain four or five weeks, and hang and smoke in the usual manner.

Thus, twenty pounds of salt are made to save 1,000 pounds of pork.

Daily Dispatch, p. 2, October 13, 1862, Richmond, VA

To Make Sage Cheese

Take the tops of sage, and press the juice from them by beating in a mortar; do the same with leaves of spinach, and mix the two juices together. After putting the rennet to the milk, pour in some of this juice, regulating the quantity by the color and taste to be given to the cheese. As the curd appears, break it gently and in an equal manner; then, emptying it into the cheese-vat, let it be a little pressed, in order to make it eat mellow. Having stood for about seven hours, salt and turn it daily for four or five weeks, when it will be fit to eat. The spinach, besides improving the flavor and correcting the bitterness of the sage, will give a much finer color than can be obtained from sage alone.

Southern Cultivator, p. 207, vol. 20, nos. 11 and 12, November and December 1862, Atlanta

Brandy from Persimmons

We find in an old magazine an account of an experiment in distilling brandy from persimmons, which may be interesting since the powers that be, seem determined that the people shall not get corned on corn. The writer prepared the persimmons in the same way as peaches are usually prepared for the still, and the result of the experiment was an average of one gallon of proof spirits of an agreeable flavor for each bushel of persimmons. Will somebody try it?—*Chron. & Sentinel.*

REMARKS—During our recent travels in North Carolina, we were struck with the great abundance of Persimmons everywhere throughout the country; and we wondered that a people so much addicted to distillation as our neighbors of the old North State, should not have turned them into Brandy, or spirit of some sort, long since. There is a great amount of saccharine matter, (and, consequently, alcoholic,) in ripe Persimmons, and as many are yet hanging on the trees in Georgia and the more Southern States, distillers can very easily try the experiment of reducing them to Brandy. We have no doubt they will make liquor of a superior quality; and we trust they will be all gathered and used instead of Corn, *every bushel of which is needed for bread.* Ed[itor] So[uthern] Cult[ivator].

Southern Cultivator, p. 208, vol. 20, nos. 11 and 12, November and December 1862, Atlanta

To Make Hominy Bread

The hominy having been properly soaked, drain off the water, and add of fresh water seven and a half pints for each pound and a half of hominy, as weighed before soaking; let this simmer for four hours—if boiled rapidly, it will become hard and never swell; the hominy will then be fit for stirabout[22] or bread. For bread, mix it gradually with the flour, making the dough in the ordinary way, and adding yeast in rather more than the usual proportion. This bread will keep moist and good for a longer time than if made entirely of wheaten flour.

Southern Field and Fireside, p. 15, vol. 1, no. 2, January 10, 1863, Augusta, GA

A Plain Custard

Boil a pint of new milk, keeping a little back to mix with a tablespoonful of flour; thicken the milk with the flour, let it cool a little, then add one egg well beaten; sweeten to taste; set it on the fire again, and stir until the egg turns, but do not let it boil. A little lemon or almond may be added.

Southern Field and Fireside, p. 15, vol. 1, no. 2, January 10, 1863, Augusta, GA

Chicken Broth

Chicken Broth may be made of any young fowl which is afterwards to be brought to table; but the best sort is to be procured from an old cock or hen, which is to be stewed down to rags, with a couple of onions, seasoned with salt and a little whole pepper; skim and strain it.

Southern Field and Fireside, p. 15, vol. 1, no. 2, January 10, 1863, Augusta, GA

Beef Tea

Cut one pound of fleshy beef in thin slices; simmer with a quart of water an hour and a half after it has once boiled and been skimmed. Season, if approved; but it wants generally only a little salt.

Southern Field and Fireside, p. 15, vol. 1, no. 2, January 10, 1863, Augusta, GA

Salad Dressing

One cup good cider vinegar, a teaspoon of oil, one of made mustard, a salt-spoon of salt, and the yolk of a hard boiled egg rubbed fine; pour over the salad, and send to the table.

Southern Field and Fireside, p. 23, vol. 1, no. 3, January 17, 1863, Augusta, GA

Batter Pudding

Five eggs beaten light; one quart of sweet milk and one pint flour. Bake ten minutes without a crust, and eat it hot, with butter and sugar for sauce.

Southern Field and Fireside, p. 23, vol. 1, no. 3, January 17, 1863, Augusta, GA

Sponge Cake

Take the yolk of five eggs, the white of one, half a pound of sugar, one teacupful of water; beat sugar, eggs, and water together, until thick as pound cake, then add six ounces of flour.

Southern Field and Fireside, p. 23, vol. 1, no. 3, January 17, 1863, Augusta, GA

Buckwheat Bread

Who loves not buckwheat pancakes, and to how many in a failure of the wheat crop, is buckwheat the staff of life? and to how many more might it be if the fact were generally known, that a most palatable bread can be made from it.

The bread is as good as the pancakes—(we say better)—far less trouble to prepare, and has no burnt grease about it to make it unwholesome. . . .

To one quart buttermilk, add a teaspoonful of soda, and flour enough to make a thin batter—put in an egg if convenient, and bake in quick oven. Try it.

Southern Field and Fireside, p. 23, vol. 1, no. 3, January 17, 1863, Augusta, GA

To Make Crackers

Take one egg, one pint sweet milk, one tea-cupful lard, a little salt, and enough flour to make a stiff dough. Rub the lard and some flour together; then add the egg and milk. Add flour and knead well till it is a very stiff dough. Then add to this one-half its size of light dough, knead them well together, and set away to rise. When light, roll out to one-eighth of an inch thick, cut in squares, prick with a fork, and bake to a crisp.

Southern Field and Fireside, p. 23, vol. 1, no. 3, January 17, 1863, Augusta, GA

Johnny Cake

1½ cups sweet cream

5 cups butter-milk

1 small tablespoonful saleratus and a little salt

Add corn-meal to make a batter as stiff as can be conveniently stirred with a spoon. It should be briskly stirred, turned into a well buttered dripping-pan, and baked in a quick but not too hot oven.

Southern Field and Fireside, p. 23, vol. 1, no. 3, January 17, 1863, Augusta, GA

To Broil Ham

Ham is better broiled than fried.—Slice it thin, and boil on a gridiron. When dished, place a fried egg on each slice. It should be broiled over bright coals, from five to eight minutes, turning it over once.

Southern Field and Fireside, p. 28, vol. 1, no. 4, January 25, 1863, Augusta, GA

Nonpareil Sauce

Take a slice of boiled ham, as much breast of roasted fowl, a pickled cucumber, a yolk of a hard-boiled egg, one anchovy, a little parsely [*sic*], and a head of shallot, chopped very fine; boil it a moment in good catsup, and use it for meat or fish.

Southern Field and Fireside, p. 28, vol. 1, no. 4, January 25, 1863, Augusta, GA

Cabbage

Large, full-grown cabbages and savoys will require half an hour or more in boiling. Strip all the outside leaves to the white ones; then shave the stalk, and score it a little way up. Boil with good bacon. Cold cabbage may be fried with ham.

Southern Field and Fireside, p. 28, vol. 1, no. 4, January 25, 1863, Augusta, GA

Cabbage was a popular vegetable across the South, valued for its ease of cultivation and nutritional value as well as for its taste. Early summer cabbage, pictured in Henderson, *Gardening for Profit*, 143.

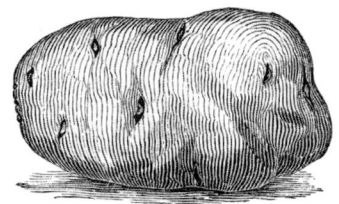

By the middle of the war, wheat flour was hard to come by for many Southerners, and some made use of garden potatoes as an alternative base for bread. The recipe for Potato Bread gave clear instructions aimed at readers who might never have made such a bread before. Potato illustration in Burr, *Field and Garden Vegetables*, 61.

To Make Potato Bread

Boil the potatoes, not quite as soft as usual, then dry them a short time on the fire, peel them while hot, and mash them as fine as possible; next put a small quantity of pearlash to new yeast; while it is working briskly, add as much flour as can be worked in, mix the whole well together, but do not add any water to it. After the dough is thus prepared, let it stand an hour and a half, or two hours, before it is put into the oven; observe, it will not require so long baking as regular flour bread.

Southern Field and Fireside, p. 28, vol. 1, no. 4, January 25, 1863, Augusta, GA

Corn Bread

Scald the meal, make a tolerably stiff dough, press or roll it to half an inch in thickness, bake one side at a time, in front of the fire, after being put on a board or sheet of tin.

Southern Field and Fireside, p. 28, vol. 1, no. 4, January 25, 1863, Augusta, GA

Johnny Cake

Three pints of Indian-meal, one egg, and a spoonful of sugar. Mix with milk or water; spread on a tin, and bake it before the fire.

Southern Field and Fireside, p. 28, vol. 1, no. 4, January 25, 1863, Augusta, GA

Rice Cakes

A pint of soft-boiled rice, a half pint of milk or water, and twelve spoonsful of rice flour; divide into small cakes, and bake them in a brisk oven.

Southern Field and Fireside, p. 28, vol. 1, no. 4, January 25, 1863, Augusta, GA

A Rich Corn Bread

Take two quarts corn meal, one quart wheat flour, a little salt, and four eggs; add sour buttermilk enough to form a stiff batter; mix well; then add two tea-spoonfuls of soda dissolved in a little warm water. Stir it well and pour into greased pans, so that it will be about two inches thick when baked. Bake in a hot oven till done— say about half an hour.

Southern Field and Fireside, p. 38, vol. 1, no. 5, January 31, 1863, Augusta, GA

Pumpkin Pie

Halve the pumpkin, take out the seeds, wash it clean, and cut it into small pieces. These are to be stewed gently until soft, then drained, and strained through a seive.[23] To one quart of the pulp, add three pints cream or milk, six beaten eggs, together with sugar, mace, nutmeg, and ginger to the taste. When the ingredients are well mixed, pour them upon pie-plates, having a bottom crust, and bake forty minutes in a hot oven.

Southern Field and Fireside, p. 38, vol. 1, no. 5, January 31, 1863, Augusta, GA

Sweet Potato Pie

Boil the potatoes very soft, then peel and mash them. To every quarter of a pound put one quart of milk, three table-spoonfuls of butter, four beaten eggs, together with sugar and nutmeg to the taste. It is improved by a glass of wine.

Southern Field and Fireside, p. 38, vol. 1, no. 5, January 31, 1863, Augusta, GA

Tomato Pie

The tomatoes are skinned and sliced, and after being mixed with sugar, are spiced and prepared in the same manner as other pies.

Southern Field and Fireside, p. 38, vol. 1, no. 5, January 31, 1863, Augusta, GA

Orange Jelly

Squeeze the juice out of twelve Havanna oranges, and one lemon; strain through a fine linen cloth; then mix with the boiled syrup; add the clarified isinglass, filter through a fine flannel bag, and finish as before.

Southern Field and Fireside, p. 38, vol. 1, no. 5, January 31, 1863, Augusta, GA

Corn Cake

Six cups of good butter milk, one egg, salt enough, and a table spoonful of saleratus; make thin as batter for frying, beat quickly and only long enough to free from lumps; pour into buttered pans and bake half an hour. This is light, with a nice tender crust.

Southern Field and Fireside, p. 38, vol. 1, no. 5, January 31, 1863, Augusta, GA

Fast Day

We hope our readers will bear in mind that Friday, 27th inst. has been appointed by the President as a day of Fasting, Humiliation and Prayer throughout the Confederate States, his proclamation to which effect we published last week. It is becoming that we, as a people, should gratefully acknowledge the blessings of Heaven bestowed upon us during the war, and especially that we should invoke the favor of the Most High in this hour of need, while contending against a foe greatly superior in numerical strength, and who is resolved upon our subjugation, if malice and cruelty can accomplish it. Let all the Churches be filled with humble worshippers on the day set apart for this solemn outpouring of Southern hearts.

Southern Field and Fireside, p. 92, vol. 1, no. 12, March 21, 1863, Augusta, GA

Sweet Potato Waffles

Two tablespoonsful of mashed potato, one of butter, one of sugar, one pint of milk, four tablespoonsful of wheat flour; mix well together and bake in a waffle iron.

Southern Field and Fireside, p. 92, vol. 1, no. 12, March 21, 1863, Augusta, GA

Soft Cakes in Little Pans

One and a half pounds of butter rubbed into two pounds of flour, add one wine glass of wine, one of rose water, two of yeast, nutmeg, cinnamon, and currants.

Southern Field and Fireside, p. 92, vol. 1, no. 12, March 21, 1863, Augusta, GA

Jumbles

Three pound of flour, two of sugar, one of butter, eight eggs, with a little carraway seed; add a little milk, if the eggs are not sufficient.

Southern Field and Fireside, p. 92, vol. 1, no. 12, March 21, 1863, Augusta, GA

Tea Cake

Three cups of sugar, three eggs, one cup of butter, one cup of milk, a small lump of pearlash, and make it not quite as thick as pound cake.

Southern Field and Fireside, p. 92, vol. 1, no. 12, March 21, 1863, Augusta, GA

To Preserve Eggs

Provide a small cupboard, safe, or tier of shelves; bore the shelves full of holes one and a quarter inches in diameter, and place the eggs in them, point downwards. They will keep sound for several months. Other modes, such as packing in salt, etc., depend for their success simply on placing the points down; the shelves are more convenient and accessible.

Southern Field and Fireside, p. 108, vol. 1, no. 14, April 4, 1863, Augusta, GA

Preservation of Milk and Cream

Put the milk into bottles, then place them in a saucepan with cold water, and gradually raise it to the boiling point; take it from the fire, and instantly cork the bottles, then raise the milk once more to the boiling point for half a minute. Finally let the bottles cool in the water in which they were boiled. Milk thus treated will remain perfectly good for six months. Emigrants, especially those having children, will find the above hint adds[24] much to their comfort while on their voyage.

Southern Field and Fireside, p. 108, vol. 1, no. 14, April 4, 1863, Augusta, GA

Sassafras Blossom as Substitute for Green or Black Tea

If the blossom of the sassafras—which will now soon be in full bloom—be gathered and dried in the shade, be used in making tea, instead of the root, it will be found an excellent substitute for tea, which now sells at from twelve to fifteen dollars a pound. By many who have tried it, it is pronounced to be a most delicious and palatable beverage

Southern Watchman, p. 1, April 22, 1863, Athens, GA

Potatoes for Bread

When potatoes bear such a price to wheat, that, cooked, they are about half the price per pound of the flour, it is economy to add about one-fourth the weight of potatoes that is used of flour, for a batch of bread. Bread so made is pleasanter to the taste, and equally nutritious. The potatoes should be boiled with the skins on, and then peeled, mashed and stirred into a pulp, with warm water, and rubbed through a wire sieve, and then mixed with the flour and yeast added as for other bread. The bakers of New York understand the economy of using potatoes in their bread, whenever they are sold at low prices. The small potatoes, which are unsaleable for other purposes, are often sold wholesale to bakers and added to the bread.

Southern Field and Fireside, p. 127, vol. 1, no. 17, April 25, 1863, Augusta, GA

Beans

Beans make an excellent article of food for winter use, and may be prepared in a variety of ways. First, there is the old fashioned dish of baked pork and beans, good either hot or cold; and just the thing for "over Sunday." Some young house keeper may have forgotten to "ask Mother" how to cook this convenient and economical dish, and for her benefit, I will jot down my way.

Pick over and wash a quart of beans; soak them ten or twelve hours in three quarts of cold water; drain them; put them into a kettle; add fresh water enough to cover them well. When they begin to boil, drain again through a colander or coarse sieve, and cover them again with cold water. Lay a bit of pork four inches square upon them, cover them closely, and let them boil till they are tender. Add a tea spoonfull of soda, or saleratus and a little salt, if the pork has not salted them sufficiently. Stir them thoroughly, pour them out into a bake pan;

cut the rind of the pork into squares, and place it in the centre; put the whole in a moderate hot oven. Bake till a fine,[25] crisp, brown crust has formed over the top. If you have neglected to put them soaking the night previous, and wish to prepare them on short notice, they can be made nearly as good by putting them over dry, if you change the water three times instead of twice.

Southern Field and Fireside, p. 127, vol. 1, no. 17, April 25, 1863, Augusta, GA

Recipe for Making Worcester Sauce

Mrs., Dr. Gage,[26] of Union District, sent to the State Agricultural Society of South Carolina, 1858, the following recipe for making Worcester Sauce, which is said to be excellent:

Take one gallon of ripe tomatos, wash them in three quarts of water, boil it half down and strain it through a sieve. When all is drained, add two table-spoonfuls of ginger, two of mace, two of whole black pepper, two of salt, one of cloves, one of cayenne; let them simmer in the juice until reduced to one quart, pour in half a pint of best vinegar, then pour the whole through a hair sieve, bottle in half pint bottles, cork down, tightly seal, and keep in a cool place.

Charleston Mercury, p. 1, July 16, 1863, Charleston, SC

About Vinegar

Its cooling, thirst-sufficing properties render it peculiarly grateful in hot climates, and to those living upon salted meat, deprived of fresh vegetables and fruits. In

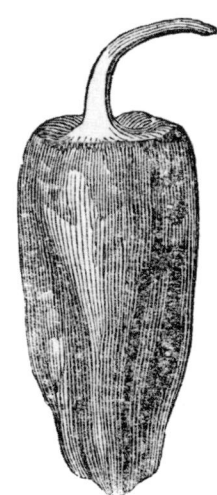

Cayenne pepper illustration in Henderson, *Gardening for Profit*, 225.

excess, it prevents digestion, and is injurious; but used with moderation, it assists and quickens digestion; keeps the stomach in tone and prevents bilious disorders; hence its generally wholesome properties make it a part of the rations furnished by most governments to their soldiers and sailors. Our own army is but badly provided for in this respect, and our brave soldiers almost invariably mention pickles as one of the most desirable things that can be sent them by their friends at home. Salt and vinegar is often one of the best things that can be given in the cases of dysentery so fatal in camps.

Southern Cultivator, p. 90, vol. 21, nos. 7 and 8, July and August 1863, Atlanta

Molasses from Watermelons!

Nothing is easier or more simple than to make molasses from the juice of watermelons. Take the juice of ripe melons and boil it in a large pot or kettle, the larger the better, until it is brought to the proper consistence, adding fresh juice from time to time as it boils away. This is all that is necessary, and this any one can do. If the business is conducted on a large scale, a simple press, similar to the old fashioned cider press, can be made to extract the juice from the pulp. After being pressed, the pulp should be put in a barrel and left to ferment. Draw off the liquid produced by the fermentation, and it will be found to be the best of vinegar.

Southern Cultivator, p. 103, vol. 21, nos. 7 and 8, July and August 1863, Atlanta

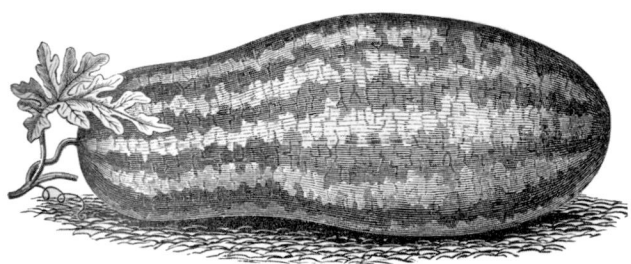

As it became harder to transport supplies of cane sugar and molasses during the war, Southerners looked for alternative sweeteners they could produce at home. The author of this 1863 article described how to produce molasses—or, at least, a thick syrup resembling molasses—by boiling down watermelon juice. Carolina watermelon illustration in Burr, *Field and Garden Vegetables*, 183.

Tomato Catsup

As the time is at hand for enjoying this favorite sauce, the following is a very good recipe for preparing it for future table use: To half a bushel of skinned tomatoes, add one quart of good vinegar, one pound of salt, a quarter of a pound of all-spice, six onions, one ounce of cloves, and two pounds of brown sugar. Boil this mass for three hours, constantly stirring it to keep from burning. When cool, strain it through a fine or coarse cloth, and bottle it for use. Many persons omit vinegar in this preparation.

Southern Cultivator, p. 103, vol. 21, nos. 7 and 8, July and August 1863, Atlanta

Dried Tomatoes

Take ripe tomatoes and scald them in the usual way, and strip off the skins, or mash and squeeze them through a sieve, then stew the pulp slowly, so as to evaporate as much as possible, without burning, then spread it on plates, and dry in a slow oven or in the hot sun. When wanted for use, you have only to soak and cook a few minutes, and serve it up just as you would tomatoes stewed fresh from the garden.

Southern Cultivator, p. 103, vol. 21, nos. 7 and 8, July and August 1863, Atlanta

To Make Good Bread

First, get good flour. Second, take one quart of flour, scald it by pouring over it some boiling water. Then for each loaf of bread you want to make, add one pint of cold water; stir in flour till it is as thick as can conveniently be stirred. Then put in one half pint of good hop yeast for every four loaves. Set it to rise over night. In the morning, make up by adding flour till it is stiff dough. Knead well, mould into loaves, and, when light, bake it well, and you will have good bread.

Southern Cultivator, p. 119, vol. 21, nos. 9 and 10, September and October 1863

Confederate Pepper

Take eight or ten pods of red pepper, boil as strong as you can make it; then add one pint of wheat and boil until it gets strong; then dry and parch it brown very slowly. Then grind, and it is fit for use.

Southern Cultivator, p. 128, reprinted from the Rokingham Register, vol. 21, nos. 9 and 10, September and October 1863, Atlanta

A company of women, in Columbus, Ga., and vicinity, claiming to be the wives of soldiers, recently addressed an epistle to Gov. Brown, in which they represented their sufferings for want of food and clothing as being very intense, and threatening that in the event their wants were not relieved, they would organize themselves into a sort of mob [or] "seizing party," and take provisions and clothing wherever they could find them. In reply, the Governor addressed the Justices of the Inferior Court of that county, enclosing the threatening epistle of the women, and requesting them to take such action in the premises as the court as might think proper.

Southern Watchman, p. 3, October 28, 1863, Athens, GA

Speaking of her mother, a noble old lady of over 60 years, our fair correspondent adds: "Mother is well and cheerful—drinking wheat coffee, without sugar—eating corn meal, instead of flour, and willing to do it the rest of her life (to use her own words), '*if we can only whip the Yankees.*'"

A people animated by such a spirit, and willing to make such sacrifices, may be overrun and temporarily depressed; but they can never be conquered or subjugated. We say, again—God bless our brave and noble Southern women! Were all our men as true-hearted and self-denying, there would be no thought even of a failure!

Southern Cultivator, p. 18, vol. 22, no. 1, January 1864, Atlanta

Syrup in Place of Bacon for Negroes

Owing to the scarcity of Bacon, and indeed of meat of all kinds, and the absolute necessity that the greater part which is made shall go to the subsistence of the army, negroes on nearly all plantations will necessarily receive but a small part of their usual allowance of animal food. Many intend to give them scarcely any bacon; but with their usual or an increased allowance of bread and the ordinary vegetables raised in plantation gardens, supply them with molasses made from Sorghum or the cane, instead of bacon. As a relish to eat with their corn bread, syrup is much liked by most negroes, and especially now when from the scanty supply of sweets the last few months their desire for it is greater than ordinary. But it is very doubtful whether syrup will at all answer as a substitute for meat for any great length of time. A working man like a working horse . . . must have something besides, and something more than the starch, oil and sugar which such a diet mainly affords, to build up his body, to repair the waste of his tissues and to give him strength and activity. Meat in some form, or some food rich in tissue-forming elements, is required. . . .

As for the white members of the family, if those in health receive a fourth even of their usual animal food for a season, with a full supply and good variety from[27] the vegetable kingdom, they will perhaps find much less inconvenience than they anticipate, and a large supply can be saved to feed our army.

Southern Cultivator, p. 20, vol. 22, no. 1, January 1864, Atlanta

Industry of Southern Women

A letter from Lincoln county, Tenn., says: "I witnessed many a scene in this rural district which the gay ladies of our fashionable cities may well ponder on, with the reflection of surprise of how little they know of the hardships which their sex are forced to undergo to sustain and support their families while their husbands and brothers are absent fighting the battles of our country. On the small farms throughout this section, all is life, activity and industry. Many a woman who never before held a plow is now seen in the corn-field—many a young girl who would have blushed at the thought before of handling a plow line, now naturally and unconsciously cries 'gee-up' to Dobbin, to the silvery tones of which the good brute readily responds, as if a pleasure to comply with so gentle a command. Many a Ruth, as of old, is seen to day, binding and gleaning in the wheat-fields. . . The picture of the rural soldier's home is at this time but a picture of primitive life."

Southern Cultivator, p. 22, vol. 22, no. 1, January 1864, Atlanta

Gravies and Fried Meats

If fried pork must be used as an article of food, to some extent, do not suffer the dripping or fat to be ever placed upon the table for gravy. Turn it out, leaving but a spoonful or two in the skillet, then pour in water or milk, and thicken while boiling, with a little flour and water rubbed till free from lumps. With the addition of salt, this makes a wholesome and palatable gravy. Gravy should be made in the same way for all fried meats. Fried meats usually, however, absorb too much fat to be strictly healthful. Meats broiled on the gridiron or baked in the oven, are more digestible.

Southern Field and Fireside, p. 5, vol. 2, no. 5, January 30, 1864, Augusta, GA

Mince Pies

Boil three pounds of lean beef till tender, and when cold chop it fine. Chop three pounds of beef suet, and mix with the meat, sprinkling in a table-spoonful of salt. Pare, core and chop fine six pounds of good apples; stone four pounds of raisins and chop them; wash and dry two pounds of currants; and mix them all with the meat. Season with a spoonful of powdered cinnamon, a powdered nutmeg, a little mace, and a few cloves, pounded, and one pound of brown sugar; add a quart of Maderia wine and a half pound of citron cut into small bits. This mixture put down in a jar and closely covered will keep several weeks. It makes a rich pie for Thanksgiving or Christmas.

Southern Field and Fireside, p. 5, vol. 2, no. 5, January 30, 1864, Augusta, GA

Mode of Preserving Apples

It is not generally known, that apples may be kept all the year round by being immersed in oats, which receive no injury from their contact.

Southern Field and Fireside, p. 5, vol. 2, no. 5, January 30, 1864, Augusta, GA

Starch or Saloon Cake

Take one cup of butter, one of sugar, one of sour milk, one teaspoonful of saleratus, one cup of starch, two cups of flour, three eggs, spice to suit your taste, bake three quarters of an hour. Add the whites of the eggs last, and stir it 10 minutes before baking.

Southern Field and Fireside, p. 5, vol. 2, no. 5, January 30, 1864, Augusta, GA

Tomato Sauce

Scald and peel your tomatoes. To nine or ten take a piece of butter the size of an egg, add pepper and salt, and a very little sugar, but no water. Cook it an hour, but stir it often.

Southern Field and Fireside, p. 5, vol. 2, no. 5, January 30, 1864, Augusta, GA

To Pickle Cabbage

Pull off the loose leaves, and cut the cabbage into shreds with a sharp knife; then sprinkle a little salt in the bottom of a keg or jar; then put in a layer of cabbage, and sprinkle salt, peppercorns, a little mace, cinnamon and allspice; then add another layer, and add spices and salt, as before. Continue these alternate layers, etc., until your jar is full. Heat your vinegar scalding hot, put in a little alum, turn it while hot on the cabbage. Turn the vinegar from the cabbage six or seven times, heat it scalding hot, and turn it back while hot, to make them tender.

Southern Cultivator, p. 36, vol. 22, no. 2, February 1864, Atlanta

Substitute for Tea

A new style of Confederate Tea, which is very much approved by those who have used it, is made by mixing half a teaspoonful of tea with a tablespoonful and a half of blackberry leaves, which have been cured by drying them on a cooking stove. The blackberry leaf can be found at any season in sheltered places, and will soon be abundant.

Southern Cultivator, p. 55, vol. 22, no. 3, March 1864, Atlanta

To Make Corn Bread

Two quarts corn meal, one quart rye, one quart of sweet milk, one quart of buttermilk, one teacup of molasses, one spoonful of salt, and one teaspoonful of soda. Beat with a spoon until well mixed. The crust, if not burned, will make excellent coffee.

Southern Cultivator, p. 55, vol. 22, no. 3, March 1864, Atlanta

Dried Potatoes

We have been shown, says the Savannah Republican, some potatoes, of the yam species, and crop of 1861, which are in a perfect state of preservation, and though hard, contain all their sweetness and nutriment. They were baked over two years ago, and then dried. Apparently they will remain sound for an indefinite time. The experiment is suggestive in this time of scarcity, and perhaps could be turned to a good account. A half bushel of potatoes thus dried could be carried readily in a soldier's haversack, and a little hot water would doubtless soften and prepare them for food.

Southern Cultivator, p. 55, vol. 22, no. 3, March 1864, Atlanta

To Make Loaf Rice Bread

Boil a pint of rice soft, and add a pint of leaven, then three quarters of the flour, put it to rise in a tin or earthen vessel until it has risen sufficiently; divide it into three parts, then bake it as other bread, and you will have three large loaves.

Southern Field and Fireside, p. 8, vol. 2, no. 18, April 30, 1864, Augusta, GA

Starvation in the Mountains

Little do the people at large dream of the sufferings of our population in the mountain counties. With most of the agricultural labor withdrawn, (for there is little slave labor there) their corn crop greatly damaged by frost last September, and the country since that time eaten up by Confederate cavalry and damaged by Federal raids, is it to be wondered that what the women and children and old men made should now be exhausted?

By letters from respectable citizens, and from conversations with reliable men from that section, who have visited this place to haul corn to the people, we learn that they are now actually suffering great privation—some of the best citizens having nothing but dry bread and others subsisting upon roots and weeds! Their means for making a crop this year are very slender—their oxen being impressed for the army and their horses and mules perished for lack of food, as well as their milch cows and hogs! Our informants do not pretend to say that all the domestic animals have perished or that all the people have been reduced to such straits, but inform us it is true of great numbers.

Southern Watchman, p. 2, May 18, 1864, Athens, GA

Our Market

If there is any thing in this town to sell, in the shape of meat or breadstuffs, we would be pleased to learn where it is. If our friends in the country ever expect to send any thing here—particularly corn, corn meal, syrup, potatoes, turnips, &c.—now is the time to do it! There is also a great demand for provender of all kinds—hay, fodder, shucks. Indeed every thing is in demand—even to fire wood. Send on quickly, or many persons and animals must perish!

Southern Watchman, p. 2, January 18, 1865, Athens, GA

Notice posted by R. Nickerson

Salt, Thread, Nails, Hand Looms and a few Sugar Mills, to exchange for bacon, corn, wheat, and wood—all of which are now wanting to supply the families of our workmen.

Athens Foundry and Machine Works

Southern Watchman, p. 3, February 15, 1865, Athens, GA

Confederate Receipt Book: A Compilation of over One Hundred Receipts, Adapted to the Times

The only Southern cookbook to be formally published during the Civil War, the *Confederate Receipt Book* plainly said it was "adapted to the times."[1] The times were hard, and the book reflects that on almost every page. Like most nineteenth-century cookbooks, it combined culinary recipes with general housekeeping hints. But unlike a traditional cookbook, this slim book—reproduced here in its entirety—focused almost exclusively on making things on the cheap, getting by without normal staples, and making the most of every crumb.

Some of the recipes were specifically intended for men in the war. For example, there are hints on preventing thirst or hunger while marching by chewing coffee grounds or by munching on toasted corn meal and brown sugar, something the author noted would have been particularly useful "to soldiers on a scout." There was also advice on purifying muddy water or on preventing blisters "on a long march" by rubbing cheap soap into sock fibers. Some of the suggested remedies were for ills particularly common to soldiers in the Civil War, like "camp itch" and dysentery.

But most of the recipes were aimed at people on the home front. This wasn't simply an economical book aimed at poor readers, but rather a guidebook for people facing a specific kind of poverty—the poverty of downward mobility. In other words, it wasn't just about making do with little, but about making do with less. The hints about making dresses and hats and kid gloves last longer, about reducing petticoats from two to one, about making "old silk look as well as new," were all speaking to women from formerly comfortable circumstances who were adjusting to dimming fortunes and dwindling supplies. The food recipes, in particular, reflect a time of shortages. Recipes like "Brewis," a mash of old crusts and hot milk, provided new ways to use up bits of stale bread. And there are all sorts of recipes for substitutes, such as instructions on making "coffee" that contained no actual coffee, and instructions on preserving meat without salt, as salt shortages worsened across the Confederacy.

But if there was no more salt, at least there was still meat. In fact, even as the *Confederate Receipt Book* focused on tumbling fortunes, it also reveals how relatively far the South still had to fall in 1863. Times were hard and getting harder, but this book shows they were hardly uniformly desperate. Note, for instance, how many recipes assumed readers would still have ingredients on hand like wheat flour, butter, and ham—all foods that poor Southerners would have been delighted to have in the best of times. And many of the new wartime recipes to produce passable substitutes for cream or coffee weren't necessarily new at all: many of them had already been in use for years by people who had never been able to afford expensive goods like imported coffee.

In fact, in the first half of 1863, the war still looked eminently winnable to many Southerners. Conditions had gotten rougher than anyone had expected, but Confederates still controlled the great majority of the South and Union forces had yet to land anything resembling a knockout blow. That would change drastically later in the war, but at the time this book was published it didn't seem absurd to include advice on topics like buying a new carpet or judging the quality of lamb. In fact, the very fact that the book was published at all in Richmond in 1863 points to a certain amount of resources and optimism.

Also keep this in mind: the *Confederate Receipt Book* was very much a wartime cookbook, but not all the problems it promised to relieve were war related. Some of the problems were simply nineteenth century related. For example, advice on curing a toothache or on softening tough meat for someone with weak and rotting teeth speak more to the abysmal state of Americans' dental health than to specific wartime troubles. Other problems—moths infesting food stores, a nagging cough, a nasty burn—were routine annoyances before refrigeration, modern medicine, or electric power.

Biscuit

Take one quart of flour, three teaspoonfuls of cream of tartar, mixed well through the flour, two tablespoonfuls of shortening, one teaspoonful of soda, dissolved in warm water, of sufficient quantity to mould the quart of flour. For large families the amount can be doubled.

Another Receipt [for biscuits]

Take two quarts of flour, two ounces of butter, half pint of boiling water, one teaspoonful of salt, one pint of cold milk, and half cup yeast. Mix well and set to rise, then mix a teaspoonful of saleratus in a little water and mix into dough, roll on a board an inch thick, cut into small biscuits, and bake twenty minutes.

Soda Biscuit

One quart of sour milk, one teaspoonful of soda, one of salt, a piece of butter the size of an egg, and flour enough to make them roll out.

Pumpkin Bread

Boil a good pumpkin in water till it is quite thick, pass it through a sieve, and mix flour so as to make a good dough. This makes an excellent bread.

Nice Buns

Take three quarters of a pound of sifted flour, two large spoonfuls of brown sugar, two spoonfuls of good yeast, add a little salt, stir well together, and when risen work in two spoonfuls of butter, make into buns, set it to rise again, and bake on tins.

Indian Bread

One quart of butter milk, one quart of corn meal, one quart of coarse flour, one cup of molasses, add a little soda and salt.

To Raise Bread without Yeast

Mix in your flour subcarbonate of soda, two parts, tartaric acid one part, both finely powdered. Mix up your bread with warm water, adding but little at a time, and bake soon.

Starchy pumpkin could be made into bread, a useful trick at times when midwestern wheat flour became costly or hard to find. Pumpkin illustration in Burr, *Field and Garden Vegetables*, 192.

Yeast

Boil one pound of good flour, a quarter of a pound of brown sugar and a little salt in two gallons of water for one hour. When milk warm bottle it close, it will be fit to use in twenty four hours. One part of this will make eighteen pounds of bread.

A Cheap and Quick Pudding

Beat up four eggs, add a pint of milk and little salt, and stir in four large spoonfuls of flour, a little nutmeg and sugar to your taste. Beat it well, and pour it into buttered teacups, filling them rather more than half full. They will bake in a stove or Dutch oven in fifteen minutes.

Republican Pudding

Take one cup of soft boiled rice, a pint of milk, a cup of sugar, three eggs, and a piece of butter the size of an egg. Serve with sauce.

A Minute Pudding

Stir flour into boiling milk to the consistence of a thin hasty pudding, and in fifteen or twenty minutes it will be fit for the table. Serve with sauce to suit the taste.

Peas Pudding

Take about three quarters of a pint of split peas, and put them into a pint basin, tie a cloth over them (to give room to swell,) put them into *boiling water*, and let them boil two hours, then take them up, untie them, add an egg beaten up, a little butter, with salt and pepper, then beat up, tie up again, and place them in the water to boil for about twenty minutes more, you will then have a well flavored and nice shaped pudding.

Plain Potato Pudding

Having pared a pound of fine large potatoes, put them into a pot, cover them well with cold water, and boil them gently till tender all through. When done lay each potato (one at a time) in a clean warm napkin, and press and wring it till all the moisture is squeezed out, and the potato becomes a round dry lump. Mince as fine as possible a quarter of a pound of fresh beef suet, (divested of skin and strings;) crumble the potato and mix it well with the suet; adding a small salt spoon of salt. Add sufficient milk to make a thick batter, and beat it well. Dip a strong square cloth in hot water, shake it out, and dredge it well with flour. Tie the pudding in, leaving room for it to swell, and put it into a large pot of hot water, and boil it steady for an hour. This is a good and economical pudding.

Potato Crust

Boil six good-sized mealy potatoes, and mash them fine, add salt, a spoonful of butter, and two of water, while they are hot, then work in flour enough for making a paste to roll out, or put in two or three spoonfuls of cream, and no butter or water. This is a good crust for hot pies or dumplings.

Paste for Pies

Excellent paste for fruit or meat pies may be made with two-thirds of wheat flour, one-third of the flour of boiled potatoes, and some butter or dripping, the whole being brought to a proper consistence with warm water, and a small quantity of yeast added when lightness is desired. This will also make palateable cakes for breakfast, and may be made with or without spices, fruit, &c.

Apple Pie without Apples

To one small bowl of crackers, that have been soaked until no hard parts remain, add one teaspoonful of tartaric acid, sweeten to your taste, add some butter, and a very little nutmeg.

Artificial Oysters

Take young green corn, grate it in a dish; to one pint of this add one egg, well beaten, a small teacup of flour, two or three tablespoonfuls of butter, some salt and pepper, mix them all together. A tablespoonful of the batter will make the size of an oyster. Fry them light brown, and when done butter them. Cream if it can be procured is better.

Cottage Cheese

This is a good way of using up a pan of milk that is found to be turning sour. Having covered it, set it in a warm place till it becomes a curd, then pour off the liquid, and tie up the curd in a clean linen bag with a pointed end, and set a bowl under it to catch the droppings, but do not squeeze it. After it has drained ten or twelve hours transfer the curd to a deep dish, enrich it with some cream, and press and chop it with a large spoon till it is a soft mass, adding as you proceed an ounce or more of nice fresh butter.

Slapjacks

Take flour, little sugar and water, mix with or without a little yeast, the latter better if at hand, mix into paste, and fry the same as fritters in clean fat.

Indian Sagamite

Three parts of Indian meal and one of brown sugar, mixed and browned over the fire, will make the food known as "Sagamite." Used in small quantities, it not only appeases hunger but allays thirst, and is therefore useful to soldiers on a scout.

Beer, Vinegar, &c.

Table Beer

To eight quarts of boiling water put a pound of treacle, a quarter of an ounce of ginger and two bay leaves, let this boil for a quarter of an hour, then cool, and work it with yeast as other beer.

Another Receipt [for table beer]

Eight quarts water, one quart molasses, one pint yeast, one tablespoonful cream of tartar, mixed and bottled in twenty-four hours; or, to two pounds of coarse brown sugar add two gallons of water, and nearly two ounces hops. Let the whole boil three quarters of an hour, and then work as usual. It should stand a week or ten days before being drawn, and will improve daily afterward for a moderate time.

Spruce Beer

Take three gallons of water, blood warmth, three half pints of molasses, a tablespoonful of essence of spruce, and the like quantity of ginger, mix well together with a gill of yeast, let it stand over night, and bottle it in the morning. It will be in a good condition to drink in twenty-four hours.

Ginger Beer

One pint of molasses and two spoonfuls of ginger put into a pail, to be half filled with boiling water; when well stirred together, fill the pail with cold water, leaving room for one pint of yeast, which must not be put in until lukewarm. Place it on a warm hearth for the night, and bottle in the morning.

Blackberry Wine

Measure your berries and bruise them; to every gallon add one quart of boiling water, let the mixture stand twenty-four hours, stirring occasionally, then strain off the liquor into a cask; to every gallon add two pounds of sugar, cork tight, and let it stand till following October, and you will have wine ready for use without any further straining or boiling, that will make lips smack as they never smacked under similar influence before.

Apple Water

Take one tart apple of ordinary size, well baked, let it be well mashed, pour on it one pint of boiling water, beat them well together, let it stand to cool, and strain it off for use. It may be sweetened with sugar if desired.

Cider Jelly

Boil cider to the consistence of syrup, and let it cool, and you have nice jelly.

To Make Vinegar

Take one pint of molasses, put it in a jug with one gallon of warm water, not boiling, let it stand for two months, and you will have good vinegar.

Another Receipt for a Larger Quantity

To eight gallons of clear rain water add three quarts of molasses, put into a good cask shake well a few times, then add two or three spoonfuls of good yeast. If in the summer place the cask in the sun; if in winter near the chimney, where it may be warm. In ten or fifteen days add to the liquid a sheet of brown paper, torn in strips, dipped into molasses, and good vinegar will be produced.

Tomato Catsup

Nice catsup may be made with four quarts of tomatoes, one pint of vinegar, three table spoonfuls salt, two of mustard, two of black pepper, three red peppers broken and half ounce alspice or mace.

Soap and Candles

Soap

Pour twelve quarts of boiling water upon five pounds of unslacked lime. Then dissolve five pounds of washing soda in twelve quarts of boiling water, mix the above together, and let the mixture remain from twelve to twenty-four hours, for the purpose of chemical action. Now pour off all the clear liquid, being careful not to disturb the sediment. Add to the above three and a half pounds of clarified grease, and from three to four ounces of rosin. Boil this compound together for one hour, and pour off to cool. Cut it up in bars for use, and you are in the possession of a superior chemical soap, costing about three and a half cents per pound in ordinary times.

Soft Soap

Bore some holes in a lye barrel, put some straw in the bottom, lay some unslacked lime on it, and fill your barrel with good hard wood ashes, wet it, and pound it down as you put it in. When full, make a basin in the ashes and pour in water, keep filling it as it sinks in the ashes. In the course of a few hours the lye will begin to run. When you have a sufficient quantity to begin with, put your grease in a large iron pot, pour in the lye, let it boil, &c. Three pounds of clean grease are allowed for two gallons of soap.

Honey Soap

Cut into thin shavings two pounds of common yellow or white soap, put it on the fire with just water enough to keep it from burning; when quite melted, add a quarter of a pound of honey, stirring it till it boils, then take it off and add a few drops of any agreeable perfume. Pour it into a deep dish to cool, and then cut it into squares. It improves by keeping. It will soften and whiten the skin.

Tallow Candles

After melting the tallow, add say one pound of quicklime to every twenty of tallow, strain the tallow, and mould the candles. If this recipe is followed, you will have a candle equal to the adamantine, free from all impurities, and giving a brilliant light.

Confederate Candle

Melt together a pound of beeswax and a quarter of a pound of rosin or of turpentine, fresh from the tree. Prepare a wick 30 or 40 yards long, made up of three threads of loosely spun cotton, saturate this well with the mixture, and draw it through your fingers, to press all closely together, and to keep the size even. Repeat the process until the candle attains the size of a large straw or quill, then wrap around a bottle, or into a ball with a flat bottom. Six inches of this candle elevated above the rest will burn for fifteen or twenty minutes, and give a very pretty light, and forty yards have sufficed a small family a summer for all the usual purposes of the bed-chamber.

Remedies, &c.

For Dysentery

Dissolve as much table salt in *pure* vinegar as will ferment and work clear. When the foam is discharged cork it up in a bottle, and put it away for use. A large spoonful of this in a gill of boiling water is efficacious in cases of dysentery and cholic.

Cure for Chills

The plant, commonly called hoarhound, is said to afford a certain cure. Boil it in water, and drink freely of the tea.

Gargle for Sore Throat, Diptheria or Scarlet Fever

Mix in a common size cup of fresh milk two teaspoon-fuls of pulverized charcoal and ten drops of spirits of turpentine. Soften the charcoal with a few drops of milk before putting into the cup. Gargle frequently, according to the violence of the symptoms.

To Relieve Asthma

Take the leaves of the stramonium (or Jamestown weed,) dried in the shade, saturated with a pretty strong solution of salt petre, and smoke it so as to inhale the fumes. It may strangle at first if taken too freely, but it will loosen the phlegm in the lungs. The leaves should be gathered before frost.

Simple Cure for Croup

If a child is taken with croup apply cold water suddenly and freely to the neck and chest with a sponge or towel. The breathing will instantly be relieved, then wipe it dry, cover it up warm, and soon a quiet slumber will relieve the parent's anxiety.

For a Troublesome Cough

Take of treacle and the best white wine vinegar six tablespoonfuls each, add forty drops of laudanum, mix it well, and put into a bottle. A teaspoonful to be taken occasionally when the cough is troublesome. The mixture will be found efficacious without the laudanum in many cases.

For Sick Headache

One teaspoonful of pulverized charcoal and one-third of a teaspoonful of soda mixed in very warm water.

Cure for a Toothache

Powdered alum will not only relieve the toothache, but prevent the decay of the tooth. Salt may advantageously be mixed with the alum.

Cure for a Burn

Wheat flour and cold water, mixed to the consistency of soft paste, is an almost instantaneous cure for a burn. Renew before the first gets dry so as to stick.

Cure for Camp Itch

Take iodide of potassium, sixty grains, lard, two ounces, mix well, and after washing the body well with warm soap suds rub the ointment over the person three times a week. In seven or eight days the acarus or itch insect will be destroyed. In this recipe the horrible effects of the old sulphur ointment are obviated.

Cure for a Felon

The *Selma Reporter* says: A poultice of onions, applied morning, noon and night for three or four days, will cure a felon.[2] No matter how bad the case, splitting the finger will be unnecessary, if this poultice be used. We have seen it tried several times, and know that the remedy is a sure, safe and speedy one.

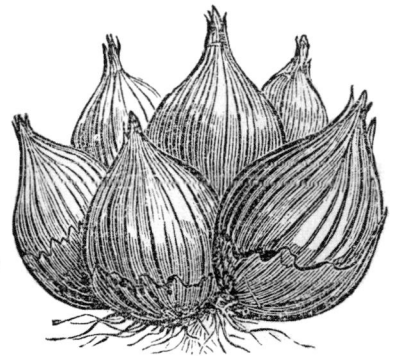

Onions were star players in a variety of Southern dishes, and they also played important parts in homemade medicines. This medicinal recipe, Cure for a Felon, promised that an onion poultice applied three times daily for several consecutive days would relieve a "felon"—that is, an infected fingertip. Illustration of a potato onion, an onion variety popular in the nineteenth century, in White, *Gardening for the South*, 259.

To Cure Corns

The cause of corns, and likewise the pain they occasion, is simply friction, and to lessen the friction you have only to use your toe as you do in like circumstances a coach wheel[;] lubricate it with some oily substance. The best thing to use is a little sweet oil rubbed on the affected part (after the corn is carefully pared) with the tip of the finger, which should be done on getting up in the morning, and just before stepping into bed at night. In a few days the pain will diminish, and in a few days more it will cease, when the nightly application may be discontinued.

To Destroy Warts

Dissolve as much common washing soda as the water will take up, wash the warts with this for a minute or two, and let them dry without wiping. Keep the water in a bottle and repeat the washing often, and it will take away the largest of warts.

Miscellaneous Receipts

Preserving Meat without Salt

We need salt as a relish to our food, but it is not essential in the preservation of our meats. The Indians used little or no salt, yet they preserved meat and even fish in abundance by drying. This can be accomplished by fire, by smoke or by sunshine, but the most rapid and reliable mode is by all these agents combined. To do this select a spot having the fullest command of sunshine. Erect there a wigwam five or six feet high, with an open top, in size proportioned to the quantity of meat to be cured, and protected from the winds, so that all the smoke must pass through the open top. The meat cut into pieces suitable for drying (the thinner the better) to be suspended on rods in the open comb, and a vigorous smoke made of decayed wood is to be kept up without cessation. Exposed thus to the combined influence of sunshine, heat and smoke, meat cut into slices not over an inch thick can be thoroughly cured in twenty-four hours. For thicker pieces there must be, of course, a longer time, and the curing of oily meat, such as pork, is more difficult than that of beef, venison or mutton.

To cure meat *in the sun* hang it on the South side of your house, as near to the wall as possible without touching.

Savages *cure fish* by pounding it fine, and exposing it to the bright sun.

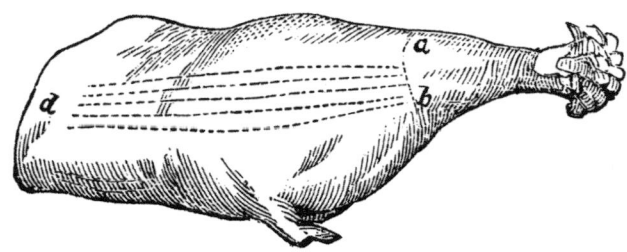

Curing meats in salt had been the primary way Southerners had preserved meat before the war. Once the Union blockade choked off salt imports, Southerners experimented with other ways to preserve a variety of meats, including venison. Venison illustration from Hill, *Mrs. Hill's Southern Practical Cookery*, facsimile of 1872 edition, 88.

To Cure Bacon with Little Salt

Take five gallons water, seven pounds salt, one pound sugar, or one pint molasses, one teaspoonful saltpetre, mix, and after sprinkling the flesh side of the hams in the salt, pack in a tight barrel, hams first, then shoulders, lastly middlings. Pour over the brine, and if not enough to cover, make another draft of the above, and repeat till all is covered, leaving the meat in brine from four to seven weeks, according to size.

To Prevent Skippers in Ham

In order to avoid the skipper,[3] and all worms and bugs that usually infest and destroy bacon, keep your smoke house *dark*, and the moth that deposits the eggs will never enter it. Smoke with green hickory, this is important, as the flavor of the bacon is often destroyed by smoking with improper wood.

Method of Curing Bad Butter

Melt the butter in hot water, skim it off as clean as possible, and work it over again in a churn, add salt and fine sugar, and press well.

To Clarify Molasses

To free molasses from its sharp taste, and to render it fit to be used, instead of sugar, take twelve pounds of molasses, twelve pounds of water, and three pounds of charcoal, coarsely pulverized, mix them in a kettle, and boil the whole over a slow wood fire. When the mixture has boiled half an hour, pour it into a flat vessel, in order that the charcoal may subside to the bottom, then pour off the liquid, and place it over the fire once more, that the superfluous[4] water may evaporate, and the molasses be brought to their former consistence. Twelve pounds of molasses will produce twelve pounds of syrup.

Substitute for Cream in Tea or Coffee

Beat the white of an egg to a froth, put to it a very small lump of butter, and mix well, then turn the coffee to it gradually, so that it may not curdle. If perfectly done it will be an excellent substitute for cream. For tea omit the butter, using only the egg.

Substitute for Coffee

Take sound ripe acorns, wash them while in the shell, dry them, and parch until they open, take the shell off, roast with a little bacon fat, and you will have a splendid cup of coffee.

To Judge the Quality of Lamb

If fresh the vein in the neck of a forequarter is bluish; if green or yellow it is stale. In the hindquarter if the knuckle is limp, and the part under the kidney smells slightly disagreeable, avoid it. If the eyes are sunken do not buy the head.

To Test Flour

Knead a small quantity by way of experiment. If good, the flour immediately forms an adhesive elastic paste, which will readily assume any form that may be given to it without breaking.

To Prepare Salt

Set a lump of salt in a plate before the fire, and when dry pound it in a mortar, or rub two pieces of salt together. It will then be free from lumps, and in very fine powder.

Soft Water

If you are troubled to get soft water for washing fill a tub or barrel half full of wood ashes, and fill it up with water, so that you may have lye whenever you want it. A gallon of strong lye put into a large kettle of hard water will make it as soft as rain water.

Nutmegs

The largest, heaviest, and most unctuous nutmegs are the best. If you begin to grate nutmeg at the stalk end it will prove hollow throughout.

Rice Glue

Mix rice flour smoothly with cold water, and simmer it over a slow fire, when it will form a delicate and durable cement, not only answering all the purposes of common paste, but well adapted for joining paper and card board ornamental work.

To Cement Broken China or Glass

Beat lime to the finest powder, and sift it through fine muslin, then tie some into a thin muslin, put on the edges of the broken china some white of egg, dust some lime quickly on the same, and unite them exactly.

Ink

To make five gallons of good cheap ink, take half a pound of extract of logwood and dissolve it in five gallons of hot water, and add half an ounce of bichromate potash. Strain and bottle it.

To Improve Pale Black Ink

To a pint of black ink add one drachm of impure carbonate of potassa, and in a few minutes it will be jet black. Be careful that the ink does not run over during the effervescence caused by the potassa.

To Preserve Steel Pens

Metallic pens may be preserved from rusting by throwing into the bottle containing the ink a few nails or broken pieces of steel pens if not varnished. The corrosive action of the acid which the ink contains is expended on the iron so introduced, and will not therefore affect the pen.

Fire Balls for Fuel

Mix one bushel of small coal or sawdust, or both, with two bushels of sand and one bushel and a half of clay, make the mixture into balls with water, and pile them in a dry place to harden them. A fire cannot be lighted with these balls, but when it burns strong put them on above the top bar, and they will keep up a strong heat.

To Purify River or Muddy Water

Dissolve half an ounce of alum in a pint of warm water, and stirring it about in a puncheon of water from the river, all the impurities will soon settle to the bottom, and in a day or two it will become quite clear.

To Give a Cool Taste to Water

A few leaves of sheep mint held in the mouth, or chewed, just before drinking water, will seemingly impart a degree of coolness to the draught.

To Prevent Thirst

Coffee grounds chewed at intervals on a march, or during any arduous service, will repress thirst and satiate the cravings of hunger. When boiled over again, and the decoction becomes cool, it will quench thirst more effectively than water.

Charcoal Tooth Powder

Pound charcoal as fine as possible in a mortar, or grind it in a mill, then well sift it, and apply a little of it to the teeth about twice a week, and it will not only render them beautifully white, but will also make the breath sweet, and the gums firm and comfortable. If the charcoal is ground in a mortar, it is convenient to grind it in water to prevent the dust from flying about. Indeed the powder is more convenient for use when kept in water.

Wax for Sealing Bottles

Take equal parts of rosin and beeswax and melt over a fire, stir in some Spanish Brown, and while hot dip in the bottles.

Cheap Blacking

To a tea cup of molasses stir in lampblack until it is black, then add the white of two eggs, well beaten, and to this add a pint of vinegar or whiskey, and put it in a bottle for use. Shake it before using.

Chinese Method of Rendering Cloth Waterproof

To one ounce of white wax, melted, add one quart of spirits of turpentine, in which, when thoroughly mixed and cold, dip the cloth and hang up to dry. Try it.

To Clean Kid Gloves

First see that your hands are clean, then put on the gloves and wash them, as though you were washing your hands in a basin of turpentine, then hang them up in a warm place, or where there is a good current of air, which will carry off all smell of turpentine. This method was brought from Paris, and thousands of dollars have been made by it.

To Bleach Straw Hats, &c.

Straw hats and bonnets are bleached by putting them, previously washed in pure water, into a box with burning sulphur, the fumes which arise unite with the water on the bonnets, and the sulphurous acid thus formed bleaches them.

To Remove Grease from Cloth

Take soft soap and fuller's earth, of each half a pound, beat them well together in a mortar, and form cakes. The spot first moistened with water is rubbed with the cake and allowed to dry, when it is well rubbed with a little warm water, and afterwards rinsed or rubbed clean.

To Remove Grease from Books

Lay upon the spot a little magnesia or powdered chalk, and under it the same, set on it a warm flat iron, and as soon as the grease is melted it will all be absorbed, and leave the paper clean.

To Make Old Silk Look as Well as New

Unpick the dress, grate two Irish potatoes into a quart of water, let it stand to settle, strain it without disturbing the sediment and sponge the silk with it. Iron on the wrong side.

Powder to Clean Gold Lace

Rock alum (burnt and finely powdered,) five parts, levigated chalk one part, mix. Apply with a dry brush.

To Keep Arms and Polished Metal from Rust

Dissolve one ounce of camphor in two pounds of hog's lard, observing to take off the scum, then mix as much black lead as will give the mixture an iron color. Fire arms, &c., rubbed over with this mixture, left twenty-four hours, and then dried with a linen cloth, will keep clean for many months.

To Make Economical Wicks for Lamps

When using a lamp with a flat wick, if you take a piece of clean cotton stocking it will answer the purpose as well as the cotton wicks which are sold in the shops.

To Dry Herbs

Dry the gathered crop, thinly spread out and shaded from the sun, tie the herbs in small bundles, and keep them compactly pressed down and covered with white paper; or, after drying them, put each sort into a small box, and by means of boards fitted in it, and a screw-press, press the herbs into cakes or little trusses. These should be afterwards carefully wrapped up in paper and be kept in a dry place, when they will retain their aroma as perfectly as when they were put into the press, for at least three years. By the common method of hanging up herbs in loose bundles the odor soon escapes.

An Illuminated Bottle

By putting a piece of phosphorus the size of a pea into a phial, and adding boiling oil until the bottle is a third full, a luminous bottle is formed, for on taking out the cork to admit atmospheric air, the empty space in the phial will become luminous. Whenever the stopper is taken out at night, sufficient light is evolved to show the hour upon a watch, and if care be taken to keep it generally well closed it will preserve its illuminative power for several months.

A Cheap Taper for a Sick Room

Take a piece of soft pliant paper, part of newspaper for example, and form a circle of it, then gather the centre together and twist it into a wick, immerse the whole in a saucer of lard and light it, and you have a taper that will last some hours.

To Prevent Blisters on the Feet

Blistering or soreness of the feet may be prevented on long marches by covering the soles of the stockings with a coating of the cheapest brown soap. Coarse cotton socks are the best for walking.

Tough Meat

Those whose teeth are not strong enough to masticate hard beef should cut their steaks the day before using into slices about two inches thick, rub over them a small quantity of soda, wash off next morning, cut them into suitable thickness, and cook according to fancy. The same process will answer for any description of tough meat.

Cheap Door Mats

Cut any old woolen articles into long strips, from one to two inches broad. Braid three of these together, and sew the braid in gradually increasing circles till large enough.

Economy in Carpets

In buying a carpet, as in everything else, those of the best quality are cheapest in the end. As it is extremely desirable that they should look as clean as possible, avoid buying a carpet that has any white in it. Even a small portion of white interspersed through the pattern will in a short time give it a dingy appearance.

If you cannot obtain a hearth rug that exactly corresponds with the carpet, get one entirely different, for a decided contrast looks better than a bad match.

Various Hints

One flannel petticoat will wear nearly as long as two, if turned behind part before, when the front begins to wear out. If you have a strip of land do not throw away soapsuds. Both ashes and soap suds are good manure for bushes and young plants.

See that nothing is thrown away which might have served to nourish your own family, or a poorer one.

"Brewis" is made of crusts and dry pieces of bread soaked a good while in hot milk, mashed up, and eaten with salt.

Charcoal powder will be found a very good thing to give knives a polish.

A bonnet and trimmings may be worn a much longer time if the dust be brushed well off after walking.

A bowl containing two quarts of water, set in an oven when baking, will prevent pies, cakes, &c., from being scorched.

Recipes for Making Bread, &c., from Rice Flour

Editors Columbus Sun: I read an article in one of your papers lately in which recipes for making different kinds of bread with rice flour were enquired for, and having a few that I think will be found very good I send them to you. They were printed in Charleston, S. C., several years ago.

Elizabeth B. Lewis

Russel County, Ala., September 8th, 1862

To Make Loaf Rice Bread

Boil a pint of rice soft, add a pint of leaven, then three quarts of rice flour, put it to rise in a tin or earthern[5] vessel until it has raised sufficiently; divide it into three parts, and bake it as other bread, and you will have three large loaves, or scald the flour, and when cold mix half wheat flour or corn meal, raised with leaven in the usual way.

Another [Rice Bread]

One quart of rice flour, make it into a stiff pap, by wetting with warm water, not so hot as to make it lumpy, when well wet add boiling water, as much as two or three quarts, stir it continually until it boils, put in half pint of yeast when it cools, and a little salt, knead in as much wheat flour as will make it a proper dough for bread, put it to rise, and when risen add a little more wheat flour, let it stand in a warm place half an hour, and bake it. This same mixture only made thinner and baked in rings make excellent muffins.

Journey or Jonny Cakes

To three spoonfuls of soft boiled rice add a small tea cup of water or milk, then add six spoonfuls of the rice flour, which will make a large Jonny cake or six waffles.

Rice Cakes

Take a pint of soft boiled rice, a half pint of milk or water, to which add twelve spoonfuls of the rice flour, divide it into small cakes, and bake them in a brick oven.

Rice Cakes Like Buckwheat Cakes

Mix one-fourth wheat flour to three-fourths superfine rice flour, and raise it as buckwheat flour, bake it like buckwheat cakes.

To Make Wafers

Take a pint of warm water, a teaspoonful of salt, add a pint of the flour and it will give you two dozen wafers.

To Make Rice Puffs

To a pint of the flour add a teaspoonful of salt, a pint of boiling water, beat up four eggs, stir them well together, put from two to three spoonfuls of lard in a pan, make it boiling hot and fry as you do common fritters.

To Make a Rice Pudding

Take a quart of milk, add a pint of the flour, boil them to a pap, beat up six eggs, to which add six spoonfuls of Havana sugar and a spoonful of butter, which when well beaten together add to the milk and flour, grease the pan it is to be baked in, grate nutmeg over the mixture and bake it.

Virginia Sponge Cake

Twelve eggs, the weight of eight eggs in sugar, and the weight of six eggs in flour. The juice of a lemon, or a table-spoonful of vinegar. Beat all well together. Put in the flour last.

Rice Flour Sponge Cake

Made like sponge cake, except that you use three-quarters of a pound of rice flour, thirteen eggs, leaving out four whites, and add a little salt.

Rice Flour Blanc Mange

Boil one quart of milk, season it as to your taste with sugar and rose water, take four table-spoonfuls of the rice flour, mix it very smooth with cold milk, add this to the other milk while it is boiling, stirring it well. Let all boil together about fifteen minutes, stirring occasionally, then pour it into moulds and put it by to cool. This is a very favorite article for invalids.

Rice Griddle Cakes

Boil one cup of whole rice quite soft in milk, and while hot stir in a little wheat flour or rice flour when cold, add two eggs and a little salt, bake in small thin cakes on the griddle.

In every case in making rice flour bread, cake or pudding, a well boiled pap should be first made of all the milk and water and half the flour, and allowed to get perfectly cold before the other ingredients are added. It forms a support for them, and prevents the flour from setting at the bottom, stir the whole a moment before it is set to cook.

Hints for the Ladies

Some of the more economical readers may be glad to have a little advice as how to freshen up a dress of which they have got tired, or which may be beginning to lose its beauty. Those which are soiled, or worn at the bottom may be made up so as to look very well at very small expense, and with little trouble. Thus, for a dress of fancy material, a band of alapaca[6] between five and six inches in width will suffice to renew it. This band should be waved at the top, and piped with a thick blue or red piping. The sleeves must have a similar reverse, and a little Swiss body, trimmed also with a piping, will complete the costume. For taffetas dresses the band should be of the same material, but black, and finished off at the top in the same manner; or, if a more simple arrangement be preferred, it may be headed with two or three rows of narrow ribbon plated in the middle. A band might be replaced with two flounces, or pinked black taffetas; these will have a better effect if placed a little distance from another, and with a heading.

If it should happen that a skirt of taffetas requires widening, and all thought of matching the dress has been given up, the only resource left is to insert plain bands. If the dress be of a deep shade, we would advise that the bands be made of black taffetas not quite eight inches wide, and put in between each breadth; in this style the skirt will have no trimming at the bottom, unless it be a band of black taffetas in wide scollops or festoons, one scollop reaching just across the breadth of the taffetas from one black band to the next; this should be headed by a narrow ruche of ribbon, and a similar ruche placed up each black band up the skirt. In setting this dress on to the skirt, care should be taken to so arrange the plates that the black band may be folded under so as not to show at the waist. A Swiss sash should be added as a finish to the body, and plain turned-back cuffs. If the dress be a light-colored plain taffetas, the best arrangement will be to make the bands of the same color, but of a deeper shade, and the little ruche should be composed of narrow guipure instead of ribbon. *Le Follet*.[7]

Maryland Recipe Manuscript,
1850s–1870

Written in elegant script on paper that is now thin and yellowed, this manuscript of handwritten recipes from the Civil War–era South has never been published before. It would be a rare and valuable source no matter where it was written, but it is especially interesting because much of it was apparently written in northern Maryland, revealing a South that extended fifty miles north of the U.S. capital. The geography of Confederate loyalty was no secret at the time: Maryland was a deeply divided border state. Some Maryland residents were loyal to the Union and felt an economic affinity with the North. But slavery was also fully legal in Maryland when the war started, and while there were more than eighty thousand free African Americans living in the state, even more people there were enslaved. Maryland slave owners supported the Confederate cause as their own, and other residents simply felt themselves to be Southerners, first and foremost. Maryland never seceded from the United States, but that was in large part because Abraham Lincoln went to great lengths to make sure it didn't, famously suspending the writ of habeas corpus to jail some Confederate loyalists without

a trial. Lincoln realized that if Maryland had seceded, it would have transformed Washington, DC, into a tiny island in a Confederate sea.

We don't know much about the writer of these recipes, but there are some hints, starting with a variety of Maryland locations. Most of the place names mentioned in the manuscript are in Maryland, including Glencoe, Annapolis, and Filston, a large farm about twenty-five miles north of Baltimore. (A generation later, the wealthy entrepreneur who invented Shredded Wheat cereal would buy the Filston estate and build a mansion on it.)[1] We know the writer spent time on the Filston farm in the 1850s and 1860s, and it's possible she lived there. The writer mentioned getting several recipes from her mother, and in one recipe she wrote "Mother / Mrs. F. Medcalf," suggesting that was her mother's name. There were a number of Medcalf families living in or around Baltimore at the time, and it seems possible that the writer was part of one of them. In addition, she indicated that she got two recipes from her grandmother in "Melrose, Mississippi," possibly meaning the grand Melrose Plantation in Natchez. From the elegant handwriting and good spelling to the references to a back parlor and a German lesson, many details in this manuscript suggest that its primary author came from a wealthy family. The costliness of the ingredients she called for supports this idea too. It seems reasonable to guess that the author was a privileged white woman who lived in Maryland and had family connections in Mississippi, possibly to a very wealthy planter family there.

It also seems clear that the writer identified with the Confederate—or as she usually wrote, Rebel—cause, celebrated with recipes like Rebel Sugar Cake, "Corn-fed" Cake (war), Rebel Pudding (war), and Rebel Wine. These titles hint at how passionately some Marylanders felt themselves to be Southerners trapped in the Union against their will. Many of the recipes in this book fit our idea of Southern food, like mint cordial, green tomatoes, biscuits, and gumbo. But others are indistinguishable from the sorts of recipes that would have appeared in Northern cookbooks in the same era. It's not even certain that there was a single writer of this manuscript. In fact, at least one of the recipes excerpted here—"Gompo Soop"—was clearly written by someone else. In that recipe the handwriting is distinct and the spelling and grammar are idiosyncratic, suggesting the writer had little formal education.

As in other nineteenth-century recipes, the cooking techniques here were sometimes a form of preservation, as in recipes for Cut up Peppers, Green Tomato Preserves, or Spiced Blackberry Syrup. But the writer also acknowledged the fact that people couldn't preserve *everything*. Milk was especially hard to keep for long. People lucky enough to own a cow could enjoy milk so fresh it was still warm from the animal's body; you'll notice that the writer in one recipe uses the phrase "milkwarm" instead of "lukewarm." But milk that wasn't extremely fresh was usually in the process of souring, and that would have been especially true in warm weather. This reality was built into many nineteenth-century recipes, with authors often calling for sour milk or sour cream in baked goods—or sometimes for milk or cream that was "*not quite sour*," as the author here called for in one of her pudding recipes. That culinary category—for dairy products somewhere between fresh and sour—is one that has completely disappeared today. Like other nineteenth-century recipe authors, this writer called for "sweet milk" when she wanted it to be absolutely fresh.

Rye and Indian Bread

Sift 2 qts of rye, and 2 qts of meal, mix them well, having scalded the meal with 2 pints of boiling milk—2 table spoonfuls of salt—stir the whole very hard. Let it stand till luke-warm and then stir in ½ pint of good fresh yeast. Knead the mixture into a stiff dough and set it to rise in a pan. Cover it with a thick cloth that has been warmed, and set it near the fire. When it is quite light and has cracked over the top, make it into 2 loaves, put them into a moderate oven, and bake two hours and a half.

Add about ½ cup of molasses.

Cousin Anna's "*renowned*" (Reading Class) receipt.

Lady Cake

1 pound of loaf sugar, 6 oz. butter, the whites of 16 eggs, ¾ of a pound of flour, mace or essence of lemon, mixed as for pound cake. Bake in a loaf or in a tin pan.

Cocoanut Pudding

Grate 1 lb of the nut, previously scraping off the black skin. Then beat ¾ lb of butter, and ¾ lb of sugar together, a little grated biscuit or stale queen-cake, wet with a little wine, a glass of rose water and some of the milk of the nut, when well mixed add the whites of 9 eggs well frothed.

Cousin Anna

Mead

2 qts of boiling water. ¾ lb of the best brown sugar. ½ pint of West India molasses. ¼ lb of Tartaric acid—stir it well and when cool strain it, bottle and cork tightly. Keep it in a cool place. Put a teaspoonful of [S]ub Car[bonate] Soda in a tumbler, and a little of the mead, then half fill it with water—stir and drink.

Mrs. Woodruf

Nutmeg Pudding

1 pound of butter, 1 pound sugar, brown. 10 yolks and 5 whites of eggs—2 nutmegs, the sugar and butter to be melted together. Then beat eggs well and separately, add the yolks first, last of all the whites. Bake it in a rich crust.

Cousin Anna's

Green Tomato Preserve—for Pies

Take green tomatoes before the frost bites them—skin them and to every 4 pounds of the tomatoes 1½ pound sugar and 1 lemon sliced[,] removing the seeds—Let it stew well[.]

Mrs. Medcalf's

Glencoe, October/54

Dewberry Bounce

Gallon best white whiskey—2 quarts of fresh dewberries[,] 2 nutmegs grated—3 cts[2] cloves whole—3 cts stick cinnamon—put all into the whiskey[,] shake them and cork the jug—keep any time.

Hettie's—November 16th 1854

Egg Nog

12 eggs—2 quarts *very* rich milk—½ pt best Jamaica spirits[,] 1 pt. brandy—2 tea spoons cinnamon—2 nutmegs—1 lb sugar[.] Beat the yolks very light with sugar and spices and scald it with your boiled milk—your spirits last—make it the day before use—and when ready to drink beat your whites and put on top.

Mrs. McCulloh's[?]

November 16th—1854

Apple Pudding

3 pints of stewed apples well mashed—melt a pound of butter—beat 10 eggs with two pounds sugar; and mix all together with a glass of brandy and wine—put in nutmeg to your taste and bake in puff paste[.]

Alie

Snuggery[,] November 21st/54

First German lesson[3]

Jellie

3 qts of water, 1 pt of white wine; 6 tablespoonsful of Brandy. 3 lb of white sugar—whites of 6 eggs slightly beaten and stirred in with the shells broken up—6 lemons peel and juice. To the quantity add four oz of Gelatine which should be soaked in cold water (one qt of the above quantity of water) for half hour. Stir the ingredients well together before it is put over the fire and then do not disturb it till it has boiled for 10 minutes, then take it off and strain it.

Back parlor, 22 December '54

Mamie Olmstead

Tappioca Pudding

7 table spoons tappioca—boil 1 qt milk, scald tapioca long enough to swell (two or three hours). 3 eggs—4 table spoons sugar—nutmeg—Bake ½ hour.[4]

Filston October 5th '55

Ginger Beer

1 pt molasses

1 pt good yeast

3 table spoons of ground ginger stirred into 2 gal[lon]s water[,] half to be hot and the other half cool—set it in a warm place to ferment and bottle it next day— cork it immediately.

[Illegible]

Filston Oct 5th '55

Sliced Cucumbers

Pare and slice your cucumbers and lay them in salt 24 hours[.] Also slice and lay in salt as many large onions as you like. Drain the cucumbers and onions[,] make a rich dressing such as you use for the table oil[,] etc. Put in cucumbers, onions and dressing alternately into jar. Boil your vinegar and fill the jar with it.

Filston Oct 5th '55

"Sliced Cucumbers" was really a recipe for simple pickles. Cucumber illustration in Burr, *Field and Garden Vegetables*, 163.

Nineteenth-century Americans used sugar pumpkin in a variety of desserts, including puddings and custards as well as pies. Sugar pumpkin illustration in Burr, *Field and Garden Vegetables*, 195.

Mint Cordial

Take the green mint. Pick all the leaves from the stems—cover it with whiskey and let it stand 24 hours—then strain it and to two quarts of liquor allow 1 lb of sugar. . . . You can use brandy if you prefer[.]

Mrs Gettings[?]—from Mrs Woollen[?]

Filston Oct 5th 1855

Potato Pudding (Mrs. Carrolls)

1 lb Irish potatoes mashed to a paste with a silver spoon—1 lb sugar, 5 oz butter creamed, the yolks of 9 eggs, and whites of four, a wine glass of maderia. ½ grated nutmeg, and a little mace. Bake it in a rich crust.

Pumpkin Pudding

1 quart stewed and strained pumpkins. 9 beaten eggs. 3 pints cream; sugar, mace, nutmeg, and ginger in powder, bake in dishes ¾ of an hour.

Cousin Anna[']s

New Year's Rusks

3 lb flour, ¾ sugar, ¼ butter, 3 eggs. Take half a pint of new milk[,] sit it on some embers, put in the butter and sugar. When melted (but observe the mixture must not be hot, only milkwarm) add it to the flour which has been sifted and in the middle pour half a pint of yeast—the eggs last—some nutmeg.

Sally Lunn

¾ pound of flour, 1 tumbler of milk, ¼ pound of butter or lard, yeast according to your judgment. 2 eggs. Beat up and put into pans to use. ¾ lb sugar[.]

Molasses Custard

1 qt milk, 3 eggs well beaten, pinch salt, sweeten to your taste with molasses—nutmeg.

Eve's Pudding

6 of the largest pippins chopped finely, 6 oz of stale bread grated, 6 oz of brown sugar, 6 oz of beef suet grated, 6 oz of raisins stoned, 6 oz of currants, 1 wine glass of brandy and wine, 1 large nutmeg, pinch of salt.

Tie the above materials in a bag, put it with boiling water boil it three hours to be served up hot with wine sauce.

Mrs. James Green

Meat Pudding

Boil the face, the haslets viz. lights, heart, lungs and a little liver—boil[e]d until they almost fall to pieces—chop up fine, and well seasoned with pepper, salt, sage and thyme and a little onion.

Mother's
Copied Filston[,] Oct. 4th 1857

Pudding

1½ pts of sour cream (*not quite sour*)
3 large table spoons of flour
¼ lb white sugar
The yellow from half a lemon.
Beat altogether with the yolks of 5 eggs[,] the whites beat very light separately and added last with 2 table spoons of brandy.

Copied Dec 24th '58
Mrs. Mandals and *delicious*

Clara's Soda Biscuit

2 pints of wheat flour—2 large spoonsful of butter—not lard—3 tea spoonsful of cream of tartar to be mixed with the butter. Then to be rubbed into the flour. Then made into a dough—by one pint of milk. You should ready 1 tea-spoonful of scalded soda and put in last. They should be made out quickly.

Silver and Golden Cake

3 cups of flour, 3 of sugar, 1 of butter, 4 eggs, 1½ cups of milk, 2 tea spoons of cream tartar, 1 [teaspoon] of soda.

If you wish to make your cake all white, use the whites of 8 eggs and make the yolks into golden cake in the same quantity as the silver.

Miss H. Allen

Lemon Syrup. Mrs. Porter's

12 lemons, 5 pounds of sugar, 3 pints of boiling water. Squeeze as nearly as possible all the juice out of the lemons, pour the water boiling over the rinds[,] let it stand a few minutes, then strain and dissolve in it the sugar by a gentle heat. Then remove the syrup from the fire and immediately stir in to it the juice.

New York Cookies

To three cups of sugar, one cup of butter or lard, one spoonful of salt, work these together then add a cup of milk or butter milk, with a tea spoon and a half saleratus[5] dissolved in it. Then put two table spoonsfull of ginger, with caraway seeds, beat all well together, add flour enough to make stiff, to roll and cut in cakes.

Miss Fannel, unknown

Oyster Batter

Drain all the liquor from the oysters[,] make a rich batter of milk, eggs and flour[,] put the oysters in, butter a dish[,] pour all in and bake it a light brown[.]

Bees-Wax

Recipe for Whitening beeswax. To make Beeswax good and clear, only requires after it is made into thin cakes, to put them in bags and boil them few minutes: adding to every gallon of water, one pint of strong lye[6] and few table spoonsfull of salt. It will be white and clear as sperm.[7]

Feb 14th '62

Sugar Cake

2 lb flour

1 lb sugar

1 lb butter or lard

4 eggs taking out the whites

Flavored with rose water or anything you like[.]

To Make Wine Cake

Half a pound of flour[,] quarter of a pound of butter, mixed well with the flour, add to it a few carroway seeds and a little lemon peel and almonds, mix it with *wine* till it is of the consistency of paste then roll it out and form your cakes with the top of a wine glass.

Old Mrs. Kittera[?]

Hallelujah Sauce

1 Tea cup full of Sugar

½ Tea cup full of Butter

1 Egg

½ Tea spoon full vanilla

½ Tea cup full Wine or Brandy

Beat up Eggs[,] butter and sugar as light as possible, then stand it in a sauce pan of boiling water about 5 or 10 minutes, then add the wine and vanilla.

Copied July 1865

Ginger Bread

1 cup sugar, 1 cup molasses, one cup butter and lard[,] 3 [cups] of Flour, ½ cup milk[,] two eggs[,] 1½ nutmegs, 1 spoon full cloves, 2 [spoons] of cinnamon, 4 [spoons] of Ginger, one spoonful soda, 2 [spoonful] of cream Tartar[.]

Copied July 1865

Rebel Sugar Cake

1 pint of sugar, ½ pint of butter[,] 2½ pints finely sifted meal, (must be sifted through mull or book muslin)[,][8] 4 eggs, nutmeg[,] 1 Tea spoon full soda. Make into *soft* dough, and bake slowly[.]

War Receipt for Coffee (Mrs. Geo[.] Brandon)

Take one pint sugar, burn it black, and 3 pints water, let it boil to a syrup[.] To 2 Table spoon full[s] of syrup put 1 table spoon full of ground coffee[.] Bottle the syrup and use as needed.

"Cornfed" Cake (war)

½ lb of butter—8 eggs, weight of 8 eggs in sugar, weight of 6 eggs in fine corn meal, 1 Teaspoonfull Soda[.] Flavor to your Taste[.]

Indian Pound Cake

1 lb Sugar[,] ½ lb Butter, 10 Eggs[,] 18 ounces of fine meal.

Indian Loaf Cake (war)

1 lb fine meal[,] ¼ lb of butter[,] ½ lb sugar[,] 3 eggs[,] 1/3 lb Raisins[,] ¼ lb Currants[.] Cut up the butter in the meal, pour over it as much *boiling* milk as would make a thick batter, when the batter is cool, whip the eggs very light—add them, then the fruit and lastly the sugar. Bake in a moderate oven 2 hours.

Rebel Pudding (war)

4 cups finely sifted meal, 1 cup sugar[,] 1 cup sour milk, 1 cup butter, 8 eggs[,] 1 Tea spoon soda[,] flour to taste, bake 1 hour[.] Eaten with sweet sauce.

Potato Pudding (war)

1 cup sweet potatoes mashed, 1 cup finely sifted meal scalded, 2 cups sugar, 1 cup of sour milk[,] ½ tea spoon soda. Bake one hour. Eaten with sweet sauce, nice pudding for those who like sweet potatoes[.]

Rebel Wine

Gather Blackberries, measure them[,] to every gallon of berries add one quart of boiling water, let the mixture stand in an open jar 24 hours[,] stirring it occasionally, then strain it. To every gallon of liquor add 2 lbs Sugar. Put in open jar for 48 hours[.] Stir it well and skim it twice each day. Stir it *thoroughly* after each skimming[.] Having remained in the open jar for 48 hours pour it into demijohns or casks and cork tightly.

Green Tomato Catsup

1 peck of tomatoes, 5 large onions[.] Cut up the tomatoes and onions, add 1 oz of Allspice[,] ½ oz cloves, ½ oz ginger, 3 oz black pepper, 3 oz mustard, ¼ lb white mustard seed, ¼ oz mace[.] (The pepper and ginger must be pounded [and] the rest of the spices must be put in whole[.]) Six tablespoons full of salt—vinegar enough to cover them, boil until the tomatoes look clean—don't slice them too thin or they boil mushy[.]

[Added in margin]: Slice the day before the tomatoes and onions[.] Sprinkle salt[,] lay 24 hours and pour off the water ½ pint[,] boil[.]

Glencoe—Mother

Mrs. F. Medcalf

Fried Oysters

Yolks of eggs well beaten—salt and pepper to your taste—drain your oysters well[,] dry them in a towel—dip one at a time into the batter then into powdered soda cracker previously prepared—repeat this process twice[,] fried in just enough batter to keep from sticking till a light brown[.]

Sister Pattie's

Boiled Yeast Pudding

1¼ flour—1 lb suet—3 table spoons of bread crumbs—Fruit of any kind ½ pound—mixed with milk to a very stiff batter and just before putting in the cloth add three table spoons of good lively yeast[,] boil three or four hours—delicious—Eat with egg sauce.

Filston 1865

Rebel Toilette Soap (war)

Take 2 or 3 lbs of nice (home made) hard soap, put it in a kettle with 4 or 5 pints of *thick* hominy water strained, let it boil awhile and then put in about 2 table spoons full of salt, after boiling a few moments longer put in a vessel to cool. Next morning cut it out and again put in with 2 pints of hominy water and boil awhile, if the soap is not hard enough put in a *little* more salt letting it boil a few moments before taking it off, then pour it out to cool or put it in moulds, cut it next day and after scraping off any sediments, put it out to dry, not where the sun is too hot. To perfume it tie up lavender or scrapings of sasafras root in a piece of muslin and let it boil with the soap when first put on.

Puffs

7 teacups of flour—2 eggs—salt—2 qts of milk[.] Bake in very quick oven—Half the quantity will be sufficient for small family.

    Annapolis

Yankee Pudding

1 cup of Indian meal, 1 large spoonful wheat flour—lump of butter or suet—1 cup of molasses[,] ginger to your taste—1 quart of sweet milk—Boil part of the milk—mix the meal with the rest—stir into the boiling milk. Let it boil until it be like *mush*—then add the suet or butter. When cold—add ginger and molasses—bake *slowly* two or three hours—it is best to let it stand about quarter of an hour before you eat—as then the suet will jelly and some of the *extra heat* remove[?]—Eat with milk[.]

Gompo Soop

Take 1 Quart of Gompo;[9] about 12 or 15 good size tomatoe[,] scald and peal them, and cut them up, in a kettel with about 3 Quart of water, then wash the Gompu and cut them in too, let them boil about a hour and take of the froth when boiling, then cut in one onion, about 6 mitter size potato, (if you like one or two carrots, one

"Gumbo," or a variation of that word, could mean several different things in the nineteenth century. Gumbo could refer to a thick soup, to powdered sassafras leaf that sometimes thickened such soups, or to okra, whose gelatinous innards also acted as a thickener. In this recipe for Gompo Soop, the anonymous writer—a different person from the writer of most of the recipes in the Maryland recipe manuscript—apparently used the word "gompo" to refer to okra. An illustration of "Okra, or Gumbo," in Henderson, *Gardening for Profit*, 209.

turnips, one handful of rice) let does boil till done, then but in a good portion of cellery, parsly, thyme and any soop plant; then take a spoon full of butter and a spoon full of flour[,] let does get brown on the stove by stirring it all time, and then take some of the soop and but into and stir it again, (it will get ticke like a mush,) but does in the [*sic*] and let it boil again[,] it gives the soop more taste, if it boils at least ⅓ hour, but dont [p]ut the flaver plant to soon in[,] it will take the flaver by boiling to long.[10]

To make dried Ochra Gumbo

Fry a chicken (half a chicken will be sufficient for half a dozen person[s]) and put it in a quart of boiling water. Having soaked the dried ochra half an hour, put it in the saucepan with the fried chicken, cover and let it boil steadily for three or four hours. Just before serving up, season [illegible] with pepper and salt and some red pepper pods. Some ripe tomatoes and minced onion is a fine addition to it. . . .

Well boiled rice is always served with it.

Chocolate Pudding

Boil one qt of milk and add 3 oz of Chocolate grated; stir it until dissolved, then take it from the fire and stir in six eggs *well beaten*, leaving out the whites of three. Make it very [illegible] and flavor with essence of vanilla. Bake as for mild[?] custard in a deep dish but do not let it remain too long in the oven as it becomes watery—Set it on ice. Before sending to the table, beat up the whites of 3

eggs—add plenty of sugar making it thick as paste and spread it on the top of the pudding. . . .

"Captain Carufs[?]"

Filston August 1st '69

Spiced Blackberry Syrup

Take one gallon of berries, put them in a bottle, with ½ qt of water, boil them fast for an hour, take them off, squeez [*sic*] them through flannel bag until you obtain all the juice, put to heat quantity 2 oz of cloves, 1 oz of alspice: let it *simmer* for an hour then strain it off again. To each pint of juice add 1 pound of sugar (loaf is best), place on the fire again and boil to a thick syrup—take it off and while scalding hot stir in ½ pint of brandy.

Melrose Mississippi

Grandma Luna's[?]

July 1862

Blackberry Cordial

Take 3 gallons of berries[,] place in a kettle with 1 gallon of water, boil *fast* for half hour, strain until you have all the juice. To every pint of juice add 1 pt of loaf sugar, for each gallon of syrup add when cold 1 pt of Brandy. Bottle and seal.

Melrose Miss

Grandma Luna's[?]

July 1862[?]

A Stew from Lewis

Have a fowl skinned and quartered, put it over the fire in a quart of water (cold), boil it full two hours, then add a handful of rice, three blades of mace, about 2 dozen peppercorns, and salt to your taste, then let all boil together for one hour more.

Sept. 11, 1863

Spanish Fritters (Good)

Mix early in the morning, (say 4½ A.M.) a quart of flour[,] one well beaten egg and lively yeast enough to raise well with sufficient milk to make a dough like muffin dough[,] adding a little salt. When well risen work in two table spoons of melted butter, [and] make into balls and fry in lard or drippings. Eat with sugar and cinnamon or wine sauce.

Cut up Peppers

1 hundred peppers *sliced* very fine
5 large head of cabbage *cut* fine also
2 [large] pieces horseradish *grated* fine
1 [large] tablespoonful of *salt*
¼ peck of onions *cut* fine
Mix well together and let them stand 4 or 5 hours. Squeeze them out and put them into a dish—Put to it 1 oz of mace, 1 oz of cloves, ½ lb white and ½ lb blk mustard seed. Put into a jar and pour boiling vinegar o[n] it and cover up *tightly*.

This is nice also for stuffing peppers.
Miss H. Sterreb[?]

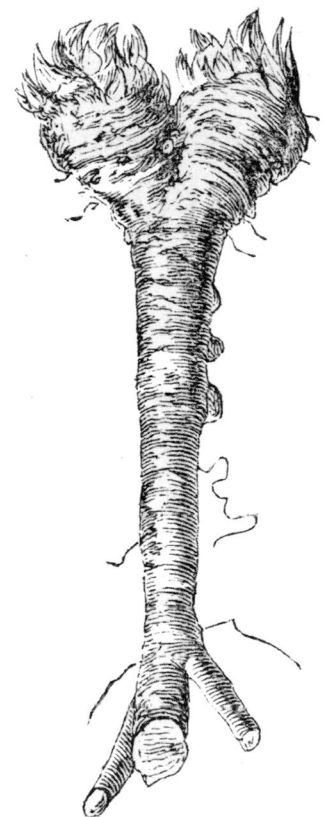

Horseradish figured in a variety of Southern recipes, especially in recipes for pickled vegetables and other zesty condiments. Henderson, *Gardening for Profit*, 184.

Maria Barringer, *Dixie Cookery: Or How I Managed My Table for Twelve Years, For Southern Housekeepers*

Published two years after the end of the Civil War but written in the middle of it, *Dixie Cookery* is widely considered the first North Carolina cookbook. It was written by Maria Barringer, a woman from a prosperous family in western North Carolina.[1] In the nineteenth century, authors routinely started books by explaining or even apologizing for bothering the world with another book, and this was especially true when the authors were women. An elite Southern woman publishing a book was no everyday event in 1867, and true to form, Maria Barringer felt the need to explain why she had written a cookbook in the first place. Downplaying her audacity in doing so, she stressed that friends "living in all parts of the 'South'" had urged her to share her recipes with a wider public. And she claimed that every other cookbook she had found was utterly "deficient in economy." The only way to have a truly economical cookbook, she felt, was to write one from scratch. Of course, this was also a smart way to play up her book's uniqueness and value.

Some of the recipes *were* economical, like Eggs and Rice, a cheap way to use up rice left from a previous meal. Other dishes, like Sausage Meat and Scrapple, would have been useful receptacles for odd scraps of meat. But this was not a book aimed at the impoverished or even at the hard up. In Barringer's recipe for Chicken Pie with Rice, for instance, she noted casually that the pie would "be sufficient for twenty persons"— a large household even by nineteenth-century standards, or one that could afford to invite a lot of guests. In general, despite her claims to be economical, Barringer called for quantities of wine, sugar, meat, butter, cream, and other costly animal products that would have seemed extravagant to most Americans. This was "economy" as defined by someone who didn't have to worry about economizing too much. If anything, the book suggests how quickly wealthy Southerners returned to abundance after the war.

Of course, *Dixie Cookery* was also unique because it was Southern, a fact Barringer broadcast with her title and with a variety of recipes like Carolina Rolls, Virginia Yellow Pickle, New Orleans Tea Cake, and Augusta Pudding. And just in case any readers might fear that Southern food meant coarse, country fare, Barringer managed to argue that her recipes were both uniquely Southern and tied to the highest cuisines of Europe. "Of course, many of our dishes are peculiar to the 'South,' as the various preparations of Rice, Corn Meal, and even our Bread-making," she wrote, but "our method of preparing Meats is more like that employed in French cookery."

As advertised, many of *Dixie Cookery*'s recipes would have struck readers as peculiarly Southern, like okra, hominy, fried squirrel, and watermelon pickles. But, just as in Mary Randolph's *Virginia Housewife*, published more than four decades earlier, there was also considerable overlap between Barringer's recipes and the kinds of recipes common in Northern cookbooks of the era. The varieties of different puddings, the doughnuts or the gingerbread, the mock turtle soup or the roast beef or the pigeon pie—all would have seemed equally at home in any cookbook from New England or the Midwest. And it's also important to remember that not all of the recipes that look Southern to us would have seemed especially so at the time. Northern cookbooks of the mid-nineteenth century also would have contained a large variety of pickle recipes, for example. And while Barringer's many recipes for oysters might strike us as a hallmark of the book's Southernness, at the time oysters were an extremely popular food in both North and South, an emblem of emerging Gilded Age cuisine more than the stamp of any one locality. In fact, Barringer's home in western North Carolina was more than two

hundred miles from the ocean and any seafood would have had a long journey before it reached her.

It's not surprising that this book was published outside of the South, since there had never been a vibrant Southern publishing industry even before the war's destruction of Southern infrastructure. But it still speaks to the rush to reconciliation that just two years after Robert E. Lee's surrender and Abraham Lincoln's assassination, a Boston press would blithely publish a book with celebratory recipes like Confederate Cakes, Richmond Cake, and Davis Jumbles. Barringer herself had special reason to celebrate Jefferson Davis, who had been president of the Confederacy. In the spring of 1865, weeks after the war ended, Davis had fled south to escape capture by Union forces. In his flight, he and the men traveling with him had stopped at the home of Maria Barringer and her husband, the Confederate veteran and lawyer Victor Clay Barringer, and asked if they could provide dinner for them. More than thirty-five years later, Barringer proudly reminisced about how she and her cook had managed to provide an appetizing meal to almost a dozen unexpected guests, one of whom was—to Maria Barringer if not to the woman actually doing the cooking—a guest of honor:

I had a few minutes talk with Ellen (the cook) who told me she had just taken from the oven a large loaf of rolls and one of our largest hams and these supplemented by poultry and vegetables and a tipsy cake pudding and fruits with cream furnished the simple dinner, ready in a half-hour after their arrival. Mr. Davis and the other gentlemen were good enough to declare they had "never tasted ham like that" which as it was of my husband's own raising and curing he much enjoyed—but I suggested their ride had doubtlessly furnished an appetite which heightened its flavor.[2]

Barringer's pride in supplying an ample meal on short notice recalls Mary Randolph's argument, decades earlier, that a preeminent sign of housewifely competence was that the table was always in readiness "as if a grand company was expected."

Although *Dixie Cookery* wasn't published until 1867, Barringer wrote much of it early in the war. In September 1862, she had noted in her diary, "Have my book on cookery all ready now for publication. Title is '*Dixie Cookery*'—Want Victor to take it to Richmond when he goes on."[3] She may have hoped to have it published in Richmond, the capital of the Confederacy, but the war probably put those publication plans on hold. Since Barringer only managed to get her book published after the war, it's interesting that she still chose to include a recipe like Blockade Coffee, an imitation brew made from parched rye or okra seeds. Wealthy southerners would no longer have needed such a recipe once the Union blockade lifted and they could once again purchase imported coffee beans. The inclusion of this obsolete recipe hints at how quickly wartime deprivations took on an air of nostalgia.

Preface

There is a very mistaken notion at the North and West, about the domestic life of Southerners, Southern women especially.

The common idea is, that we are entirely destitute of practical knowledge of household affairs. This is a great mistake. The contrary is true.

A Southern woman must know how to prepare any dish, for she finds no cooks made to order; they must be of her own training, in the minutest particulars of every department.

Northern housekeepers, in all the large towns and cities, do not have to depend on their own skill for the delicacies of every description that make up the dainties of the table, but we Southern housewives, even in our larger towns and cities, all do; and Northern visitors stand aghast at the amount of labor summoned up in the filling of our store-rooms, and it is difficult to convince them that we trust these preparations to no one else.

I found every cook-book I took up so deficient in economy, that I determined to make one for my own guidance,—the best method of enriching a larder, as well as of insuring success.

Hence, the exactness of measures given. My book is entirely practical,—nothing else. It contains no theoretic dissertations on the culinary art, but is made up of Receipts which have been my daily assistants for twelve years, in the management of my house, and the preparation of various dishes served for large and small companies.

It treats of the preparation of

Soups, Fish, Meats, Poultry, etc.;

Vegetables, Pickles, Catsups, etc.;

Bread, Pastry, Puddings, etc.;

Cakes, Preserves, Jellies, &c.;

Syrups, Creams, Cordials, &c.,

with a few miscellaneous receipts added, relating to care of stores and house generally. A regular breakfast-cake of George Washington's, obtained from a relative of his, in Virginia, will attract great attention.

I am largely indebted to an English friend for many of my preparations, and, after following these directions for twelve years, can safely recommend them. Of course, many of our dishes are peculiar to the "South," as the various preparations of Rice, Corn Meal, and even our Bread-making. Our method of preparing Meats is more like that employed in French cookery.

At the repeated solicitations of friends, living in all parts of the "South," I have decided to give this private experience of twelve years' daily practice to the public, and ask those who are interested, to look with favor on Dixie Cookery.

Maria Massey Barringer

Concord, North Carolina, June, 1867

Soups

Mock Turtle Soup

Boil a calf's head, a few slices of ham, a head of celery, and a bunch of thyme, and parsley, in two gallons of water for five hours. When they have boiled an hour, take out the head and cut up the meat into inch-square pieces. Let the soup boil half an hour longer, strain it and return the meat to it. Season with the juice of a lemon, and salt and pepper. An hour before dinner, put in a thickening of browned flour and butter and water. A few minutes before serving, throw in egg-balls made of grated yolks of hard-boiled eggs, a little flour and beaten yolk of egg about the size of partridge eggs. Lastly, put in a half a pint of good wine and a tablespoonful of browned sugar, and send to table immediately.

Squirrel Soup

Cut up two young squirrels, and put them in a pot with five quarts of cold water. Season with salt and pepper. Let them boil until the meat is very well done, and remove it from the liquor, and cut it up into small pieces. Put in the soup a quarter of a pound of butter mixed with a little flour, and a pint of cream. Throw in the cut meat, and just before you serve it add the beaten yolks of two eggs and a little parsley. Chicken soup is nice made in the same way, with the addition of a pint of green corn cut from the cob, and put in when it is half done.

Oyster Soup

Strain the liquor from two quarts of oysters, add to it an equal quantity of water. Put it on to boil, and skim it. Then throw in a little white pepper, a head of celery cut in small pieces, and a third of a pound of butter with two teaspoonfuls of flour rubbed in it. Boil it five minutes longer, and put in the oysters and a pint of cream, and after one more boil pour into the tureen, in which have some toasted bread cut in dice, and a little finely-cut parsley.

Ochra Soup

Take three pounds of fresh lean beef, or a fine fat chicken, and simmer in a gallon and a half of water for two hours. Skim off the fat and season with salt and pepper. Cut up a small portion of the meat, and return it to the soup. Add a teacupful of sliced green ochra or a half a teacupful of dried ochra, and a teacupful of tomatoes peeled and sliced. Boil until the meat is in shreds, and the vegetables are all to pieces.

Vegetable Soup

Put a pint of Lima beans, a half a dozen large tomatoes, two teacupfuls of corn cut from the cob, a few snap beans, and two teaspoonfuls of dried ochra, into five quarts of water, with three slices of lean ham. Boil for two hours, and season with salt and pepper. Remove the ham before sending to table. Thicken with yellow of egg and a little flour.

A nice winter-soup is made by boiling a few slices of lean ham, half a pint of dried Lima beans, a few heads of celery cut up, and turnips and potatoes sliced thin. A fourth of a teacupful of dried ochra will be a nice addition, and a grated carrot, or half a teacupful of stewed tomatoes, preserved in cans, will improve the color. If thickening is required, add some made of browned flour and water. Two tablespoonfuls of pepper-sauce will improve it. Put it in after it is in the tureen.

Fish

To Bake a Shad

Prepare a stuffing of bread crumbs, salt, pepper, butter, and parsley, and mix this up with beaten yolk of egg, fill the fish with it, and tie a string around it. Pour over it a little water and some butter, and bake as you would a fowl. A shad will require from an hour to an hour and a quarter to bake.

Rock fish is baked in the same way, but requires a longer time to cook.

Stewed Oysters

Take the liquor from five hundred oysters, and strain and boil the one-half of it. Add three-quarters of a pound of butter to the boiling liquor, and when it is melted put in the oysters. As soon as they have commenced boiling, take them out, and throw them in cold water to give them firmness. Whilst the oysters are in the cold water, stir into the boiling liquor a pint of sweet cream.

When the mixture boils again, return the oysters to it, and simmer a few minutes until they are thoroughly heated, and they are ready to serve.

Scalloped Oysters

Fill a buttered dish with alternate layers of oysters, hard-boiled eggs, grated bread-crumbs, pepper, butter, and salt, taking care to have a thick layer of crumbs on top. Place in a hot oven, and bake from twenty to thirty minutes. You may add spice if you like it. No oyster liquor need be put in, as there will be enough when they are cooked.

Fried Oysters

Select the finest sized oysters, drain them, and season with salt and pepper. Beat up an egg, and dip them first in it, and then in corn-meal or grated cracker, and fry in hot butter. Serve on a hot dish.

Oyster Pie

Strain the liquor from the oysters, and put it on to boil with butter, and pepper, and a thickening of bread-crumbs and milk well beaten together, and after boiling a few minutes, throw in the oysters. Let them remain five minutes, take them off, and when warm add the beaten yolks of three eggs. Line a buttered dish with a rich paste, and fill with white paper or a clean napkin, to support a lid of paste, and bake it. When lightly browned, take off the lid, remove the napkin, pour in the oysters, set a few minutes in the oven, and send to table hot.

To Pickle Oysters

To the liquor of one hundred oysters, add one teacup of vinegar. Boil and skim it, and put in the oysters with a tablespoonful of salt, and the same quantity of pepper, and let the whole simmer a few minutes together.

In cold weather, they will keep several days.

Lobster Salad

Make a dressing of the yolks of four hard-boiled eggs, some salt and pepper, a little oil and mustard, and some vinegar.

Make these ingredients into a smooth paste, about the consistency of thick cream. Mash the coral meat of the lobster, and with a little cold water, just enough to soften it, and cut up a head of lettuce into small pieces, and mix with it. Season the lettuce and meat with Cayenne pepper and a little salt, and mix them with the dressing just before sending to table.

The different condiments must be in such proportion that no one shall predominate.

To Fry Clams

After opening them, wash them in their own liquor, drain them, and make a batter of an egg, flour, and pepper. Dip them in this, and fry in hot butter.

Eggs

Oyster Omelet

Beat six eggs well, and add by degrees a gill of cream, and pepper and salt to your taste. Have ready one dozen large oysters cut in halves; pour the eggs into a pan of hot butter, and drop the oysters over it as equally as possible. Fry to a light brown and serve as an omelet. It must not be turned.

Eggs and Potatoes

Remove the skins from some boiled Irish potatoes, and when perfectly cold cut them up in small pieces about the size of a grain of corn, and season with salt and pepper. To a quart of potatoes thus prepared, take the yolks of six eggs, and the whites of three, and beat them well together. Have some butter in a frying-pan, and when it is melted put in the potatoes. When they are quite hot stir in the eggs, and continue stirring so as to mix them well with the potatoes, and until the eggs are set. Then pepper, and send them to table in a hot dish.

Eggs and Rice

Take six eggs and beat them well. Have a quart of cooked rice well boiled and steamed, and when perfectly dry, stir in the eggs and season with salt, and serve on a hot dish. The proportion of egg is one to every tablespoonful of rice. Cold rice is nice dressed in this manner for breakfast. If you use rice cooked, the previous day stir in a little butter with it when you put it in the kettle to soften.

Eggs and Beef

Chip some dried beef, and pour boiling water over it to freshen it. Pour off the water and put a little butter into the skillet with the meat. When it is hot stir in three or four eggs until they are well mixed with the meat; pepper, and send to the breakfast-table hot.

To Preserve Eggs for Winter Use

Pack them with the small ends downwards, and put in alternate layers of salt and eggs until the vessel is full. Or pour three gallons of hot water on a pint of lime, and a half a pint of salt. When it is cold, pour over the eggs and keep in a cool place. One cracked egg will spoil them all. The best test of the freshness of eggs is dropping them into a pan of cold water. Those that sink are fresh enough to pack away.

Sauces

Drawn Butter

Mix well together a quarter of a pound of butter, and one tablespoonful of flour. Put a pint of water into a rice-kettle, and when it boils stir in the flour and butter. Season with salt and white pepper, and celery if in season, removing the stalks of celery before sending to the table. It will require but a few minutes' boiling, and must be stirred constantly.

Celery Sauce

Cut up a large bunch of celery into small pieces. Use only that which is blanched, throwing aside the green tops. Put it into a pint of water and boil until it is tender. Then add a teaspoonful of flour and a lump of butter the size of an egg, mixed well together. Season with salt and white pepper, and stir constantly until removed from the fire. It is nice with boiled poultry.

Oyster Sauce

Set the oysters in their liquor over the fire for a few minutes until they look plump. Then remove them from the liquor and stir into it some flour and butter rubbed together; some salt and pepper. Stir it well, and when it has boiled ten minutes throw in the oysters, and add a glass of white wine, if you like it, and serve immediately. This is a nice accompaniment to boiled fowls.

Caper Sauce

To a pint of drawn butter add one tablespoonful of fresh butter, two of capers, and two of vinegar, or the juice of a lemon. Throw in a little salt and pepper, and after stirring over the fire for ten minutes pour into the sauce-tureen, and send to table.

Pickled nasturtiums are an admirable substitute for capers, and pickled cucumbers, cut fine, may be used.

Tomato Sauce

Stew a dozen large tomatoes with Cayenne pepper, and salt until they become like a marmalade. Pass them through a sieve to remove the seeds, and stir until it is of the consistency of very thick cream. Then add a half a pint of nice broth and a little butter. Or if you have no broth, a little warm water, and an ounce and a half of butter, with two tablespoonfuls of grated cracker, or bread may be stirred in just before sending to table. In seasoning this sauce use very little pepper. It will be a nice accompaniment to beef-steak, or beef a-la-mode, or cold roast beef.

Mint Sauce

Take the leaves of young mint and cut up finely, and to three tablespoonfuls of chopped mint add one of sugar, and vinegar sufficient to moisten the mint and sugar well. Put in a little salt, and serve with roast lamb.

Meats, Poultry, Etc.

To Boil Pigs' Feet

First clean them well by dipping them in scalding water, and scraping off the hairs and hoofs, after which put them into weak salt and water for a day. They are then ready to boil for souse.

If, however, you wish to keep them for frying, or stewing, they may be preserved in this weak salt and water for three or four weeks. If the weather is warm, the salt and water may require to be changed. They must be soaked in fresh water all night, before boiling them: Boil them in cold water until tender.

To Boil a Ham

Soak the ham overnight, and put it into cold water and let it cook slowly, very slowly, for four or five hours in a covered vessel. Skim it, leaving a small piece upon the knuckle, which carve handsomely, and serve with a paper frill tied around the knuckle-bone, or some fine bunches of curled parsley. If the ham is more than a year old, soak it well, and boil it for six or seven hours—changing the water three or four times.

To Roast a Pig

Rub the inside of the pig with pepper and salt, and fill the body with a stuffing of bread, butter, parsley, sage, and thyme, softened with a little hot water, and beaten yolk of egg, and sew it up with a strong thread. Put the pig on the spit, first flouring the skin, that it may be crisp. Put a pint and a half of water into the dripping-pan, a spoonful of lard, and a little salt, and baste the pig frequently with this, and turn often, so that every part will be well done. When the skin begins to get stiff, grease it with butter or lard, and baste it no more after this, or it will blister. A pig will require from three to four hours to roast. Chop up the heart and liver, previously boiled in water, and add to the gravy in the dripping-pan, with salt, thyme, and brown flour, and water, as a thickening. Apple-sauce, cold slaw, and cranberries, are the usual accompaniments of roast pig.

Roast Beef

Season the beef with pepper and salt, and skewer it well to the spit. Put a pint of water and a little lard in the dripping-pan. Turn the meat frequently. Baste it with the liquid in the dripping-pan, and a short while before it is done, dredge a little flour over it. When the beef is nearly done, pour the gravy into a skillet, and thicken it with a little brown flour and water rubbed together. If too fat, remove the top by skimming it. It will be most likely to suit all tastes if one-half of the meat is well done, and the other side less cooked, so as to furnish rare slices for those who prefer it thus. Grated or scraped horse-radish is nice with beef thus cooked.

To Roast a Goose

Have the goose prepared the night previous to cooking. Fill the body with a stuffing of bread, sage, thyme, a little onion, and some mashed Irish potatoes, and a very little butter. Add salt and pepper and yolk of egg, and baste the same as a turkey. Pour off most of the fat that drips from the goose, or the gravy will be too rich. The gravy is the same as for turkey. Apple-sauce to be served with it.

Illustration of a trussed goose, from Hill, *Mrs. Hill's Southern Practical Cookery*, facsimile of 1872 edition, 91.

To Bake a Beef's Heart

Cut it open, remove the ventricles, and let it soak an hour in lukewarm water, to free it from the blood. Wipe dry with a cloth, and parboil in a little water for twenty minutes. Make a rich stuffing, fill the heart with it, and secure it with a string. Let it bake an hour and a half, or two hours, with a half a pint of water, in the oven or dripping-pan. The gravy will not need any thickening, but will be improved by a glass of wine. Serve in a chafing-dish, and with currant, or any acid jelly.

Beef a-la-Mode

Take part of a round of beef, bone it, and make incisions, which are filled with a stuffing of bread, butter, thyme, pepper, salt, a little minced onion, and yolk of egg. After the meat is stuffed, bind it with tape, and put in an oven, with water enough to cover it, and let it stew slowly for three hours. Keep a lid on the oven whilst it is stewing, and if more water is needed, add boiling water. The gravy will require no thickening, but a glass of wine will improve it.

French Steak

Cut thin slices of cold roast beef, and put in a chafing-dish; season with salt, pepper, walnut catchup,[4] a little vinegar, a little warm water, and plenty of butter, with some browned flour rubbed into it. The meat should be entirely covered with the gravy. Light the lamp and put on the lid of the chafing-dish, and let it steam thus, until the gravy is reduced two-thirds. A nice breakfast dish.

To Fry Liver

It should be cut across the grain in slices half an inch thick. Then put into a deep plate, and pour boiling water over it. Let it lie thus for a few minutes, drain it, and season with pepper and salt. Dip each piece in flour, and drop in hot lard. Let it be thoroughly done, but not hard. Make a gravy as for beef, and pour over it.

To Fricassee Chickens

Cut up the chickens, and put to soak in cold water for an hour; then throw them in weak salt and water, and let them soak another hour. Put them into a pot, with water enough to cover them, some salt, and pepper, and half a pint of cream or some milk. Add a tablespoonful of butter mixed with flour, and stew all together for an hour.

Before it is dished, stir in the beaten yolks of two eggs, and a little finely-cut parsley or celery.

To Fry Chickens

Cut up the chickens, and let them lie in salt and water twenty minutes; drain them, and season with salt and pepper. Dip each piece separately in flour, and drop into a frying-pan of hot lard. When well browned, turn the other side to fry. Take up the chicken, and pour into the pan a little warm water, and a thickening of milk and flour, some salt, and a little butter. Let it boil a few minutes, and pour over the chickens.

Chickens fried in batter are prepared in the same way, dipping them in a batter instead of flour, before frying them. The batter made of two eggs, a little salt, a teacup of milk, and flour enough to make a thin batter. Lard is nicer for frying them than butter.

Chicken Pie with Rice

Cut up three young chickens into joints, and drop them into weak salt and water for a half an hour. Have ready two quarts of rice boiled, but not steamed, into which stir a pound and a quarter of butter, a quart of milk, a little salt, and six well-beaten eggs. Put into your baking-dish half the quantity of this mixture, and place the chicken and a few slices of ham in it. Then pour in the remainder of the rice and egg, and rub a little flour and milk smoothly together, and put on the top, to make it brown nicely. This pie will be sufficient for twenty persons.

To Roast Venison

Make a dough of flour and water, and roll it out an inch thick. Rub the meat with lard, and wrap the dough around it. When half done, remove the dough, and baste the meat frequently with butter, and water, and claret wine, and dredge with flour. It will require five or six hours to roast. Serve currant jelly with it.

Make a sauce by skimming the fat from the gravy in the dripping-pan, and adding some butter with brown flour mixed in it, pepper, salt, and currant jelly, to your taste. Cold roasted venison makes fine French steak.

Roasted Hare

Having trussed the hare, prepare a rich stuffing of corn and wheat bread, mixed and rubbed fine, butter, pepper, salt, thyme, and beaten yolk of egg. Stuff the body of the hare and tie it up, and rub the skin with butter, and roast before the fire, as sucking pig is done.[5] It will require from two to three hours to cook. Serve with currant jelly. Add wine to the gravy, if you like it.

Rabbit Stew

Cook them with a little chopped onion in a stewpan, with water enough to cover them, and butter and cream, pepper and salt, added when they are nearly done. Or add nothing but butter and wine to the gravy.

Wild Ducks

After they are cleaned, and ready for cooking, wrap them in a clean cloth, and bury twelve hours in the earth, to remove the strong flavor of this bird. They are usually cooked without stuffing. Three-quarters of an hour will be sufficient to cook them.

When you dish it, draw a sharp knife three times through the breast, and pour over a gravy of a little hot butter, the juice of a lemon, a sprinkling of Cayenne pepper, and a wine-glass of port wine. This is poured over as they go on the table.

Fricassee of Squirrels

Put two young squirrels into a pot with two ounces of butter, one or two ounces of ham, some salt and pepper, and just water enough to cover them. Let them stew slowly until tender. Take them up, and pour half a tea-cup of cream and a beaten yolk of egg into the gravy, and when it has boiled five minutes, pour over the squirrels in the dish. Some persons prefer a wineglass of red wine, and omit the cream and egg.

Fried Squirrel

Cut up and season with salt and pepper, and dip each piece in beaten yolk of egg and grated cracker, and fry in hot lard until of a nice brown.

Squirrel Pie

Cut them up, and parboil in water, with a little salt in it, for half an hour. Then proceed as in chicken pie.

Pigeon Pie

Having picked and cleaned five pigeons, stuff them with a stuffing of grated cold ham, some salt, and grated cracker, some pepper and butter. If asparagus is in season, the green tops may be substituted for the cracker. Pour milk and water into the dish until the pigeons are nearly covered. Put a lid of paste on the top, and bake an hour. If you wish the pigeons very tender, parboil them twenty minutes, and use the water in which they are boiled to make the pie.

To Stew Pig's Feet

Boil four feet, take out the bones, and put them in a vessel with a little vinegar and water, a lump of butter the size of a goose egg, and some salt and pepper, and stew for a half an hour, and serve on a hot dish. Or they are nice dressed as terrapins.

Sausage Meat

To eighty pounds of chopped meat, which should be one-third fat and two-thirds lean, add two pounds of fine salt, one pint of pulverized sage, six ounces of ground pepper, and eight tablespoonfuls of brown sugar. Mix all well together.

Scrapple

Take the scraps of pork and the heads, and boil in water until the meat is tender. Pick out the bones and chop it fine. Strain the liquor, and pour it back into the pot. Put in the meat, and season with sage, and salt, and pepper, to the taste. Stir in corn meal until it is of the consistency of thick mush. Let it cook about twenty minutes, stirring constantly. Remove from the fire and put in deep pans, and fry in thick slices.

A Nice Breakfast Relish

Chip some smoked beef, and drop into boiling water to soften. Let it lie ten minutes, and then put it into a skillet with a little boiling water, and stir gently for twenty minutes. Pour off the water, put in a little butter, and some pepper, and pour in a half a teacup of cream, five minutes before taking from the fire.

To Pickle Beef's Liver

Wash the livers, and put them into a strong brine, and let them lie three weeks. Then hang and smoke them, as beef is done, until properly dry.

They make a nice relish for breakfast by stewing them for half an hour in water, and dressing them with cream and cut parsley. They must be shaved thin like chip beef, and soaked ten minutes in warm water before stewing.

Another way is to warm it up in a little butter, after it is soaked fresh.

Vegetables

Asparagus

Put the stalks into bundles; cut them the same length, tie up with strings, and boil in hot water without salt for three-quarters of an hour. Remove the strings, and serve on buttered toast; pour over some pressed butter, and season with pepper and salt.

You may omit the toast, and add a little vinegar to the butter. The stalks must be scraped below the green head before boiling, and kept in water until ready to cook. If your bed does not yield a sufficient quantity of asparagus for a meal at one cutting, bury the cut stalks in the asparagus bed, pinned up in a cloth, until you have a dish full.

Beans

String, and break them in halves; boil in salt and water, and throw in a piece of soda the size of a pea, if they are old, or you wish them a fine color. Boil them for an hour and a half; pour off the water, and dress with butter and cream, and sprinkle over some pepper. . . .

Lima Beans

Let them boil about an hour, and when the water is poured off, season with salt, pepper, and butter. Send to table hot. Dried Lima beans must be soaked over night, and boiled two hours, or until they are soft, and should have some cream added to the dressing.

Cold Slaw

Take vinegar and water in equal proportions (unless the vinegar is very strong); add butter, the size of an egg, and a little flour. Pour into a saucepan over the fire, and stir until it is thick; then pour in the beaten yolks of two eggs, and some salt. When it has been on the fire ten minutes more, stir in the cabbage, nicely shredded with a cabbage-cutter.[6] The cabbage must be taken up, as soon as it is hot.

You may add a saltspoonful of mustard to the sauce, if you like it.[7] Salt the cabbage.

Warm Slaw

Make a sauce of beaten yolk of egg, a teacup of vinegar, a teacup of sour cream, and butter the size of a walnut; and when it begins to thicken, put in the cut cabbage, and stir until it is hot. Add salt and pepper, to the taste.

Cucumbers

Remove the rinds in long, thick slices. Cut them on a cabbage-cutter in very thin slices, and lay them into cold water,—ice-water, if you can get it. Drain off the water, and lay into a dish, with small, thick lumps of ice through them, and strong vinegar poured over. Season with pepper and salt, before putting them into the dish.

Corn

Remove the silk, and drop into boiling water with a little salt in it, for half an hour. If it is old, it will take an hour. Lay a napkin on a dish, put in the corn, and fold the napkin over, to keep it hot.

Corn Oysters

Cut the corn through the grain, and use a knife to scrape the pulp from the cob. Make a batter of two eggs well beaten, two tablespoonfuls of flour, a little salt, pepper, and some milk, with a quart of the pulp. Beat the whole well together, and drop a spoonful at a time into hot lard, and fry brown.

Green-Corn Pudding

Pulp the corn in the same way, as for corn-oysters. Take two eggs, a quart of milk, some flour, and salt, and the corn, and beat it well. It must be of a consistency to pour easily. Grease the dish with butter, pour in the pudding, and bake with a quick heat for half an hour. Six ears of corn will be sufficient for a quart of milk.

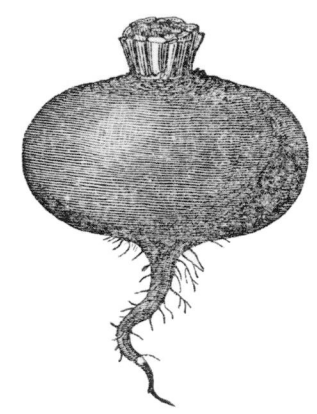

This image shows a "blood turnip beet," a vegetable nineteenth-century Americans valued for its vivid color as well as its sweet taste. From Henderson, *Gardening for Profit*, 126.

Beets

They are usually plain boiled, and dressed with melted butter and vinegar, pepper and salt. But they are sweeter, roasted in the fire as potatoes, or baked in an oven or stove, and then dressed as above.

Egg Plant

Cut in slices half an inch thick, sprinkle thick with salt, and let them stand a few minutes to extract the bitter taste. Wash in cold water; wipe them dry. Season with pepper. Dip in flour, and fry in butter, or dip in yolk of egg and grated cracker.

When wanted for breakfast, some persons cut them the night before and sprinkle with salt, and soak in the morning in fresh water for an hour before frying.

Maria Barringer casually mentioned fried eggplant as a possible breakfast food, hinting at how different breakfast was in the nineteenth century. At the time, Americans regularly ate a variety of meats, vegetables, and desserts at the morning meal. Eggplant illustration in Burr, *Field and Garden Vegetables*, 599.

Stewed Irish Potatoes

Slice thin, and boil in water till tender; pour off the water and put in some butter, salt, pepper, and rich cream and a dust of flour. Before taking up, stir in the beaten yolk of an egg, with some chopped parsley. It is a nice breakfast dish.

Sweet Potatoes

Bake them slowly in an oven, or peel them, and slice in large slices and put into a baking dish, with plenty of butter, a little water, and some sugar, and serve in the dish in which they are cooked. There must be plenty of butter on them when sent to table.

To Stew Tomatoes

Wash, and pour boiling water over them; peel off the skins, and cut them up. Season with pepper and salt and butter, and cook in their own juice a half an hour. Thicken with bread-crumbs, and, after ten minutes, take them up.

Hominy

Soak it over night and boil for three or four hours, if large hominy; and if small it will cook in an hour. Dress with butter and salt.

Spinach

Boil it in salt and water, pour over melted butter and vinegar, and sprinkle on some pepper, and serve with poached eggs, laid over the top of the spinach.

Ochra

Boil the young pods in water until tender, and dress with melted butter, vinegar, pepper, and salt.

If you wish them for winter use, slice them very thin, and dry on dishes in the sun, and put away in paper bags.

Squashes

Cut them up, and remove the seeds, and cook in hot water until tender. Then mash them, and dress with butter, salt, and pepper.

They are nice, cut in thick slices, and fried as egg-plant.

Winter Squash

Cut the end off, and take out the seeds, and set it into the stove to bake until tender. Then take it out, put in plenty of butter, and stir through the squash, and return to the oven for ten minutes. Send to the table in the skin in which it is baked.

Parsnips

Scrape and split them, and put into a pot of boiling water, until tender. Dress with plenty of butter, salt, and pepper. Or you may parboil them, and dip into beaten egg and grated cracker, and fry in hot lard.

Winter crookneck squash illustration in Burr, *Field and Garden Vegetables*, 219.

Turnips

They are dressed like parsnips. But a nicer way is to grate the raw turnips, and stir into a sauce of egg, vinegar, butter, and flour, and when it has boiled till of the consistency of cream, put in the turnips, give it another stir or two, and take up at once. This is called turnip-slaw.

To Boil Rice

Pick and wash a teacupful of rice, and put into a rice-kettle, with a pint of cold water; cover close, and let it steam a few minutes after it is tender, so that every grain will stand alone. It will cook in twenty minutes over a bright fire.

To Cook Macaroni

Put the macaroni into a pot of boiling water, with a little salt in it, and let it cook ten minutes. Then pour on fresh hot water and milk in equal quantities, and boil ten minutes more. Then put it into a deep dish, with alternate layers of butter and grated cheese, until the dish is full, having macaroni on the top, with a little butter on it without cheese.

Bake in an oven or stove for half an hour.

Pickles and Catchups

Carolina Yellow Pickle

Six ounces of turmeric tied in a bag, six ounces of white pepper, three ounces of white mustard-seed, one ounce and a half of white pepper. Put these ingredients into vinegar, and let it stand two weeks before the cabbage is put in.

Quarter the heads of cabbage, sprinkle with salt, and let them stand twenty-four hours. Then scald in the same salt and water which has formed a pickle around them, and after, wiping dry, put into the vinegar.

Virginia Yellow Pickle

Two and a half gallons of good vinegar, seven pounds of brown sugar, one pound of white mustard-seed, one of ginger, one half pound of white pepper, one quarter of a pound of turmeric, one box of mustard, and two ounces of nutmeg, mace, celery-seed, allspice, and grated horse-radish. Mix the turmeric with a small portion of vinegar, as you do mustard, and add to the spiced vinegar, or tie it up in a thin bag. Slice and scald two dozen large onions; sprinkle them with salt, let them stand a day, then drain well, say for six hours, and wash them in vinegar, and throw into the jar of spiced vinegar with half a dozen lemons or limes sliced thin. Select firm heads of cabbage, split them in halves, or quarter them, scald them in brine that will bear an egg until they are half done, drain them, and squeeze the moisture out with a napkin, and lay in the sun for one day. Put them in plain vinegar for a fortnight, after which they must be drained and sunned another day, before they go into the spiced vinegar. This vinegar may be prepared at any season, and the cabbage added when you choose. One jar of vinegar will make three of pickled cabbage. The spices must all be pounded (but not finely) before putting into the vinegar. It will be ready for use in a week. Keep the jar covered tightly.

Small Cucumbers

Gather them from two to four inches long, and drop into strong vinegar, with mustard-seed, pepper, and celery-seed, in it. Tie them close.

Cherry Pickles

Wash the cherries, leaving the stems on. Put them into a jar, with alternate layers of sugar, cloves, and cinnamon, and pour cold vinegar over them.

Cabbage Pickle

Cut up the cabbage on a cabbage-cutter, sprinkle with salt, let it stand twelve hours, drain it, and press out any moisture that remains. Put it into a jar, with layers of white mustard-seed between, and fill with cold vinegar.

Nasturtiums

Drop them into a jar of strong vinegar, as you gather them, and tie up the jar close.[8]

Onions

Peel small white onions, pour boiling milk and water over them, and when cold, put them into a jar with white mustard-seed and horseradish, and pour boiling vinegar over them.

Ripe Tomatoes

Take small, round tomatoes, and prick them with a needle, and let them lie a week in salt and water. Then wash them well, and drain them for ten hours. Put into a jar, with white pepper sprinkled over, some mustard-seed, and one or two pods of red pepper sliced. Pour strong, cold vinegar over them, and they will be ready for use in a few days. Keep them covered close.

Green Tomatoes

Slice thin on a cabbage-cutter, sprinkle with salt, and let them stand six hours. Drain off the water, and press out the remaining moisture. Cut, salt, and drain some onions in the same way, and put into the jar alternate layers of tomatoes, onions, sliced green peppers, spices, and a little brown sugar, in the proportion of a teacupful to every gallon of tomatoes. Pour cold vinegar over them. About one-fourth of the pickle should be onions.

Walnut Pickles, Black

Gather the walnuts, whilst soft enough to run a pin through them; put them into an iron pot, and boil in water until the hull comes off easily. Put into a tub of cold water; hull them, and wash them, and put them into jars. Pour moderately strong salt and water over them, and let them remain in this a week, changing the brine once during this time. At the end of this time, scald them in weak vinegar, and let them stand in this four days; then pour it off, and, to a peck of hulled walnuts, take a quarter of a pound of cloves, a teacup of mustard-seed, two spoonfuls of black pepper, a pint of grated horseradish, two pods of red pepper, some sliced onions, and garlic, and put in with the walnuts, and pour over them cold vinegar.

Sweet Pickle Peaches (excellent)

Pare the pickles and cut them in halves, and to two pounds of fruit, take one quart of vinegar, and one pound of sugar. Put the sugar and vinegar over the fire, skim it, and when it has simmered fifteen minutes, put on the peaches, and let them remain until they are slightly cooked, but not soft. Boil cinnamon and mace in the syrup. Cloves are nice, but discolor the fruit.

Spiced Peaches

Take nine pounds of clingstone peaches, ripe, but not soft, pare and halve them, or leave them whole. Make a syrup of four pounds of brown sugar and a pint of good vinegar, some mace and cinnamon, and skim it well. Let it cook a quarter of an hour, and then throw in the peaches, a few at a time, so as to keep them as whole as possible, and when clear, take them out and lay on dishes, and put in more; when all are done, pour the syrup over the peaches.

Sauce of Cherries or Damsons, for Meats

Allow half a pound of brown sugar to every pound of fruit, and to every seven pounds of fruit a pint of strong vinegar. Put all in together, and let them cook slowly until they are done. Then take the fruit from the syrup and put on dishes. Let the syrup boil longer until it is rich, adding cloves and four sticks of cinnamon. Pour over the fruit in jars, whilst hot.

Watermelon Sweet Pickles

Two pounds of watermelon or muskmelon rinds boiled in pure water until tender. Drain them well. Then make a syrup of two pounds of sugar, one quart of vinegar, half an ounce of mace, an ounce of cinnamon, and some roots of ginger boiled until thick, and pour over the melons

Pickled watermelon rinds were a popular food both North and South in the mid-nineteenth century. Citron watermelon illustration in Burr, *Field and Garden Vegetables*, 184.

boiling hot. Drain off the syrup, heat it until boiling hot, and pour over the melons three days in succession. They are very nice, and will keep two years.

White Walnut Catchup

Gather the walnuts when soft enough to run a pin through, put them in salt and water for ten days; then pound them in a mortar or pot, and to every dozen walnuts put a quart of strong vinegar and stir it occasionally. Then strain it through a bag, and to every quart of liquor put a teaspoonful of pounded mace, the same of cloves, and a few slices of onion. Boil it half an hour, and when cold, bottle it. If you use black walnuts, remove the hulls in the same way as for pickles.

Cucumber Catchup

Pare and cut the cucumbers into very small square slices, the size of a grain of corn, and add onions cut in the same way, in the proportion of one onion to every half dozen cucumbers. Mix them and salt them well, and let them stand ten or twelve hours. Then drain them well through a sieve or colander. Season with white or black pepper to your taste, and put in alternate layers of the fruit and white mustard-seed, until your jars are three-fourths full. The jars must be small, as this catchup spoils by exposure to the air. Fill the jars entirely to the top with vinegar. The vinegar must be the very best cider vinegar. White wine dissolves the fruit. Some persons prefer the catchup with wine in it. Madeira wine is the best, in the proportion of a pint to every gallon of vinegar. Seal up the jars well, and every few days examine them. When you see the cucumbers rising above the vinegar, open the jar and press them down, and fill up with vinegar, and seal tightly again. Keep them in a cool place during the warm weather.

Tomato Catchup

Take a peck of ripe tomatoes, wash and cut them in pieces, and put in a porcelain kettle, and boil until they are quite soft. Then mash them well and strain through a hair sieve. Season with salt and cayenne pepper, and white mustard-seed, and let it boil till half of it is boiled away. Let the bottles in which you intend to pour it be set on the back part of the stove and gradually heated, and pour the catchup into the bottles when quite hot,[9] but not boiling. Cork and seal well, and keep in a cool place, until the warm weather is over. You may add powdered cloves and black pepper, if you like them, but they will discolor the tomato juice.

Bread, Pastry, Puddings, Etc.

Milk Biscuit

Take one pound of flour, one quarter of a pound of butter, eight tablespoonfuls of yeast, and one half a pint of new milk. Melt the butter in the milk, put in the yeast and some salt, and work into the stiff paste. When light, knead it well, roll it out an inch thick, cut out with a tumbler, prick them with a fork, and bake in a quick oven.

If butter is not abundant, you may take an eighth of a pound of lard, and the other butter.

Plain Biscuit

One pint of flour, a tablespoonful of lard, and a little salt, with water enough to make a soft dough. Work it long and well with the hands. On this depends the lightness and excellence of the biscuit. Bake in a quick oven.

Crackers

Mix two teaspoonfuls of cream of tartar, and three-fourths of a teaspoonful of soda, with one quart of flour, and a piece of butter the size of a goose-egg. Make these ingredients into a stiff dough with cold water, and beat and work the dough well. Roll it out, and cut into cakes with a tumbler.

Rice and Flour Muffins

Half a teacup of flour, a teacup of bursted rice,[10] a pint and a half of milk, and three eggs. The batter must be as thin as for pancakes. Bake with a quick heat.

Very Fine Corn Muffins

Put a tablespoonful of lard into a pint of sifted corn meal, and pour over these a pint and a quarter of boiling water. Stir it until it is lukewarm, and then put in six well-beaten eggs, and a little salt. Bake in small pans well greased.

Light Corn Bread

Take two quarts of corn meal, and pour boiling water on one-half of it. Mix up the rest with cold water, and when it is all worked together and lukewarm, put in three tablespoonfuls of yeast, and one of salt. Work it well, and set it to rise in a wooden bowl. When it begins to open on top, grease the oven, and put it to bake. Bake slowly for some hours, until well browned.

Corn Meal or Flour Crisp

One pint of meal or flour mixed with warm water and a little salt, and a small piece of lard. Make these ingredients into a soft dough, and bake on a journey-cake board before a hot fire, until it is of a fine brown on each side. After it is done, take it up, cut it open, and remove the soft part entirely, so as to leave the thin crusts, which put down before the fire again, and burn until perfectly crisp, without scorching.

A Virginia Sally Lunn

Three pints of flour, six eggs, four ounces of butter, a pint and a half of yeast, and one pint of milk. Beat all these ingredients together, pour into the buttered mould in which it is to be baked, and let it stand over night, if you wish it for breakfast.

Brown Bread

Take two quarts of corn meal and scald it, and when cool, add one quart of rye flour, and mix with cold water until stiff enough to make into a loaf. Put in a little salt, and bake two hours in a hot oven. This quantity will be sufficient for two loaves.

Carolina Rolls

Take half a pint of yeast, one quart of water, milk-warm, and flour enough to make a light sponge, and next morning add half a pint of cold water, and half a pound of butter. Stir it well, and add flour enough to make it tolerably stiff. Let it stand one hour, and bake in a hot oven, after moulding into small cakes.

Velvet Cakes

One quart of flour, three well-beaten eggs, one quart of milk, and eight tablespoonfuls of yeast. Beat all well together, and add a little salt. Let it rise in a warm place, and when ready, cream, a tablespoonful of butter and beat it in, and bake in cakes on a griddle. Put in the butter half an hour before baking. Bake when light.

Flannel Cakes

Warm a tablespoonful of butter in a quart of milk, put in a little salt, and stir in two tablespoonfuls of yeast, and flour enough to make a thin batter. Then add two well-beaten eggs. Let it rise, and after five hours' standing, bake on a griddle in cakes the size of a tea-plate. The griddle should not be greased after the first baking.

Buckwheat Cakes

Take a pint of milk and warm it, and put in a teacupful of buckwheat flour, a little salt, two tablespoonfuls of yeast, and two beaten eggs. Set it to rise, and bake when light. Or you may take a pint of buckwheat flour, a teacup of wheat flour, and half a teacup of meal, and mix with lukewarm water, until it is a thick batter. Add a tablespoonful of yeast, and set it to rise. After an hour, pour in a little milk, until of the consistency of waffle-batter, and let it stand two hours in a warm place. Do not grease the griddle but once. Serve with melted butter in a boat.

Fine Waffles

One pint of sweet milk, half a teacup of buttermilk or clabber, two eggs, a pint and a half of flour, and a piece of lard the size of a guinea egg, melted and put in the batter. Beat well for fifteen minutes. Grease the waffle irons, fill them with batter, and bake on a bed of bright coals, turning the irons so that both sides will be browned. Butter as you remove from the irons. If you have no sweet milk, it will do to make them entirely with buttermilk.

Soaked Crackers for Tea

Boil some milk and pour over some crackers, put in some butter and salt, and cover close until tea is ready. Keep them in a warm place. Serve in a deep-covered dish.

General Washington's Breakfast Cakes

Make a thick mush with corn meal and water, add some salt and a little butter, and drop in little cakes half an inch thick on a hot griddle.

N.B. Received from one of his relatives.

Pancakes

Take a pint of flour, a little salt, four well-beaten eggs, and milk enough to make a very thin batter, and beat well, and bake on a greased griddle, turning the cake so that both sides are browned nicely. Grease the griddle every few times.

Corn Gruel Batter Cakes

To a pint of thin gruel, luke-warm, add two eggs well beaten, some salt, and two tablespoonfuls of cold rice. Bake on a greased griddle.

Milk Toast

Toast some slices of bread until of a light straw color. Boil a teacup of milk and a spoonful of butter, with a little salt, and when it has boiled a few minutes, pour over the toast. If cream is abundant make it half cream.

Puff Paste

Sift a pound of flour, and take out a quarter of a pound for rolling. Divide a pound of butter or three quarters of a pound of lard into four equal parts. Put one part of the shortening into the flour, and with a little water, make it into a stiff dough. Roll it out, and flake it with part of the shortening. Fold over the sheet of paste, roll it out again, and spread over another portion of butter or lard. Roll and fold thus three times. Handle it as little as possible, and put in a cold place until ready for use. This quantity is sufficient for four pies. This paste must be baked with a quick heat, say for ten or fifteen minutes. Or you may take two pounds and a half of flour, two pounds of butter, one pint of water, with two eggs broken in the water.

Mince Pies

Boil four pounds of lean beef and chop it fine. Pick and chop three pounds of suet, wash two pounds of currants, and one of raisins, grate the peel of two lemons and add the juice, an ounce of sliced citron, and twelve large apples chopped fine. Mix these ingredients with three pounds of sugar, half a pint of wine, and the same of brandy, and a little sweet cider, and nutmeg and mace to your taste. Bake this mince-meat in puff paste, with a lid of paste on top.

Rhubarb Pie

Peel the young stalks, cut them in small pieces, and stew till very soft, with a very little water. Mash it into a marmalade, sweeten with sugar, and set away to cool. Bake a lower crust and fill with the stewed rhubarb. They are not nice after the first day.

Apple and Peach Pie

If made of early green apples, they must be stewed with a little water, sweetened with sugar, and nutmeg grated over the top. Bake without a lid of paste.

Winter apples are pared, cored, sliced thin, and put into a dish lined with paste, with the juice and grated rind of a lemon, and a little sugar, and very little water. Bake with a cover of paste. Peaches are pared and sliced, sugared, and put into a pie-plate lined with crust, with a tablespoonful of water. Cover with paste.

Apple Pies without Apples (very good)

One cup of sugar, two cups of water, one cup of bread-crumbs, one egg beaten light, and one teaspoonful of tartaric acid. Soak the bread-crumbs in the warm water and rub them smooth, and put in the other ingredients, and season with lemon or nutmeg to your taste, and bake with a crust above, as an apple-pie.

Sweet Potato Pie

Boil the potatoes, skin and slice them, and put into a deep dish with a few sliced apples. Fill the dish with apples and potatoes, and pour over some wine, sugar, butter, nutmeg, and a little water. Bake with a crust.

Icing for Pies

Just before they are quite done, wash over the top of the pie with the beaten white of an egg on a feather, and sift white sugar finely powdered over the egg. Or use only plain water, and sift over white sugar. Or you may beat up the yolk of an egg, and put a piece of butter the size of a walnut (melted) into it, and wash over the tops of the pies with it, sifting white sugar powdered over it.

Stewed and Baked Apples

Pare and core some firm acid apples. Stick cloves in them; fill the vacancy left by the core with sugar, and some thin strips of lemon-peel, if you have them, and put into a baking-pan, with just water enough to keep them from burning. Bake them until they are tender, but not until they break. When they are cold, eat them with whipped cream heaped over them for dinner, or plain cream for tea.

To stew apples, pare and core them, and leave them whole. Make a syrup of loaf-sugar and water, boil and skim it; and when it has boiled twenty minutes, drop in the apples and some slices of lemon, carefully removing the lemon-seed, or some strips of lemon-peel cut thin. If the apples are not very firm, you can take them up on dishes to cool, after they have been in the syrup a few minutes, and then return them to the syrup, and cook until tender. They are very nice, and may be prepared the day before they are to be served.

An Apple Charlotte

Take slices of light bread, and dip them in boiling milk, and lay them in the bottom of your baking-dish. Pare and chop your apples into fine pieces. Then put in alternate layers of apples and batter, sugar and spices, until the dish is full. Put bread-crumbs, soaked in boiling milk, over the top, and bake from three to four hours, until it is a perfect jelly.

It is usually served hot for dinner, but may be eaten cold.

Apple Float

Take a quart of stewed apples, mash them fine, and press them through a sieve, and season with loaf-sugar and flour, with lemon. Stir into the apples the well-beaten whites of four eggs, and pile up the apple thus prepared on a glass bowl half filled with rich cream and milk. Serve in saucers.

Wine Custard

Beat eight eggs very light, leaving out the whites of three. Take half a pound of sugar, and a pint of wine, and beat with the eggs for a few minutes. Pour the mixture into a hot kettle, and stir constantly until it boils. Then pour the mixture out, and beat until cold. Flavor with lemon, and grate nutmeg over. Serve in glasses. The wine must be a light color, and the kettle not very hot. This quantity is sufficient for six persons.

Syllabub

One quart of cream, one gill of wine, the juice of three lemons, the beaten whites of six eggs, and sugar to your taste. Froth these ingredients in a syllabub-churn, and put into glasses.

Ambrosia

Grate the white part of the cocoanut, sweeten with a little sugar, and place in a glass bowl, in alternate layers with pulped oranges, having a layer of cocoanut on top. Serve in ice-cream plates or saucers.

Augusta Pudding

Nine tablespoonfuls of flour, ten eggs, and one quart of milk. Boil the milk, and pour over the flour, and let it stand till it is cool, and then put in the eggs, which have been beaten separately and very light. Bake it in a tin mould or dish, and in a quick oven. Serve with cream sauce.

A Baked Rice Pudding

To three pints of milk, two-thirds of a teacup of rice (before it is cooked), a piece of butter the size of a small Walnut, three tablespoonfuls of sugar, and a little lemon or orange-peel. Bake in a slow oven till it is done.

A Simple Bread Pudding

Fill a deep dish with slices of sponge cake, or buttered light bread, and sprinkle raisins, grated nutmeg, and sugar on each slice. Make a custard of six eggs, a teacup of sugar, and two quarts of milk, and pour over until the dish is full. Bake a short time,—for a quarter of an hour, if it is a quick oven. Dry acid preserves may be substituted for the raisins.

Dried Fruit Pudding

Boil the fruit until nearly done, and chop it fine. Save a teacupful of the juice for sauce. Make a batter of light bread soaked soft in water or milk, put the fruit into it and stir well, and pour into a bag and boil until done.

Make a sauce of melted butter, sugar, and a little flour, with enough of the apple-juice to flavor it richly, and nutmeg and spice to your taste.

Tapioca Pudding

Pour a quart of warm milk over eight tablespoonfuls of tapioca that has been previously washed through several waters. When it is soft, add three tablespoonfuls of melted butter, five well-beaten eggs, sugar, wine, and spice to your taste. Bake in a buttered dish.

Corn-Meal Pudding without Eggs

Take seven heaping tablespoonfuls of meal, half a teaspoonful of salt, two tablespoonfuls of butter (or one of butter and one of lard), one teacupful of molasses, two tablespoonfuls of ginger or cinnamon, and pour into this mixture a quart of boiling milk. Mix it well, and pour into a buttered dish. Just as you set it into the oven, stir in a teacupful of cold water, which will have the same effect as eggs. Bake for three quarters of an hour.

Stale Bread Pudding

Tie a loaf of stale bread in a cloth, and boil it an hour, and serve with any kind of liquid pudding-sauce.

This is very simple, and suited to delicate persons.

Quaking Pudding

One pound of suet, one pound of raisins, a pint of milk, six eggs, and as much flour as will make a thick batter. Boil it for three hours.

Cream Sauce

Boil half a pint of cream, thicken it with a teaspoonful of flour, and put in a large lump of butter. Sweeten to your taste, and when cold add wine or brandy.

Sauce for Puddings

Two teacupfuls of sugar, one tablespoonful of butter, and one wineglassful of wine, melted together, and a tablespoonful of flour mixed in a cup of cold water and poured in. Season with nutmeg.

Brandy Sauce

Boil some lemon rinds and a gill of milk together until the milk is flavored, then stir in three beaten eggs, and sweeten with sugar to your taste. Stir constantly until it is as thick as thin cream, but do not let it boil, and then stir in two wine-glassfuls of brandy.

Irish Potato Pudding

One pound of mashed potatoes, three quarters of a pound of butter, three quarters of a pound of sugar, seven eggs beaten light, a gill of brandy and one of rose-water. Beat the butter and sugar together, and add the other ingredients, and whites last of all. Bake in paste.

Cocoanut Pudding

Stir a pound of loaf-sugar and a quarter of a pound of butter to a cream. Take the yolks of twelve eggs and the whites of six, and when beaten separately and light, add them to the butter and sugar, and then put in one pound of grated cocoanut. Lastly put in four tablespoonfuls of rose-water, four of cream, and the juice of two lemons. Bake in puff-paste, and sift loaf-sugar over after it comes from the oven.

Lemon Tarts

Beat three quarters of a pound of butter and the same of sugar together until light, then stir in the beaten yolks of twelve eggs, the juice of one lemon and the grated rinds of three, and bake in puff-paste.

Sweet Potato Pudding

Take two pounds of boiled potatoes and rub through a colander. Beat six eggs and mix them with the potatoes, and add half a pound of butter, the same of sugar, one pint of cream, the juice and rind of a lemon, brandy and nutmeg to your taste, and bake in paste.

Molasses Custard

To five eggs beaten light, take two tumblers of molasses, two tablespoonfuls of butter, and one grated nutmeg. Beat all well together. This quantity will make two custards. Bake in rich paste.

Ground Rice Pudding

Mix six ounces of rice-flour with a pint of milk until it is a smooth batter. Put a pint of milk over the fire, and when it has boiled, stir into it the rice batter, and six ounces of butter. Boil it a few minutes until well mixed, and stir it constantly. Remove it from the fire and put in six ounces of sugar, and set it away to cool. When it is lukewarm, add six eggs beaten light, a little wine, some rose-water, the juice and grated rind of a lemon, or some essence of lemon, and let it stand until cool before you put it into the paste to bake. Or you may bake it in a buttered dish without paste, and grate loaf-sugar on the top when cooked.

A Boiled Peach Pudding

Make a batter of five eggs and three pints of milk, and beat well. Stir in some stewed dried peaches just before putting on to boil. Put into boiling water and cook for three hours, turning frequently to keep the peaches from settling on one side. Serve with cream sauce.

Cakes

Fruit Cake

Cream one pound of butter, and stir into it ten well-beaten eggs, a pound of sugar, and a pound of flour. Stone and cut fine three pounds of raisins, stem and dry two pounds of currants, and slice one pound of citron fine, and add to the batter. Grate one nutmeg and put in, and if the cake is to be used shortly after baking, add a pound of almonds blanched and cut fine. If kept any time the almonds impart a rancid taste to the cake. A small portion of the flour must be reserved to dredge the fruit with, to prevent it from sinking in the batter. Bake slowly for six or seven hours.

Black Cake

One pound of flour, one pound of sugar, one pound of butter, two pounds of currants, two pounds of raisins, twelve eggs beaten light, and spice to your taste.

Clove Cake

Three pounds of flour, one pound of butter, one of sugar, three eggs, two tablespoonfuls of cloves, and some molasses mixed in.

Cream Cake

Four teacups of flour, three of sugar, one of butter, one of cream, five eggs, and three fourths of a teaspoonful of soda. Rub the butter and sugar together, mix in the other ingredients, and bake as pound cake.

New Orleans Tea Cake

Three pounds of flour, a pound and a half of sugar, three quarters of a pound of butter, two tablespoonfuls of caraway-seed, one small teaspoonful of soda, and half a pint of milk. Roll out, and bake in small cakes.

Spanish Bunns[11]

Stir three quarters of a pound of butter into seven wine-glassfuls of warm milk (not hot), add a pound and a half of flour, nine eggs, three wineglassfuls of yeast, and one nutmeg. Let it stand two hours, and then add a pound and a half of sugar.

Sugar Biscuit

One pound of flour, a quarter of a pound of butter, the same of sugar, half a pint of rich milk, a teacupful of yeast, and half a teaspoonful of soda.

Doughnuts

Mix together six pounds of flour, and a pound and three quarters of sugar. Stir a pound of butter into enough of warm milk to make up the flour into a stiff batter. Add seven well-beaten eggs to the batter, and a teacupful and a half of yeast, and set it to rise. When it is light, knead in flour enough to make a soft dough, some powdered cinnamon and mace, and set to rise again. When it is very light, roll it out thin, cut it in shapes, and fry in hot lard. Sprinkle cinnamon and loaf-sugar over them whilst hot.

Florida Cake

Mix together two pounds of flour, two pounds of sugar, a pound and three quarters of butter, and seventeen well-beaten eggs. Flavor with nutmeg and cloves, and a glassful of brandy, and stir in a pound of currants picked and washed and dredged with flour, and a pound of raisins, stoned, cut in halves, and floured.

Frontier Cake

A pound and a half of sugar, half a pound of butter, two pounds of flour, and eight eggs beaten separately and light. Mix two teaspoonfuls of cream of tartar with the flour, and when all the ingredients are well beaten together, put in a teaspoonful of soda dissolved in a little hot water, and pour into your moulds to bake.

Soft Gingerbread

Three teacupfuls of molasses, two of buttermilk, one of butter, one egg, and as much flour as will make a thick batter. Add a tablespoonful of powdered ginger, and a teaspoonful of soda dissolved in warm water. The batter must be so thick it will not run. Put it into pans, and smooth the top with a knife.

Hard Gingerbread

Four pounds of flour, a pound and a quarter of butter and lard mixed, four teacupfuls of sugar, one of ground ginger, half a teacup of cream, some powdered cloves, and molasses sufficient to make a soft dough.

Diet Bread

A pound of flour, a pound of sugar, nine well-beaten eggs, leaving out four of the whites, a little mace, and some rose-water.

Confederate Cakes

One pound of flour mixed with a quarter of a pound of butter. Three quarters of a pound of sugar beaten with two eggs. Flavor with rose-water and brandy and spice. Make the whole into a soft dough, and bake in small cakes.

Jackson Jumbles

A teacupful of sugar, one of butter, one of sour cream, three eggs, and a teaspoonful of soda, stirred into sufficient flour to make a soft dough. Bake in a quick oven.

Davis Jumbles (very fine)

One teacupful of grated loaf-sugar, one cup of butter, and the white of one egg beaten light. Mix to a tolerably stiff dough with flour, and if you like, add a tablespoonful of thick cream, and as much soda as will lie on a sixpence. Roll the dough in thin sheets, and cut in round cakes or rings. Dip the cakes in grated loaf-sugar before baking.

North Carolina Jumbles

One pound of flour, the same of sugar, and an equal quantity of butter. Mix these ingredients with three well-beaten eggs, a wineglassful of rose-water, and some essence of lemon. Roll into thin sheets, and cut in rings, and dip in loaf-sugar before baking.

Cocoanut Macaroons

Take equal parts of grated cocoanut and powdered white sugar, and mix the beaten whites of two eggs until they form a thick paste. Bake on buttered paper until of a pale-brown color.

Norfolk Tea Cake

One pound of flour, the same quantity of sugar, half a pound of butter, and six eggs, with flavoring of lemon or vanilla.

Palmetto Cake

One pound of flour, the same of butter, a pound and a quarter of sugar, twelve eggs, two grated cocoanuts, and two pounds of citron sliced and floured as for fruit cake. Beat well and bake as pound cake, but it will require a longer time in the oven on account of the fruit.

Richmond Cake

One tablespoonful of butter and one teacupful and a half of white sugar, beaten together to a cream, two eggs well beaten, one cupful of milk, with a teaspoonful of soda, dissolved in hot water and added to it, and a pint of flour with two teaspoonfuls of cream of tartar mixed in it. Beat all well together, and flavor to your taste.

Rice Flour Sponge Cake

Take three-quarters of a pound of rice flour, one pound of white sugar finely powdered, and ten eggs. Beat the yolks with the sugar, and the whites alone. Add the flour and whites alternately, a little at a time. Season with brandy, and bake in shallow pans.

Boiled Icing for Cake

Take the best refined loaf-sugar, break it into small lumps, and pour over it some cold water, taking care to use no more than will be just sufficient to dissolve it. Mash the lumps with the back of a spoon, and set over the fire and boil without stirring until the syrup is the consistency of honey. In the meantime beat to a stiff froth the whites of three eggs, allowing this number of eggs to every pound of sugar. Strain the boiled syrup into a bowl immediately upon removing it from the fire, and in a few minutes stir in gradually the beaten whites of eggs, and some lemon-juice or essence. Beat it until very smooth and light, and put in a few drops of indigo squeezed through a muslin bag, to make it a pearly white. If the icing is too thin, set the bowl in an oven of boiling water, over a few bright coals, and stir it whilst it boils, taking care it does not adhere to the side of the bowl. Or you may omit a portion of the whites of the eggs. If too thick from standing, add some beaten white of egg, a small portion at a time, until of the proper consistency. Put on this icing while it is warm.

Preserves and Jellies

Crab Apples

Put them into your preserving-kettle, with cold water enough to cover them, and let them boil until the skin breaks. Then take them out one by one and skin them, and remove the seeds with a penknife. Make a syrup of a pint of water and a pound of sugar to every pound of fruit, and when it is clear, drop in the apples and let them boil until they are transparent.

Pine-Apple Marmalade

Pare and grate the pine-apple, and take equal parts of fruit and sugar and put into your preserving-kettle, and cook slowly until it is clear. It is very nice and keeps well.

To Preserve Green-Gage Plums

Weigh the fruit and put into the kettle with alternate layers of vine-leaves. Fill the kettle with cold water, and let them simmer until the skin begins to crack open. Then remove from the fire and pare them with a knife, leaving the stems on. Measure the parings, and for every pint deduct a pound from the weight of the fruit. Scald the fruit again after it has been pared. Make a syrup of a pound of sugar to every pound of fruit with a very little water, and when clarified, drop in the fruit and cook slowly until clear. Then remove from the syrup, and add another pound of sugar to the syrup, and boil for half an hour.

If you do not wish to take off the skins, prick them with a pin.

Green Lemons

Cut them in halves, take out the pulp, and cut in fancy shapes. Put into your preserving-kettle and cover with water, adding a little alum to green them. Boil until clear, and then take them out and drain them on a cloth. Clean the kettle, and put them in with their weight in sugar, and stew them slowly until the syrup is rich.

Green Peppers

Leave the stems on them; remove the seeds, and put them in salt and water for three days, changing the water every day. Then green them in a kettle with cold

PLATE IV.

A painted plate showing plums, in this case with some damage from insects, in Isaac Pim Trimble, *A Treatise on the Insect Enemies of Fruit and Fruit Trees* (New York: W. Wood, 1865), plate opposite p. 29, Michigan State University Special Collections.

water, vine-leaves, and a little alum; simmer thus for two hours. Then put them into fresh water for three days, changing the water every day. Then boil in a syrup of a pound of sugar to the same weight of pepper and a little water, for half an hour. Fill the inside with candied sugar.

Green Tomatoes (very fine)

Take them while quite small and green, and put them into cold clarified Syrup, with an orange cut in slices to every two pounds of tomatoes. (In making the syrup, take the weight of the fruit in sugar.) Simmer them gently over a slow fire for two or three hours. Grate the rinds and add the juice of two fresh lemons to every three pounds of preserves, and put in some bruised ginger in bags. If you wish the preserves to be very superior, take the tomatoes from the syrup when they have been over the fire for three-quarters of an hour, and add a quarter of a pound more of sugar for every pound of fruit, and, when boiled and skimmed, drop in the tomatoes and boil till the syrup seems to have penetrated them. In about a week, heat the syrup boiling hot, and pour over them, and seal up immediately. They resemble limes, thus prepared.

Water-Melon Rinds

Cut in strips and shapes, and remove the green skin, and boil in water till tender, with a teaspoonful of soda and a dozen peach-leaves to every two quarts of water. Then take out the rinds and soak them in alum-water an hour, and afterwards boil gently in strong ginger tea

for an hour. Make a syrup of equal weights of the sugar and rinds, and a little water, clarify it, and boil and skim it. Then put in the rinds with some ginger-root tied in a muslin bag, and when hot take them out on dishes to cool, and when cold return to the syrup and cook until soft. Pour the syrup over, and after a few days boil the syrup with the juice of a lemon, or flavor with essence of lemon, and pour over the rinds whilst it is hot. They are then ready to put into jars.

Orange Marmalade

Put the rinds of the oranges into a kettle with cold water, and boil until soft enough to run the head of a pin into them easily. Then take them up on a plate, and with a penknife remove the white part of the rind so as to leave the yellow part of the rind as thin as possible. Quarter the oranges and pulp them, removing the seeds and core, and weigh them with the skins, and to every pound of the fruit allow a pound of loaf-sugar. Make a syrup of the sugar, and half a pint of water to every pound of it, and boil and clarify, and throw in the rinds, and when tender add the pulp, and boil all together for half an hour.

Lemon marmalade is made in the same way, allowing a pound and a half of sugar to every pound of fruit.

Strawberries

Gather the berries in dry weather, pick out the firmest and largest, and stem them. If you stem them as you remove from the vine they will be nicer. To every pound of berries take a pound of white sugar. Dissolve the sugar in wine, allowing a wineglassful to a pound, and clarify and boil it. Then pour in any juice that runs from the strawberries, and skim it well. When boiling, put in the strawberries, and to every pound of fruit as much pulverized alum as will lie on the blade of a penknife. Let them boil a few minutes and they are done. Try them by taking one from the syrup and cutting it in halves. Do not stir them. Remove carefully from the syrup and boil it longer. Have small jars or pint tumblers of common glass heated until so hot you cannot hold them in your hand, and when the syrup has been taken from the fire a few minutes, fill the jars with the fruit, and pour over the syrup, and seal up tightly.

Very Fine Apple Jelly

Wash and quarter the fruit without paring it, and put into a kettle and cover with water. Boil till perfectly soft. Then strain the juice off, and to every pint of it allow half a pound of sugar. Don't put in a spoon after the sugar is dissolved. Boil for nearly an hour, or until it jellies. When done, strain through a thick cloth. If the jelly is not firm, put in some lemon-juice and heat it over, or some gelatine. If you wish it very light, take light-colored fruit, and make only a small quantity at a time. Quince jelly is made in the same way.

Currant Jelly

Pick off the stems, bruise the fruit, strain off the juice, and to every pint of juice take three-quarters of a pound of sugar. Stir together until it is dissolved, place over the fire skimming it well, and when it has boiled for fifteen minutes it will be done. Try it by putting some in a saucer, and when it is cold, if it is not firm enough, boil it longer. Fill up small common glass tumblers with it, and seal up immediately.

Pigs'-Feet Jelly

To one quart of stock take half a pound of loaf-sugar, one pint of wine, one wineglassful of brandy, the rind and juice of two lemons, a few sticks of cinnamon broken up, a little mace, and the whites of three eggs strained, not beaten, and the shells broken up; mix all these ingredients well together, and boil for forty minutes. Do not stir it. Then throw in a pint of cold water, and let it boil ten or fifteen minutes longer. Strain through a flannel bag with a thin layer of cotton at the bottom of it. If you have no lemons, use a part of a tumbler of strong white vinegar, and use the essence of lemon. If the stock has not kept well, boil it over, and strain it before making the jelly.

Bread Jelly

Boil a quart of water, and, when cold, put into it a small loaf of bread sliced thin and toasted brown. Set it on some coals in a covered vessel, and boil gently until you find it has become a perfect jelly. Strain through a thin cloth, and set away until wanted. When it is to be taken, sweeten with loaf-sugar, and flavor with lemon, and warm a teacupful of it at a time.

Syrups, Creams, Ices, Cordials, Etc.

Raspberry Cream

Rub a quart of raspberries through a sieve to take out the seeds, and then mix it well with some cream, and sweeten with sugar to your taste. Put it in a bowl and froth with a syllabub churn,[12] taking off the froth as it rises. When you have as much froth as you want, put the rest of the cream into a deep glass bowl or dish, and put the frothed cream on it, as high as it will stand.

Orange Syrup

Squeeze the juice and strain it, and to every pint of it add a pound and a half of powdered sugar. Boil it slowly and skim it well, and when the scum ceases to rise, take it from the fire, let it grow cold, and bottle it. Secure the corks well. It is a nice flavoring for pudding-sauces, or custards, or punch.

Lemon Syrup

One quart of water and three pounds of sugar boiled and skimmed well, and when of the consistency of honey and quite hot, stir in three-quarters of an ounce of tartaric acid previously rubbed well in a mortar with twenty-five drops of essence or oil of lemon. It will require but twelve drops of the oil of lemon, or even less will do. The essence is best, as the oil is seldom very fresh. The essence and acid must be well mixed. A small quantity in cold water is a good substitute for lemonade of fresh lemons.

Lemon Juice

Boil together three pounds of loaf-sugar, three quarts of water, and a quart of strained lemon juice until the scum rises and the syrup is quite rich. Then strain and bottle it.

Strawberry Syrup

Mash, and strain the juice, and to every pint of it put a pound of sugar, and boil it till quite a rich syrup is formed. Then bottle and cork it.

Mountain Nectar

Put six pounds of sugar, four ounces of tartaric acid, and two quarts of water; put all into a porcelain kettle, and let it come almost to a boil, but not quite to the boiling-point. Then take it off and stir in the whites of four well-beaten eggs. Strain it, and when it is cool, flavor it richly with essence of lemon. It will keep for months. Two tablespoonfuls of this mixture, and two-thirds of a glass of ice-water, to be put into a goblet, and when ready to drink, a small quantity of soda stirred in, which will make it effervesce finely.

Pine-apple Cider (very fine)

Cut the rind of one large pine-apple or two small ones, into small pieces; put them into a pitcher with two quarts of water. Tie a piece of thin cloth over the pitcher, and let it stand to ferment. Then strain it and sweeten to your taste. Put into bottles, cork tightly, wire them well, and lay on the side. It will be ready for use in forty-eight hours.

Raspberry Vinegar

Squeeze the juice from three pints of raspberries, and mix with one pint of the best white vinegar and a pound of loaf-sugar. Simmer in a jar or pitcher, set in boiling water for an hour, skim it, and bottle when cold. Put a teaspoonful of this into half a pint of spring water.

Muscadine Wine

To one gallon of grapes mashed, take one quart of cold water; then strain immediately, and to every gallon of juice take three pounds of white sugar. Let it stand in a

Scuppernongs, a variety of muscadine grape, are native to North America. Sugary sweet and thick-skinned, scuppernongs thrive in the South's heat, and Southerners often used them to make wines and cordials. Scuppernong grape illustration in White, *Gardening for the South*, 374.

jug with the cork loose, to ferment. When it has done fermenting, strain again through flannel, and bottle and seal.

Ginger Beer

Put into a vessel two gallons of boiling water, two pounds of common white sugar, two ounces of ginger bruised, and two ounces of cream of tartar or a sliced lemon. Stir them until the sugar is dissolved, let it stand until as warm as new milk, then add two tablespoonfuls of good yeast poured on to a piece of bread. Cover the whole over with a cloth, and let it stand undisturbed for twenty-four hours. Then strain it and put into bottles, only filling them three-quarters full. Cork the bottles well, and tie the corks, and in two days, in warm weather, it will be fit to drink. This quantity will make thirty-six bottles.

Blackberry Cordial

Mash and strain the berries, put on the juice to boil, skim it well, and to every gallon of juice put three pounds of sugar and a quart of spirits; bruise some cloves and put in, and when cool bottle it.

Cherry Cordial

Boil and skim the juice, and to every gallon of it take two pounds of sugar. Dissolve the sugar in a little water, and when it comes to a boil strain it and mix with the juice, and to this quantity add half a pint of spirits. Bottle when cold.

Blackberry Wine

To every gallon of berries, after being well mashed, a quart of boiling water. Let it stand twenty-four hours, then strain, and add three pounds of loaf-sugar to every gallon of juice. Let it stand until it is done fermenting, for three or four weeks, with the bung laid on loosely. At the end of three or four weeks, stop it tightly, and set away for some months, and then bottle it. Strawberry wine [is] made in the same way, except that no water is added to the juice.

Porter Beer

Take one bottle of porter, five bottles of water, a pint of molasses or a pound of brown sugar. Make a strong ginger tea and mix all well together. This quantity will fill seven bottles. Put three or four raisins in each bottle, fill them, cork and wire them, and lay on their sides in a cool place.

Corn Beer

Take a pint of corn, boil it until soft, and add to it a gallon of water sweetened with a pint of brown sugar. Cork it tightly and set it in a warm place, and put into it a small quantity of yeast if the weather is cold. In warm weather omit the yeast. Add a few roots of bruised ginger, and a few sliced lemons. The same corn will answer for a year. When you pour out a pitcherful of beer, put in one of sweetened water.

Strawberry Ice-Cream

Mash a pint of berries, and strain the juice into a pint of cream, and sweeten very sweet, and freeze it. Or, flavor with the syrup.

Carolina Ice-Cream

Make a thin custard of a quart of new milk and three well-beaten eggs, the whites and yolks whipped separately. Dissolve a heaping teaspoonful of arrowroot in cold milk, and stir it in the custard while it is scalding. Let the custard simmer, but not boil. Sweeten to your taste, then strain it, and add the flavoring after it is cold, just before it is put into the freezer.

Wilmington Ice-Cream

Take two quarts of milk, or cream if you have it, and boil, and thicken it with three tablespoonfuls of arrowroot. Sweeten with one pound of loaf-sugar, and pour the whole over the beaten whites of eight eggs. Then strain it, and when cold, add the flavoring. If you wish vanilla flavoring, boil half a bean in the milk. Corn-starch will take the place of arrow-root. In straining, a milk-strainer is sufficiently close to use.

Fruit Ice-Cream

Mix the juice of the fruit with enough sugar to sweeten the cream, which need not be very thick.

Lemon-Ice and Fruit-Ices

To a quart of lemonade, add the beaten whites of six eggs cut to a froth, and freeze it. Any other fruit can be used, straining the juice, and sweetening it before putting in the eggs.

Sherbet

Take nine oranges and three lemons. Grate off the yellow from the rinds, and put into a gallon of water, with three pounds of loaf-sugar, and boil to a candy-height. Then take it from the fire and add the pulp of the oranges and lemons, and keep stirring it until almost cold, it is then ready to freeze.

Miscellaneous Receipts

Blockade Coffee

Scald some rye in boiling water, and let it simmer for twenty minutes until it is slightly soft. Then remove from the fire and wash it in cold water, and parch as brown as coffee. To three tablespoonfuls of the ground rye take one tablespoonful of coffee, or a saltspoonful of the essence of coffee, and put into a tin pot, and pour over a quart of boiling water, and let it boil slowly for more than an hour. Let it settle and pour off, and you will find it quite clear without eggs, and very good. Okra seeds parched and ground, and mixed with coffee, in the proportion of one-fourth coffee to three-fourths of okra, is a very nice beverage, and a good substitute for coffee.

Egg-Nogg

Beat separately the yolks and whites of six eggs, and stir into the yolks sufficient powdered loaf-sugar to make it pleasantly sweet, and beat them till very light, and flavor with a little lemon-juice and nutmeg. Beat in six tablespoonfuls of brandy. Boil a quart of thin cream or new milk. Fill the goblets half full of the sugar and eggs, after stirring in the beaten whites just before putting into the glasses. Put a teaspoon in each goblet, and place them on a waiter so they can be distributed immediately after the milk is poured in. Pour the boiling milk into a pitcher, and fill up the goblets with it as you hand them around. Stir the milk and egg well together before drinking.

Rose Brandy for Flavoring

Nearly fill a glass jar with rose leaves, and pour over French brandy enough to fill it quite up. Let it stand twenty-four hours, and pour into a thin muslin and press the leaves well. Return the strained liquid to the jar, and put in fresh leaves, and repeat this every day until you have a strong preparation. It is nice for cakes.

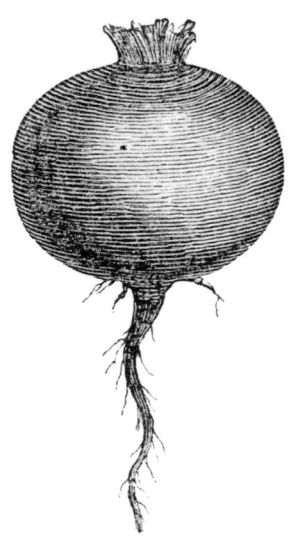

Radishes were a common ingredient of "Pickle-Lily," sometimes spelled piccalilly or picillilla, a pungent condiment combining a variety of pickled vegetables and spices. Illustration of radish in Henderson, *Gardening for Profit*, 231.

To Dry Peaches

Pare and slice them very thin. Their nicety and fine color will depend upon drying quickly, and the thinner and smaller the slices, the sooner they will be ready to put up. Dry on poplar boards with a rim around the edge, and never leave them out after sunset. A still nicer way is to make a syrup of a pound of sugar, and water enough to dissolve it, and when it has boiled, drop in the sliced peaches and cook until half done. Remove from the syrup with a perforated skimmer, and put on dishes in the sun until partly dry, and then on boards until perfectly dry. These peaches make nice pies in winter.

To Make Pickle-Lily

Scald some vinegar, and season with salt, pepper, cloves, mace, and allspice, and when highly seasoned and cold, pour into jars. Drop into this vinegar as they ripen, small cucumbers, tender radish-pods, young beans, and very small onions. Cork close.

Annabella P. Hill, *Mrs. Hill's New Cook Book: A Practical System for Private Families, in Town and Country*

Like many women in the nineteenth century, Annabella Hill married young and bore many children. Born Annabella Dawson in Georgia in 1810, she married a man named Edward Hill when she was seventeen years old. She eventually had eleven children, five of whom died in childhood.[1] By the mid-1840s, Edward Hill had become a judge and the family was living in a small town called LaGrange, Georgia, while also managing a plantation in the country nearby. They almost certainly owned slaves.[2] The early 1860s were hard for Hill. Her husband died in 1860, and then two of her three remaining sons were killed in the war. In 1865 she had to sell her house in LaGrange, although she stayed in town long enough to finish her cookbook, which was first published in 1867.[3] By 1870, she had sold the plantation and was working in Atlanta as the principal of an orphan school.[4]

Although Annabella Hill claimed her cookbook focused on postwar economy, her recipes reflect the cooking style of the antebellum South, and antebellum Georgia in particular.[5] Her experience planning and eating meals in the prewar Deep South shine through in recipes like Scraffle, Souse, Samp, Chitterlings, Succotash, Greens, Grits, Fried Okra, Hopping John, Pepper Vinegar, Chow, and Ground Pea Candy—which would have been similar to peanut brittle.[6] She connected other recipe titles to the war, like Confederate Fruit Cake, Southern Rights Cake, Secession Biscuit, or General Gordon Cake, named after the Confederate general John B. Gordon, born from just one county away from Hill's western Georgia home. But some of her other "political" recipes titles could have appeared just as easily in a Northern book, like Railroad Cake, a popular cake name all over the country in the mid-nineteenth century, or Taylor Pudding, named after the Mexican War hero and later U.S. president Zachary Taylor.

Hill was clearly sympathetic towards young housekeepers who were ignorant of basic housekeeping, as she had been as a teenaged bride herself. And she felt that the situation for most young white Southern brides had only gotten worse since she was young. As she wrote, "'Mother,' even if within accessible distance, is too much occupied with the accumulated cares of her own establishment to be able to devote much time and attention to a separate one; while 'mother's cook' and 'trained servants' are remembered as among the good spirits that ministered to the luxury and ease of by-gone days," a description of slavery that was steeped in nostalgia.

Hill's recipes were quite explicit compared to many other cookbooks of the era, and they would have been helpful to the inexperienced. But despite her claims about postwar austerity, she made all sorts of assumptions about social class in her recipes. In fact, some of her entries read more like instructions on gracious living than recipes. Describing Breakfast Fruits, for example, she wrote, "Remove the first course, and the white cloth; if the table is not a handsome one, it should be covered with a wine cloth, under the white tablecloth; always send colored doylies with fruit. Grapes may be tastily arranged with their leaves. Finger-bowls should be placed before each person, to be used after the fruit course is finished." In fact, Hill's general concern with food's appearance and presentation also speaks to her economic privilege. "To look well," she wrote, cauliflowers "should be very white." Crimson radishes were desirable because they were "highly ornamental." And red peppers were good for ketchup simply because they made it "beautiful." She also casually called for ingredients and supplies that would have been out of reach of most Southerners, like big pots of boiling lard in which to fry vegetables or a plentiful supply of ice at a time when most ice would have been harvested in New England and available only to a privileged few in the South.

For the most part, though, Hill really did seem to assume her reader would be doing the cooking herself, and she treated cooking as an honorable skill, calling it a "science" all young women should learn. In fact, her cookbook opened with a vigorous call from E. W. Wilson for Southern white women to become more involved housekeepers and cooks. Faced with the "present crisis" of Reconstruction, Wilson believed, all Southern women should learn to cook, even privileged white women who had considered that work beneath them before the war. "As woman has been queen in the parlor," Wilson predicted optimistically, "so, if need be, she will be queen in the kitchen." Before the war, a big part of the social identity of elite white women had been their supposed delicacy and unsuitability for physical labor. Wilson held up a new feminine ideal, one where women's domestic labor was part of their moral contributions to the household and the basis of their physical health and happiness. "Reverse the present order of things," Wilson begged. Instead of looking forward "as slaves to the task" of housekeeping, he wrote, white women should think of labor as "honorable" and idleness as shameful. These new ideals about the prestige of housework drew on the arguments of earlier domestic reformers like Catharine Beecher while also anticipating the arguments home economists would be making in large numbers by the early twentieth century.

Like many other nineteenth-century women who knew they would be expected to serve as nurses in times of family sickness, Hill readily talked about cooking as a tool for treating the sick. Her long section on cooking for invalids included recipes for classic sickroom dishes like gruel, mush, and wine, which would have been common in other cookbooks of the era. But at least some of her invalid cookery advice seems distinctively Southern, as when she recommended squirrels as a mild meat perfect for people with weakened constitutions. Besides sickroom cookery, Hill also touched on the treatment of wounds and other emergencies like snakebites and fires and the severing of an artery.

Finally, Hill included a section on recipes for homemade medicines. In these recipes she made heavy use of opiates, including in recipes destined for babies and children. For example, for a child with the whooping cough she recommended "Hog's lard and molasses in equal quantities with a little laudanum." When someone had scarlet fever she advised rubbing the patient's body from head to foot with fat bacon. Obviously, her remedies don't have much in common with modern medicine, and it can be tempting to laugh at nineteenth-century ignorance. But at a time when epidemic diseases regularly raced through American populations, killing as they went, family members were desperate to do something to help their loved ones; laudanum, at least, would have eased a child's suffering. Hill must have tried some of these recipes on her own children, and sometimes she probably credited a homemade medicine with restoring a child to health. But despite whatever nursing she may have tried, five of her children died. Like other nineteenth-century Americans tasked with nursing the sick, Hill was giving the best advice she could based on the knowledge she had.

Introduction

The book which meets the wants of the times deserves a place in every household, and the writer who, in these degenerate days, contributes to the pleasures, and at the same time advances the real welfare, of the race, deserves a place in the Calendar with all the benefactors of the age. [This book] comes up to the standard here laid down.

In reading the advertisements in our daily papers, the eye frequently falls upon something like this:—"*Wanted, A good Cook.*" This is a universal want, and one that must, to some extent, be supplied. We are an eating race, and people will eat; they have been educated to eat. Indeed, hitherto we have lived by this process, and even now there appears no sign among the improvements of the age, of such a reformation as will dispense with "table comforts." Happy is that family that has this want gratified. I do not mean that we are an Epicurean race; so far from it, indeed, that there are no visible tendencies in that direction, and it is hoped none will ever appear. But man is an animal, and all animals must eat; and although it is written of him, "Thou shalt not live by bread alone," yet, a bountiful Providence has decreed seed time and harvest, bread earned by the sweat of his brow, and a table of plenty. . . .

The days for romance have passed, if they ever existed; the night for the dream visions of elegance and luxury in connection with a life on indolence has suddenly given place to the day of enterprise and industry. A crisis is upon us which demands the development of

the *will* and *energy* of Southern character. . . . As woman has been queen in the parlor, so, if need be, she will be queen in the kitchen; as she has performed so gracefully the duties of mistress of the establishment in the past, so she will, with a lovelier grace, perform whatever labor duty demands. She has learned that the services of a good cook, that queen of the kitchen, are essential elements in the health, the good temper, the enjoyment and peace of every family; that the art of Cooking is the parent of all other arts and eating and drinking the highest of all animal enjoyments. The race of good cooks among us is almost extinct. What shall be done to bring back the good old times, when a knowledge of the good housewifery demanded for the health and comfort of every family was not considered too low for the attention of any lady? . . .

Will not the ladies, whose opinions and actions form public sentiment, lead off in a culinary reform, which will correct the errors of the past, and introduce a system of industry and economy to meet the present emergencies? Reverse the present order of things. Make idleness and indolence disreputable, and labor and usefulness honorable. Pluck from the hand of the destroyer the premium awarded to idleness and give it to industry. . . . Those now entering and soon to enter upon the full duties of life, should not do so with mistaken views as to the responsibilities they will have to meet, and the manner of discharging the obligations of the domestic sphere. They should not look forward as slaves to the task, or as idle pupils to the recitation. Labor promotes health, and health fosters contentment. So, to be both healthy and happy, we should be both usefully and profitably employed. . . .

Our authoress [Hill] has proved herself to be mistress in literature, as well as queen in the kitchen. Her versatility of talent qualifies her for the position which her sense of duty urged her, against her inclination, to assume; namely, to assist all who may desire knowledge and improvement in the important art of cooking.

The instructions here presented are the result of a life of experience, observation, and reading. No untried theory is offered, nor have we here a system too luxurious for the poor, or too economical for the rich. The wants, tastes, and abilities of all are consulted, so that the poor may luxuriate on delicious soups every day made from the savings which a wasteful housekeeper would consider utterly worthless. If our Southern women are going to meet the present crisis as they have all the trials of the past (and none can doubt but they will), they will find this book a companion of invaluable service, and a constant adviser, whose opinions may be trusted as entirely reliable. Adopt the system here presented, and you will soon find your husband delighted with the improvement in your style of living, and it will not be long before he will compliment you on the economy of your new regulations.

E. W. Warren, Macon, GA

Dedication

To young and inexperienced Southern housekeepers I desire to dedicate this work. . . . Thousands of young women are taking upon themselves the responsibilities of housekeepers, a position for which their inexperience and ignorance of household affairs renders them wholly unfitted. Formerly "mother" or "mother's cook," or one whom the considerate mother had trained to fill this important office in the daughter's *ménage*, was, with many, the only authority considered necessary in the conduct of culinary operations. Now, however, things are changed. "Mother," even if within accessible distance, is too much occupied with the accumulated cares of her own establishment to be able to devote much time and attention to a separate one; while "mother's cook" and "trained servants" are remembered as among the good spirits that ministered to the luxury and ease of by-gone days.

Youth and inexperience are lamentable drawbacks which cannot be set aside by the brave hearts that would overcome the trials that assail them in the outset of their domestic career; and they must content themselves to "begin at the beginning"; to learn the rudiments of the science first, and by the exercise of common sense and a laudable ambition they may hope to become (through experience) thorough good housekeepers. It is with the earnest hope of benefiting this class that I have yielded to the importunities of many friends and consented to place in their hands the results of an experience of thirty years, trusting that it may prove to many an unerring guide through the labyrinth of domestic duties.

The rules that I give are collected from experience and other "reliable" sources, and if faithfully and attentively practiced will insure success. To experienced housekeepers, the directions may seem *tediously minute*. I have examined a great many Cookery books. In a majority of them too much is taken for granted, and much of the very information that a *novice* most needs is omitted, as facts with which every one is familiar. In preparing this receipt Book, a vivid recollection of my own utter ignorance of household affairs at the time that I assumed the duties of mistress of a family, suggested the idea of taking but one thing for granted, viz.: that the majority of those for whom this book is principally intended know as little as I did, and stand as greatly in need of the aid and instruction that I would gladly have received. That they will be found in the pages of this book I sincerely believe, and although devoid of the vanity of supposing that my contemporaries in age can profit by the directions herein contained, I should confess to defeat and disappointment, should they fail to supply that absence of practical knowledge which is the source of so many failures and disappointments to those who are just taking the initiatory steps in housekeeping.

Mrs. A. P. Hill

Soups

Gumbo

Fry a young chicken; after it gets cold, take out the bones. In another vessel fry one pint of young, tender, cut up ochra and two onions. Put all in a well-cleaned soup-kettle; an iron stew-pan lined with tin or porcelain is best. Add one quart of water; stew gently until done; and season with pepper and salt. Another way of preparing Gumbo, is: Cut up a fowl as if to fry; break the bones; lay it in a pot with a little lard or fresh butter. Brown it a little. When browned, pour a gallon of water on it; add a slice of lean bacon, one onion cut in slices, a pint of tomatoes skinned, two pints of young pods of ochra cut up, and a few sprigs of parsley. Cover closely, removing the cover to skim off all impurities that may rise to the top. Set the soup-kettle where the water will simmer gently at least four hours. Half an hour before the soup is put in the tureen, add a thickening, by mixing a heaping tablespoonful of sassafras leaves, dried and pounded fine, with a little soup. Stir this well into the soup. Serve with a separate dish of rice.

Gather the leaf-buds of the sassafras early in the spring; dry, pound, sift, and bottle them. Miss Leslie recommends stirring the soup with a sassafras stick, when the powdered leaves cannot be procured. The sassafras taste is very disagreeable to some persons, therefore should be omitted when this is the case.

Asparagus Soup

Boil the asparagus with any kind of fresh meat or fowl, or the broth in which they have been boiled. To a quart of this liquor add a heaping teaspoonful of flour stirred into a teacup of cream, added just before serving. A hundred points of asparagus will answer for three pints of broth; cut them into pieces two inches long; boil half an hour; salt and pepper to taste.

Corn Soup

To a small hock bone of ham, or slice of good ham, add one quart of water. As soon as it boils, skim it well until the liquor is clear; add one large teacup and a half of grated corn, one quart of sweet milk, and a tablespoonful of butter, into which has been rubbed a heaping teaspoonful of flour; salt and pepper to taste.

Green Pea Soup

The pods of peas make an excellent soup after the peas are shelled out. Boil the hulls and peas in separate vessels. Strain the water in which the hulls were boiled through a colander. Return the liquor to the pot and make the soup by any of the foregoing receipts, and add the peas a quarter of an hour before serving; add crackers in the bottom of the tureen. Instead of boiling the pea-hulls in water alone, add a little fresh meat or a slice of ham; butter may be added with a small quantity of flour rubbed into it if liked.

Ochra Soup

Make a broth of fowls or fresh meat; veal is best. To a gallon of this add three dozen young, tender pods of ochra; cut up thin; boil gently and slowly three hours, stirring occasionally. Remove the meat, and season with salt and pepper. Rice and tomatoes may, if liked, be added in small quantities. This should make three quarts of soup.

Chicken Soup

Cut up a grown chicken as for frying; boil gently in three quarts of water, and remove all scum carefully. To half a gallon of soup add half a pint of rice, a few sprigs of chopped parsley; pepper and salt to taste. Boil until the chicken is done. Add half a pint of sweet milk and one tablespoonful of arrow-root, stirred into a spoonful of butter. If for a sick person, omit the butter. The meat may be used in the soup if preferred, but picked carefully from the bones; if not used in the soup, make it into salad or hash. Old fowls, when in good condition, are best for soup. Never put bones or gristle in the soup tureen. Corn starch, or wheat flour, will answer for thickening.

Pigeon Soup

Take six pigeons, partridges, or other birds; clean nicely and cut up. Put the gizzards, necks, and livers, with the other parts of the birds, into half a gallon of cold water. Boil until done. Take up the pigeons; pick all the meat from the bones; strain the broth through a sieve; return it to the pot, and thicken with half a pint of bread crumbs. Season with mace, allspice, and cloves; put the last in whole; salt and pepper. Add the meat, which must be picked up very fine. After the soup is in the tureen, add four hard-boiled eggs grated. A dozen berries of allspice, eight of cloves, is sufficient.

Chicken and Oyster Soup (a superior receipt)

Cut up a full-grown fowl as for frying. Clean the giblets nicely, and put all in the soup-kettle with just enough water to cover them; let it simmer gently; remove all the scum. When the chicken is tender, take it up, strain the liquor and return it to the kettle. Add a quart of sweet milk to a quart of broth; if there should not be as much broth as is needed, pour in sufficient boiling water; Add a quart of oysters with their juice, and two or three blades of mace. A tablespoonful of butter, one of arrowroot, wheat flour rubbed into the butter, and one gill of hot cream; stew gently five minutes. Cream must always be boiled before being put into soup or gravy. Use the chicken for salad.

Fish

To Fry Fish

Use for this purpose a frying-pan, spider,[7] or iron oven. If the frying-pan is preferred, half fill the vessel with lard; but if a larger and deeper vessel is used, have lard enough to cover the fish. The lard should be sweet and clean, and free from salt, as rancid lard imparts a disagreeable taste, and salt will prevent the article from browning. It is important to know when the lard is hot enough. If not hot enough, the fish will be pale and sodden. A good and easy way to ascertain this is to throw a small piece of bread into the vessel. If it fries crisp, the lard is ready; if the bread burns, it is too hot. As soon as the fish is done, remove it to a soft cloth before the fire; turn once. This will absorb the grease; the grease otherwise would settle upon the lower pieces. Fish, to be in perfection, must be fresh. To ascertain this, examine the gills and eyes; the former should be of a bright red, the latter bright and lively, and the flesh firm. The least taint about fish renders them worthless. Pond fish have an earthy, muddy taste. To extract this, soak them in salt and water.

To Fry Fillets of Fish

Cut them in slices half an inch thick; fry them plain, or in thin batter, or roll in Indian meal. Whole fish may be fried or boiled in plenty of boiling lard; when done, skin them, and serve immediately in a hot dish; use piquant sauce.

To Fry Shad

Clean them thoroughly; cut in slices of proper size to help at the table. Wipe each piece dry. Beat one or two eggs well together, and with an egg-brush put the egg evenly over the fish; or the pieces may be dipped in the egg. Be sure that every part is covered by the beaten egg. Roll them in bread crumbs. Shake off the loose crumbs, and fry in hot lard. Fry the thick parts a few minutes before putting in the thin. Have plenty of lard to cover the fish. Do not put it in until the lard boils, or it will not be firm and crisp. If there are eggs or roe, fry them. Shad and other fish may be rolled in corn meal, sifted fine, or in flour, before being fried. Either way is good. This receipt will answer for frying any kind of fish. Very small fresh water fish may be cooked whole, and simply rolled in Indian meal, or fried plain.

Trout, black-fish, mullet, whiting, perch, sturgeon, and drum, are all excellent cooked by either of the above receipts. Large fish should be cut into steaks or fillets.

To Broil Smoked Fish

Wash it well in cold water; wipe it dry; broil on a hot gridiron, turning two to three times, when thoroughly hot; pour on it melted butter; pepper well; garnish with parsley and lemon. A good breakfast dish. It is a good plan to let fresh fish lie several hours in the seasoning, before broiling; each slice, if the fish is large, may be seasoned with butter, pepper[,] salt, a little minced onion, or eschalot;[8] wrap in buttered paper separately and broil; turn out of the paper and serve with sauce.

To Stew Catfish, Eels, Perch, Etc.

After cleaning well, place the fish in the kettle; strew over two large onions, cut up fine; pepper and salt to taste; cover with warm water; set the kettle where it will simmer gently. Cut up very fine, four or five large sprigs of parsley; add this to the fish. Pour into the stew-pan one pint of sweet cream or rich sweet milk; add to this a teacup of butter into which has been rubbed a tablespoonful of flour; place it on the fire for five minutes, shaking the pan frequently. Take up the fish and pour the gravy over it.

To Souse Fish

Boil the fish until done; add a little salt. Take equal quantities of the water it was boiled in and good vinegar. Season highly with pepper, cloves, allspice, and mace; boil the spices in the water until their strength is extracted. Cut off the head and tail of the fish; cut the rest in pieces; pack close in a stone jar and pour over the vinegar. It must stand a day or two before using. Keep the jar, well covered, in a cool place. Should more vinegar be needed, add it cold.

Shrimp Patties

Chop or grind one soup-plate of peeled shrimps; moisten with water one tumblerful of grated light bread, first removing the crust; mix well with the shrimps until a smooth paste is formed; add a *heaped-up* tablespoonful of butter, a teaspoonful of mixed mustard, salt, cayenne, and black pepper to taste, and half a grated nutmeg; make into small cakes and fry in butter or lard, a light brown color.

To Cook Frogs

Only the hind legs of the large green kind are used; skin them; season with salt and pepper, and broil or fry them; the meat is beautifully white; the taste delicate.

Mock Oysters

Take brains from the head of hogs, as whole as possible; remove the skin and throw them into salt and water; let them remain in this two hours; then boil them, until done, in sweet milk; take them up in an earthen bowl or dish, and pour over weak vinegar to cover them; prepare sufficient vinegar to cover them, by adding to it cloves, allspice, and cinnamon to taste; season well with pepper, using part red pepper; scald this vinegar; pour off the weak vinegar; cover with the spiced vinegar. Eat cold, or stewed with crackers as oysters.

Meats

To Know When Hams Are Sound

Stick a sharp knife to the bone in the thickest part of the ham, and also run it around the knuckle. If there is any taint, you can detect it by smelling and examining the knife.

To Glaze a Ham

Brush over the ham (using a feather or a brush) with the yolk of an egg; cover thickly with bread crumbs. Go over it with thick cream; put it in the stove or oven to brown; put the glaze on half an inch thick; if necessary go over a second time.

To Boil Corned Beef

Soak the beef over night in plenty of water to cover it well. At nine o'clock the next morning, wash the piece well, put it in the pot and cover with cold water; boil slowly; skim frequently. If it is to be served cold, let it remain in the pot until it becomes so.

To prepare it for luncheon or as a supper dish, remove all the bones when thoroughly done, pick the meat as for salad and pack in a deep dish, putting in alternately fat and lean. Skim the liquor, removing all fat; boil this broth until reduced one half; pour into the dish as much of it as may be needed to fill all the spaces left in packing the meat; lay over this a flat cover that will just fit it, place a heavy weight upon this. It is best to prepare this dish in cold weather or put upon ice the dish it was prepared in. Serve it upon a plate or round dish, and garnish with green sprigs of parsley, or celery; serve with it chow, picillilla[9] or any good pickle. French mustard is excellent eaten with it.

To Boil Cow-Heel

After being well cleaned boil them until the bones can be removed easily; skin them and serve with parsley and onion sauce.

Clean the feet by immersing them in boiling water; let them remain long enough to loosen the horny part; run a knife around and under the horn; force it off, scrape and wash well. This is an economical dish, nutritive and agreeable, when well prepared it is good fried, after being boiled, or stewed and dressed with cream and butter; cut it in pieces of convenient size for serving.

Scraffle[10]

Boil a fresh-killed hog's head tender. This is made in the winter during what we at the South call "hog-killing." Take it up and remove all the bones; chop the meat very fine and season it with salt, pepper, and sage, as sausage meat; strain the liquor; wipe out the pot nicely; return the broth to the pot; there should be about a quart of this. Put the meat back and stir into the broth fine corn meal until the mass is the consistence of soft mush; let this simmer half an hour, stirring frequently; pour the mixture into pans three or four inches deep. When cold slice in thin slices, roll in corn meal or flour, and fry in boiling lard, a light brown. This keeps as well as souse; it should be well protected from dust and air.

Souse

The feet and ears of the hog are best for this, though the upper part of the head is often used, removing the fat where there is too much. To prepare the feet, scald them well; scrape off the hair. Some persons roll them in hot ashes; I prefer the boiling water, as the other plan frequently scorches the skin, and souse should be very white. Scrape them, removing the horny part; when all

are well cleaned, lay them to soak a day and night. Put them to boil in plenty of cold water; skim the pot well; simmer them gently. When the bones can be removed easily, take them up, and as soon as they can be handled, pick the meat from the bones; season the mass highly with salt, pepper and vinegar; pack it in pans, and lay over each a clean cloth dipped in vinegar; dip the cloth in vinegar every day, and it may be kept for some time in that way or it may be packed in jars and covered with half vinegar and water.

Pepper-Pot

Clean four calf's feet and two pounds of tripe; boil them tender; cut up the tripe in small pieces, pick the bones from the feet; return the tripe and meat to the pot, pour over the broth after skimming off the fat; add two white skinned onions sliced, half a dozen of Irish potatoes peeled and sliced, a teaspoonful each of parsley, thyme, and marjoram; stew until the vegetables are tender; season highly with black and Cayenne pepper, and salt to taste. Make a rich gravy of part of the broth, a spoonful of butter into which has been rubbed a dessert-spoonful of flour, and a tumblerful of hot cream.

To Make Hash

Meats that have been once done, only require to be warmed over. To cook them again renders them tough and insipid. Cut up the vegetables to be used for seasoning—onions, potatoes, tomatoes, etc., as may be preferred. Put the butter, flour, salt, pepper, and vegetables (or spices if preferred as seasoning) into the stew-pan with all the cold gravy that may have been saved; essence of ham answers a good purpose; a few inches of portable soup[11] is very good if there should not be sufficiency of gravy; a teacup of boiling water for a pound of meat; very little water should be used. Cover the stew-pan and let this stew gently a quarter of an hour, shaking the stew-pan frequently. Have the meat minced fine, removing all bones and gristle; add to the gravy, stirring it in well. Let it remain until the meat is thoroughly hot, and serve. Use catsup upon the plate for extempore dressing. Very little cooking is necessary and very little gravy. When there is stuffing, a small quantity may be used.

Mrs. J.'s Receipt for Scotch Hash

Mince corned beef as fine as possible, also a good portion of onion chopped fine; season highly with Cayenne pepper; add a tablespoonful of butter; add boiling water, not quite enough to cover the meat; let this become very hot. Beat two eggs well in a common sized pie-pan; stir the meat to the eggs and put it in the stove-oven until a light brown crust is formed. A few minutes will form the crust, if the oven is as hot as it should be. Serve immediately. A good breakfast dish.

Chicken and Oysters

Truss a young fowl as for boiling; clean the inside well, removing all clotted blood. Chop as many oysters fine as will fill it; close the apron well with a few stitches. Stew in a double kettle, or put it in an unglazed jar; cover it well, and, putting it in a kettle of boiling water, keep it boiling an hour and a half, or until tender. Serve with a sauce made of the gravy from the stew, a little of the oyster liquor, butter and flour to make it rich enough and of proper consistence.

Beef Tongue and Mushrooms

Soak a pickled tongue; lard it across. Season highly with pepper, salt, and spices; onion and parsley cut up fine. Lay it in a stew-pan, cover with water, and put over it slices of bacon or pork. Stew gently until tender. Fry a pint of button mushrooms in butter (be particular to prevent the butter from burning). Take the tongue up, and put the mushrooms in the stew-pan, and stew five or six minutes; pour over the tongue. Serve hot.

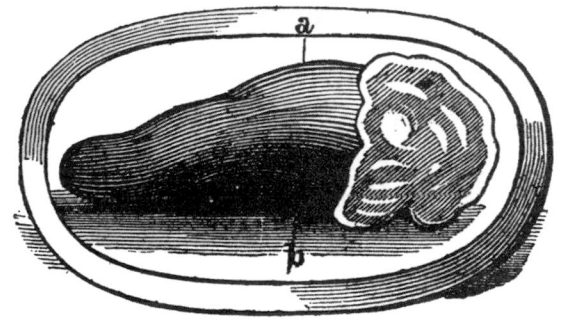

Beef tongue appeared regularly on tables in the Civil War era, but it fell out of favor in the decades that followed. In Annabella Hill's recipe, she instructed cooks to stew a pickled beef tongue with onions and bacon before topping it with sautéed mushrooms. Hill, *Mrs. Hill's Southern Practical Cookery*, facsimile of 1872 edition, 79.

Beef Liver

Wash it well; remove the veins; parboil it an hour before it is to be cooked. Pour the liver and water into a vessel, let it set until nearly cold; slice it in pieces an inch thick; season them with salt and pepper. Cut half a dozen slices of fat bacon; remove the skin; put them with a table-spoonful of lard into the frying-pan; when the lard is hot, roll the slices of liver in flour, shake them slightly and put them to fry; turn frequently. Take the bacon up when crisp; they will be ready to take up before the liver. Take the liver up when done; dredge a little flour into the pan; pour in a small teacup of boiling water; let all boil up until the gravy thickens sufficiently, and pour into a sauce-boat. It should not be poured over the liver. Serve the liver and bacon together upon the same dish. Calf and hog's liver are better than beef, and may be prepared in the same way. Butter may be used for making gravy, if preferred to the lard.

Roasting Meat

This style of dressing meat is less practised in the common everyday cooking than it should be. It is certainly of all others the most elegant. To even approximate perfection in the art, practice is absolutely necessary. Although there are a variety of contrivances for roasting, very many families are unprovided with any kind of apparatus for conducting the business. A very cheap and simple arrangement, and which will answer the purpose as well as more costly and complicated machinery, is to roast by the string. Procure a piece of iron or steel eighteen inches long, with a hinge in the middle, to fold

Annabella Hill praised the many advantages of roasting meat over a fire. For inexperienced cooks, she outlined a "very cheap and simple" method of roasting meat by hanging it over the fire with string. Illustration from Hill, *Mrs. Hill's Southern Practical Cookery*, facsimile of 1872 edition, 80.

it out of the way when not in use. It should be strong enough to meet any demands made upon it; at one end there should be a plate of iron three inches long and two wide, with screws inserted to fasten it to the mantelpiece. This should be done securely. At the other end a twirling hook, or common ring and hook; take a twine or twisted woollen string long enough to bring the articles to be cooked before the full influence of the fire. A hook should be securely fastened to each end of this string; catch one hook to the twirling hook, the other insert in the meat. Run a skewer through the feet of poultry and catch one hook to the skewer. If the roast is a piece of beef, veal, etc., when it is half done turn it. If it be necessary to expose one part to the fire more than the rest, prop it with a paddle or board, resting one end of the paddle against a smoothing iron (or a brick will answer) placed directly behind the roast, and at just sufficient distance to rest the broad part of the paddle against the roast. A sharp stick must not be used, as the least puncture will let out the juices.

This plan is for a permanent arrangement. For temporary use, a wooden peg driven over the fireplace will answer. (I shall be glad to see the roaster substituted for that most popular of all kitchen utensils, the frying pan.) A tin screen will greatly increase the heat, and thus save fuel. It should be so placed as to guard the roast from currents of air. The most convenient pattern I know is one made of tin three feet wide, one and a half feet deep, with a shelf in it. It may be put upon rollers. This will also answer for a plate warmer.

A Haunch of Venison

This being a dry meat requires a great deal of basting. I have been informed by old hunters that on this account it is best to roast it very soon after being killed. Protect the fat with oiled paper, keep the string well greased to prevent its scorching; a twisted woollen string is less liable to burn than a cotton one. Twelve pounds will require three hours before a solid, brisk fire. Currant jelly may be served in the gravy or sent to table as an accompaniment; any acid jelly will answer; crab apple or grape jelly is very good. Wine may be added to the gravy if liked. . . .

Kid

This animal is in its greatest perfection at five months old. The meat is delicate and juicy, and deserves to be more popular. Roast as you would lamb; serve with the same accompaniments and sauce. The head is excellent stewed or baked, and also makes fine soup. The meat is good eaten cold with French mustard.

A Roasted Rabbit—Whole Except the Head

This is best stuffed. While roasting baste frequently with butter; dredge it with flour and manage as with any other roast. The head and liver may be boiled; split the head, take out the brains, mash them with the liver, and add to the gravy. Wine and jelly are by some persons liked in the gravy. If a little thickening is needed to the gravy; set the dripping-pan upon the stove and make the gravy to taste.

To Bake a Pig

All meats are better for being kept several hours after being killed, except pig. Dr. Kitchiner says, "it loses part of its goodness every hour after being killed; if not fresh, no art can make the crackling crisp." If intended to be baked whole, it should not exceed a month old, and should be fat and plump. Kill it early in the morning, if for dinner. Immerse it in hot water (but not boiling) a few minutes; then scrape off the hair, repeating the process until every part is white and clean; force off the horny part attached to the feet. Cut off the feet at the first joint; do this carefully, with a sharp knife. They are often very carelessly chopped off, leaving the bone projecting beyond the meat. Mrs. Hale gives excellent directions for thoroughly cleaning a pig: "Take the wax out of the ears; the dirt from the nostrils, by using a small skewer (or piece of wire) covered with a bit of thin rag, which you must wipe often upon a coarse towel or dish rag; take out the eyes with a sharp knife or fork; clean the tongue, gums and lips, by scraping with a sharp knife; wipe them; be careful not to cut them; run your hand up the throat; take out all the clotted blood and loose pieces found there, and lastly cleanse the other end of the pig, by putting a skewer covered with a cloth through from the inside; wipe the inside clean with a damp cloth; make a slit in the abdomen, and take out the entrails; wash it in two or three waters; wipe it dry, and wrap it immediately in a cloth to protect it from the air."[12] Prepare the stuffing of bread crumbs, moistened with water, seasoned with onion and sage; a tablespoonful of butter; pepper and salt to taste; mash the bread smooth; beat into it two eggs, and put the mixture to fry until as thick as mush; then with a spoon, and while hot, put it inside the pig; a few stitches will prevent the stuffing from falling out; the thread must be removed before sending it to the table. If to be baked in a brick oven or stove, lay it in a large pan that will hold it comfortably; if in an iron oven, put a trivet upon the bottom; pour in a pint of warm water, and brush it all over with sweet olive oil, or good fresh butter. Besides my own experience, I have the very high authority of Dr. K for saying that nothing

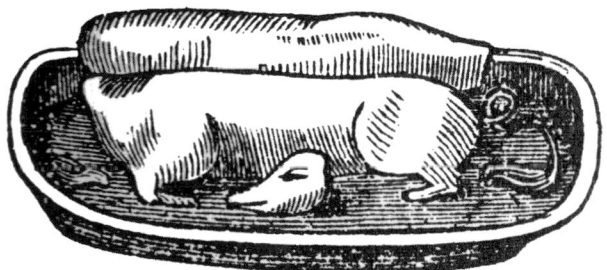

In this illustration for baked pig, the head was served beside the rest of the body. In contrast to modern styles of butchery and cooking that tend to downplay the animal origins of meat, such a presentation would have played those origins up. It also would have also given diners the chance to eat the cheeks and tongue and other parts of the pig's head. In fact, according to Annabella Hill's instructions, the brains would already have been incorporated into the gravy and the ears would be presented separately for easier eating. Hill, *Mrs. Hill's Southern Practical Cookery*, facsimile of 1872 edition, 105.

answers for basting pig so well as salad oil. Says he, "rub a little sweet oil on the skin with a brush or goose feather; this makes the crackling crisper and browner than basting it with its own drippings, and is the best way to prevent its blistering." The crackling or skin must be nicely crisped and delicately browned, without being either blistered or burned. After oiling it, baste with salt and water twice; then with salad oil or fresh butter. Stew the harslet; chop fine and season with pepper and parsley; serve in a separate dish; thicken the gravy slightly with a paste made of flour and water. If too rich, pour off part of the grease. Send to the table in a tureen. Apple sauce is a good accompaniment; also grated horseradish, or mustard pickle. When done, take off the head; cut it in two; part the whole body; put the brains in the gravy; lay the pig in the dish, back to back. The ears should, while baking, be covered with oiled paper, or they will become too hard before the rest of the pig is done. Cut them from the head, and lay upon the dish as may be preferred. The head may also be placed as in the plate, or as one may fancy. Lay the stuffing around and under the pig, or upon a separate dish; put some of this upon each plate.

Wild Fowls

Are usually trussed with the head on, as in the plate, turned under the wing; run a bird skewer through the thighs, and tie the legs. Pheasants, woodcocks, or snipes, are all trussed, and served in the same way upon toast. Baste well with butter; pour part of the gravy upon the toast; send the remainder in a sauce-boat. Woodcocks

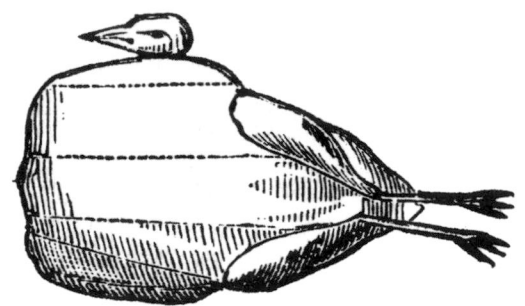

Beyond ducks and geese, "wild fowl" was a category that included pheasant, grouse, quail, woodcock, snipe, plover, and a variety of other game birds. Hill, *Mrs. Hill's Southern Practical Cookery*, facsimile of 1872 edition, 92.

and plovers are excellent picked and not drawn, wrapped in thick brown paper, and roasted on the hearth in hot ashes.

A Brisket of Beef

Joint the bone, by sawing through it without cutting the outside skin. This is done for the convenience of carving. It may be stuffed with oysters, or any rich stuffing, first removing the small bones, and supplying their places with stuffing. . . . The heart and liver are excellent stuffed and baked. Remove the ventricle from the heart; clean well, and slightly parboil it, and also the liver; then stuff them. To make a good stuffing, take equal quantities of the kidney, suet and bread crumbs. Chop the suet fine; season highly with parsley, pepper, red and black; salt to taste; ginger and lemon peel if liked; work it up with a raw egg. Send the gravy to the table just as it comes from the meat, unseasoned, in a hot tureen.

Cow-Heel

After being well cleaned, boil them until the bones can be removed easily. Cut each heel in four parts; dip them first in beaten egg, then roll in bread crumbs or corn meal, and fry in hot lard until a golden color; very little cooking is necessary; or fry them plain until slightly brown. French mustard is good eaten with them, or any of the store sauces. Season extempore.

Venison Steaks

Cut the steaks from the haunch or saddle, half an inch thick; fry in half lard and butter. Never leave them a moment after putting them in the pan, but turn constantly. Season with salt and pepper when half done; a very few minutes will be required to cook them, but they should be thoroughly done. Take up the steak into a hot covered dish; dredge a little flour into the gravy, stir it in smoothly; pour in half a tumbler of boiling water; let it boil up once, then immediately pour in a wine-glass of good Madeira wine; pour over the steak. If preferred, mushroom or tomato catsup may be used in place of the wine. Serve with cranberry jam or any pleasant acid jelly.

Pork Chops

Quarter the animal, remove the chine bone, cut the blade bone from the ribs (chops are taken from the fore quarter); cut the ribs into pieces two or three inches long, one bone to a chop; if very fat, remove a part of it. Sprinkle a little finely pulverized sage over each piece; fry a light brown; serve without gravy. Fried apples, tomato sauce, or dried apple sauce are good accompaniments.

Lamb's Fry and Pluck

The small bowels, sweetbreads and kernels compose the fry; the lights, liver and heart make the pluck. Clean and soak them well, cutting open the intestines with sharp scissors. When clean, cut them into small pieces, roll in flour, and fry a golden color. Put all into a stew-pan, cover them with boiling water, and stew until tender. Season with red and black pepper, salt to taste, onions and tomatoes.

Chitterlings

Take the intestines and maws selected for chitterlings (and take those only which are in good condition); cut them open with a sharp knife. Hog chitterlings are best—indeed the only kind in general use. Turn and wash them in several waters; scrape them; lay them to soak in weak salt and water two days, changing the water and washing them well; when changed, in fresh cold water. Boil them until tender; pack them in a jar. Pour over weak vinegar to cover them; renew the vinegar as may be necessary. Cut them in pieces if large; roll in corn meal or bread crumbs, and fry until hot in boiling lard, or dip them in thin batter and fry until the batter is a golden color; very little cooking is required. This is a popular dish, very rich; but should be attended to by a very neat, careful person, and not suffered to lie a moment that can be avoided after being taken from the animal until they are cleaned and in soak. The water should be changed often and the vessel in which they are put to soak washed clean each time of changing. Seasoned like oysters, they make a good mock oyster.

Pork Sparerib—Is Excellent Broiled

Baste constantly with butter. Very few persons baste it sufficiently, hence it is not unfrequently brought to the table dry and tasteless.[13] It requires neither gravy nor seasoning.

To Broil Chickens

The fowl must be fat and young; no other kind is fit for the gridiron. After it is picked, open it by cutting down the back; remove the intestines; wash it well; keep it at least twelve hours, if the weather will admit. Warm and grease the gridiron; lay the fowl down with the inside next to the fire. Have a small oven lid, washed upon the inside perfectly clean, and wiped dry until it will not smut; put this upon the chicken; weight this down with a flat-iron. Broil slowly. When done—and it is seldom well done—pour over the fowl melted butter. Stew the giblets half done; then pepper them well, and finish upon the gridiron.

To Barbecue Any Kind of Fresh Meat

Gash the meat. Broil slowly over a solid fire. Baste constantly with a sauce composed of butter, mustard, red and black pepper, vinegar. Mix these in a pan, and set it where the sauce will keep warm, not hot. Have a swab made by tying a piece of clean, soft cloth upon a stick about a foot long; dip this in the sauce and baste with it. Where a large carcass is barbecued, it is usual to dig a pit in the ground outdoors, and lay narrow bars of wood across. Very early in the morning fill the pit with wood; set it burning, and in this way heat it very hot. When the wood has burned to coals, lay the meat over. Should the fire need replenishing, keep a fire outside burning, from which draw coals, and scatter evenly in the pit under the meat. Should there be any sauce left, pour it over the meat. For barbecuing a joint, a large gridiron answers well; it needs constant attention; should be cooked slowly and steadily.

Meat Pies

Considering the popularity of these dishes, few make their appearance upon the table unless *illy prepared*. In nine cases out of ten they are either tough and leathery, or so rich that it is beyond the capacity of a stomach of good powers to digest. The top crust (usually) is hastily baked, scorched and blistered; the bottom crust not baked *at all*, or *insufficiently*, and thoroughly saturated with rich gravy. These are the *extremes*; but how few avoid them! Where the meat is cooked in the pastry, I think they cannot, under any kind of management, be healthful, particularly for children and dyspeptics; but with care and judgment they may be made savoury and relishing.

A less objectionable way of preparing them is to bake them in a mould; stew the flesh or fowl, add the seasoning, and pour it into the pastry after it is done. . . .

An Oyster Pie

Make a light puff paste dough; cover it, and set it in a cold place an hour; line a drum-shaped mould with the paste; brush the edge next to the bottom, on the inside, with the white of an egg; lay upon the bottom a piece of the dough rolled around to fit, and let it turn up half an inch upon the inside; press it against the sides upon which the white of the egg is, so as to cement them together. Lay across the top of the mould, crossed in different directions, large broom straws, washed clean. This will support the lid, and prevent its falling in. While the pastry is baking get the oysters ready; put enough to fill the mould in a stew-pan; they must be well covered with their own liquor. Grate in the yolks of two hard boiled eggs; rub into a large tablespoonful of fresh butter a dessert-spoonful of flour; put this to the oysters. Stew five or six minutes, or until the oysters begin to shrink; add a wine-glass or rich, sweet cream. As soon as the mould is ready, take off the top crust; remove the pastry from the mould, and put it in a handsome circular, deep dish. Pour in the oysters; replace the top crust, and serve hot. If left standing too long, the bottom crust will imbibe so much of the gravy as to make it heavy and sodden. Some persons like this pie seasoned with mace—use it if relished. Instead of the straws to support the lid of the mould, slices of light bread are sometimes used to fill it. When the crust is done, remove the bread and pound it fine for soups, puddings, etc., etc. Send part of the gravy to table in a gravy-boat, using only enough in the pie to moisten the meat well.

Pease Pudding

Soak nice white peas (of the kind called Cornfield) several hours in plenty of water; tie them in a cloth, allowing room to swell; boil; when tender, turn them out; mash them; season with pepper and salt; tie in a scalded cloth; boil half an hour. From time immemorial this has been considered a proper accompaniment to boiled pork.

Virginia Chicken Pudding

Stew two young chickens cut up as for frying; season well with butter, pepper, salt, parsley, and onion shred fine. Make a batter of a quart of milk, six eggs beaten well; stir to the eggs smoothly nine tablespoonfuls of flour; thin with the milk. Take the chicken from the stew-pan when tender, leaving out the necks; place the pieces in an earthen dish; pour over the batter, and bake until the pudding is firm. It should not be suffered to stand long before being eaten, or it will be tough. A tureen of rich sauce should accompany it, using as much of the broth in which the chicken was stewed as is needed for the foundation of the gravy; add catsup of any kind. Instead of chicken, or combined with chicken, oysters, beef steak, veal, or any kind of game, may be used.

Confederate Candles

To two pounds of tallow add a teacup of strong lye (from hickory or ash ashes); simmer over a slow fire, when a greasy scum will float on top; skim this off as long as it rises; this grease will make soap. Mould your candles as usual.

Sauces, Stuffings, and Gravies

"The most homely fare may be made relishing, and the most excellent and independent improved by a well-made sauce."

Celery Sauce

Boil the white parts of six stalks of celery (first cutting them in small pieces) in two tumblerfuls of the broth the meat was boiled in, or any pale broth (veal is best), or boiling water alone will answer. Add salt to taste; cover the stewpan and let it simmer gently until tender. Rub a heaped teaspoonful of flour into a piece of butter the size of a hen's egg; strain the water from the celery upon this.[14] Remove the celery from the stew-pan, wipe it out, return the broth, add a tumbler of sweet cream or rich fresh milk; let this simmer gently five minutes, and serve. When fresh celery cannot be obtained, use the extract or the seeds bruised; tie them in a thin muslin cloth that they may be easily removed.

Oyster Sauce

A tumblerful of oysters; strain the liquor, pick out all the shells. Put the liquor in a stew-pan with one or two blades of mace; salt to taste. To a piece of butter as large as a hen's egg, rub a teaspoonful of flour; add this to the liquor with a tumblerful of sweet cream or milk. When this is just ready to boil, put in the oysters, first mincing them. Simmer gently until the oysters are well scalded, and pour into a gravy tureen. When made of canned oysters, stew entirely in milk or a pale broth.

Caper Sauce

Melt a quarter of a pound of butter, into which two teaspoonfuls of flour has been rubbed; add two tumblers of sweet milk, or half water (all milk is best). Add six or eight tablespoonfuls of capers.

Mock caper sauce is made by adding pickles cut up; radish pods or nasturtions are good as substitutes for capers.

Sauce for Boiled Fowls

Beat the yolk of an egg; add to it a tumbler of melted butter, one wineglass of sweet cream; stew five minutes. Season any way liked. This makes a nice sauce for pork chops, if seasoned with sage.

Mint Sauce

Three tablespoonfuls of fresh mint chopped fine, five tablespoonfuls of vinegar, two teaspoonfuls of sugar dissolved in the vinegar. Serve with roast lamb or chops.

Mustard Sauce

Stir to a teacup of vinegar a teaspoonful of mustard, one of salt, two of loaf sugar pulverized, one tablespoonful of butter; put all into a stew-pan, and let it simmer until boiling hot. Beat in a bowl the yolks of two eggs; stir the vinegar to them, stirring slowly and constantly. Return the mixture to the fire, and when boiling hot, pour into a tureen and serve. This is a good sauce for broiled meats, hashes, ragouts, or game. If fresh olive oil is used instead of butter, this makes an excellent sauce for salad or cold slaw.

Pickle Sauce

Into a tumblerful of melted butter stir a large table-spoonful of chopped mustard pickle, with a tablespoon-ful of the vinegar; stir three minutes, or until thoroughly hot.

Curry Sauce

Add to a pint of broth or melted butter an even table-spoonful of curry powder; wet into a paste with cold water; or boil in the broth an apple or an onion cut up; when soft enough to mash fine, strain; wipe out the stew-pan; return to the stew-pan, and add the curry powder; simmer two minutes. Parboil the onion before adding it to the broth; this is more delicate than to add it raw.

Sauce for Barbecues

Melt half a pound of butter; stir into it a large table-spoonful of mustard, half a teaspoonful of red pepper, one of black salt to taste; add vinegar until the sauce has a strong acid taste. The quantity of vinegar will depend upon the strength of it. As soon as the meat becomes hot, begin to baste, and continue basting frequently until it is done; pour over the meat any sauce that remains.

Stuffing for Pig

Use equal quantities of cold hominy (or rice) and flour; mince a few eschalots or an onion, a few sprigs of parsley, a little sage, salt and pepper; make this into a dough; bake it a light brown; while hot, mash it with sufficient butter to make it rich enough; stuff while hot; or use for the dough half flour and half corn meal.

Potato Stuffing

Bake or boil dry Irish potatoes; mash and strain them through a colander; mix with them an equal quantity of bread crumbs; grate, and add three hard-boiled eggs; mix with a large tablespoonful of butter. If not suffi-ciently moist add a little cream; season to taste—a deli-cate and delicious stuffing. When batter-bread muffins, etc. are used, save some for stuffing; corn meal batter-bread makes a fine pig stuffing. Meats are sometimes added to stuffing. Sausage-meat is considered good to add to stuffing for baked turkey, also grated ham, or tongue. All stuffings made of cold breads, and moist-ened with milk or water, are richer for being fried a few minutes after they are mixed and seasoned, stirring con-stantly. Stuffing should not, as a general thing, be bound together with raw egg; it is lighter without.

Stuffing for Fish

Butter slices of stale bread upon both sides; saturate them with wine, catsup, or cream, as preferred. Cut again in smaller slices, and lay inside the fish; this also makes a good stuffing for game.

Vegetables

Succotash

Boil butter-beans shelled (dried or green) half an hour; salt the water; then add half as much green corn cut from the cobs. Boil the cobs a few minutes when the beans are first put to boil. Take out the cobs; add the corn; to half a gallon of the succotash add a paste made of two tablespoonfuls of flour, and water sufficient to form the paste; season with salt and butter enough to make it as rich as may be liked. This is also very good boiled in the broth in which poultry has been boiled, or cooked with a small piece of pork. Succotash may be made of dried beans, and corn dried for winter use; soak them an hour before using. Dried beans are excellent baked with pickled pork.

Brocoli

Gather hard heads; peel the stalks; boil in salted water briskly, leaving the vessel open twenty minutes, or until tender; take them up and pour over melted butter. Serve hot.

Hot Slaw

Cut the cabbage in four quarters; after washing it carefully, parboil ten minutes. Take it out of the water; cut in thin slices; put it in a stew-pan; season with salt; add a wineglass of hot water, an even tablespoonful of butter; cover the stew-pan, and let the cabbage stew until tender; stir it frequently from the bottom. When tender, which will probably require an hour's steady stewing, add as much vinegar as will give the mass a pleasant acid taste.

Cauliflower

Remove all green leaves. To look well this vegetable should be very white. Boil it in water salted, or half sweet milk; when tender, put over it, while hot, slices of butter, putting some on the inside. This vegetable is fine in soups, to season meat sauces, for salads and pickle.

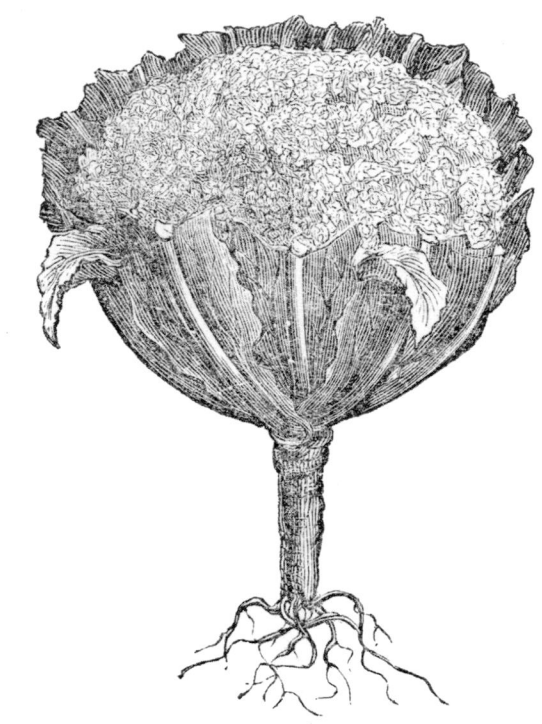

Annabella Hill instructed cooks that cauliflower should "be very white" in order to be part of an elegant presentation on the table. Image of cauliflower from Henderson, *Gardening for Profit*, 136.

Carrots

Carrots require longer cooking than any other vegetable. When young, they only require to be washed before being cooked. Old carrots should be cut into slices, and stewed until tender; season with salt and butter. Carrots are good in soup, and are better grated; they give a rich color to soups.

Cucumbers

Gather them early in the morning; put them in water. An hour before they are to be served, peel and cut them in thin, round slices; cover with cold water until a few minutes before sending to the table. Pour off this water; add a third as much white onion, cut in thin slices, as cucumber. The onion should be skinned and kept in cold water until used; season with salt, pepper and vinegar. Cucumbers may also be stewed as squashes, and seasoned with butter, or sliced length-wise, rolled in corn meal, salted and fried.

Samp

Take the corn when the grains are full, but milky; with a sharp knife shave off the corn to the cob; be careful not to cut the cob (that would injure the taste of the corn); scrape out the milk. Put it all in a stew-pan; pour over four times its bulk of boiling water; add salt to taste. Let the mass boil four hours, covered; boil slowly. Eat with butter; or pour into pans; cut in slices, when cold, and fry. Stir frequently when the corn is nearly done.

Green Corn Fritters

Six ears of boiled corn grated, three eggs; beat the yolks; mix with the corn; season with pepper and salt; add two even tablespoonfuls of sifted flour; beat the whites to a stiff froth, and add last. Fry as fritters, in hot lard. Serve upon a napkin laid upon a flat dish.

Green Corn Pudding

Two well beaten eggs, two tumblers of grated corn, half a tumbler of milk, tablespoon a little heaped of butter, pepper and salt to taste.

Egg-Plant

The purple is best. Peel and parboil them; mash fine; season with salt, pepper, and a little onion, if the flavor is not disliked; add butter to make it moderately rich. Put this mixture in a deep earthen dish; grate over it bread crumbs, and bake a light brown color.

To Fry Plain [Eggplant]

Peel the egg-plant; cut it in thin slices; strew salt between the slices; let them remain an hour; parboil them five minutes; roll each slice in flour or corn meal; fry a golden color in boiling lard; turn the pieces once; serve upon a napkin.

Greens

Kale, or cole, mustard, cabbage sprouts, turnip tops, to any of which may be added a few beet tops, the young shoots of the poke plant, all make good spring greens. Pick and wash them; let them lie in cold water at least an hour before they are used. Put them on in plenty of boiling water, salted; boil briskly twenty minutes; they will sink to the bottom when done. Take them up in a colander; press the water from them; put upon a hot dish; cut across the leaves in several places with a sharp knife; pour over melted butter; dress with poached eggs, either placed upon the dish of greens or served in a separate dish. They are not good unless served hot. Some persons prefer greens boiled with pieces of bacon or hock bone of ham. No matter in what way they are cooked, poached eggs should accompany them.

To Bake Mushrooms

Rub off the skins of the large flaps with salt and a piece of coarse clean cloth; trim the fringe from the small ones; cut off the stalks; lay them upon their back in an earthen dish. For a pint, use a large tablespoonful of fresh butter, with an even tablespoonful of brown flour stirred to it; put some of this upon each mushroom; bake until tender, which will require from twenty to thirty minutes. Serve upon toast, first dip the toast in boiling water.

Ochra

Gather only the young pods. They should be very little washed, and not suffered to remain a minute in water, and never trim them until after they are washed, as they lose much of the fine mucilage that makes the vegetable so valuable. It may be used in soup, or to make gumbo (which is a thick soup), and stewed, fried, etc., and may be dried and preserved as a winter vegetable. Receipts for soup and gumbo have already been given.

To Stew Ochra

Cut it in round slices; put it in a stew-pan; for a quart, add a wineglass of hot water, a tablespoonful of butter, into which has been rubbed an even teaspoonful of flour; salt and pepper to taste. Cover the stew-pan, shake it occasionally, and stew until tender; serve in a hot covered dish. A few tomatoes and a little onion stewed with the ochra is an improvement. This is excellent used as a sauce for plain boiled rice.

To Fry Ochra

Boil a quart; strain it well from the water; mash it smooth; season with salt and pepper. Beat in one or two eggs, and add flour (about half a tumbler or sifted flour) to make the batter stiff enough to fry as fritters. Serve on a flat dish upon a napkin. They should not be piled; send in as fast as fried.

Ochra and Tomatoes

Use half of each; season with salt and pepper; skin the tomatoes; slice the ochra; add a little onion; add a little sugar to the tomatoes. Stew without water, three quarters of an hour; add a piece of butter the size of a walnut to each quart of the mixture, when first put in the stew-pan.

To Scollop Potatoes

Boil, and mash them with the end of a rolling-pin until perfectly smooth; season highly with salt, pepper, butter, and two or three hard-boiled eggs chopped fine (three eggs for a quart of mashed potatoes); fill an earthen dish with it. Bake long enough to form a slight crust, and just before being sent to table.

To Fry Sweet Potatoes

Take large potatoes, peel and slice them; fry them in hot lard, turn often, salt each piece slightly; serve on a napkin. A good breakfast dish.

Hopping John

Pick out all defective ones from a quart of dried peas; soak them several hours in tepid water; boil them with a chicken or piece of pickled pork until the peas are thoroughly done. In a separate stew-pan boil half as much rice dry; take the peas from the meat, mix them with the rice, fry a few minutes until dry. Season with pepper and salt. This may be made of green English peas.

Pumpkin

Cut the pumpkin open; take out the seed, but do not scrape the inside; peel the rind off; cut in small pieces. Put them to stew in a covered vessel, with very little water[;] stir often from the bottom, to prevent its scorching. When done it may be kept several days in a cool place; use an earthen vessel. Dress with butter and a little sugar and ginger, as a stew, or fry with a little sweet lard, or use for making puddings and custards.

Parsnip Fritters

Boil enough parsnips to make two tumblerfuls, when mashed and rubbed through the colander; season with salt and pepper; add one well-beaten egg, and flour enough to hold it together (half a teacup full will be sufficient); fry in thick cakes. Serve as fast as they are fried. The sugar parsnip is best.

Radishes

Are served in a raw state. Gather them early in the morning; break off part of the long tap-root, and cut off all the top except an inch or two; wash them well, and keep in ice-cold water until it is time to serve them. Put them upon a salad bowl, with lettuce, cresses, etc., or in glass stands. The crimson ones are highly ornamental. Radishes are more digestible if grated and seasoned with salt and pepper; used as a salad.

To Bake Tomatoes

Peel and mince enough to fill a quart dish; season them with sugar, mace, pepper, salt, and a little minced onion. Put a layer of bread crumbs upon the bottom of the dish; then a layer of tomatoes, a little butter, another of bread crumbs, until the dish is full; bread crumbs must be strewn thickly over the top; lay over bits of butter. Bake in a moderate oven, two hours.

Tomato Leather

Mash fine; strain through a sieve; add a little sugar; grease panes of glass; spread over the mixture, and dry. This can be used in soup or stews.

Mrs. A.'s Receipt for Green Tomato Sauce

Slice thin a peck of green tomatoes. Make the winter's supply just before the frost falls upon them. Put the tomatoes in layers, with salt, twenty-four hours; drain through a sieve. Boil in a gallon of good apple vinegar an ounce each of mace, allspice, black pepper, half an ounce of cloves, a tablespoonful of celery seed, two of mustard seed, half a dozen pods of green pepper, and a pound of brown sugar. After the spices are well scalded in vinegar, strain it on the tomatoes; return all to the stew-pan; scald them well, but no more. When cold, mix in a small box or mustard bottle, and cork well.

Chetney Sauce (imitation)[16]

Eight ounces of tart apples, the same of salt; a quarter of a pound each of tomatoes, raisins, and brown sugar; a tablespoonful of Cayenne pepper; garlic and onion, tablespoonful each. Bruise these, and cover with three quarts of good apple vinegar. Grate the rind of four lemons; add the juice, removing the seed. Put in a jug, set near the stove, and shake well twice a day for a month. Strain the juice through a flannel bag without squeezing. This makes an excellent fish sauce, using a teaspoonful to a tumbler of broth or melted butter. Bottle and cork well. What remains in the bag answers well for "devils," grills, barbecues, etc.[17]

Pepper Catsup

Take any quantity of red or green pepper pods; slit the pods; boil in sufficient water to cover them. Stir and mash them while boiling; strain through a colander, then through a sieve. To two quarts of this pulp, add one quart of vinegar, two or three garlic buttons minced fine, a small onion cut up, one tablespoonful of salt, one of cloves, the same of allspice. Boil one hour; if too thick, add more vinegar. The red pods make a beautiful red catsup.

Cucumber Catsup

Grate two dozen grown cucumbers and six silver-skinned onions; sprinkle half a tumbler of salt upon them. Prepare them in the evening, and early in the morning lay them on a sieve and let them drain. Soak a teacup of white mustard seed; drain them from the water, and add to the cucumbers a wineglass of whole pepper-corns. Put them in a jar; cover with vinegar. Keep in a wide-mouthed jar in a cool, dry place; cork well.

Lemon Catsup

Roll well half a dozen lemons to increase their juice; grate off the peel; squeeze out the juice; remove the seed; add a tablespoonful of grated horseradish, the same of ground ginger, half as much mace and cinnamon, one grated nutmeg. Pour over a pint of vinegar; scald five minutes. When cold, strain and bottle. Use to flavor piquant sauces.

Pudding Catsup

Mix together half a pint of noyau [recipe below], a pint of Sherry or other white wine, the yellow peel of four lemons pared thin, and half an ounce of mace. Put the whole in a large bottle, and let it stand for two or three weeks; then strain it, and add half a pint of capillaire [recipe below], or strong sugar syrup of curacoa. Bottle it, and it will keep three or four years. It may be used for several dishes, but chiefly for pudding sauce, mixed with melted butter.

Noyau

Blanch and beat a pound of bitter almonds or peach kernels; mix with the grated rinds of three lemons three pounds of loaf sugar, one tumblerful of honey, one gallon of brandy, one quart of rose-water; put in a jug, and cork tight. Shake it well every day for a month. Then strain it; add another quart of rose-water; mix well; bottle and cork, and cement the stopper. Keep in a dry, cool place.

Capillaire

Eight pounds of loaf sugar pulverized; wet with three pints of water, and three eggs well beaten. Let it boil up twice; skim and strain it; flavor with two wineglasses of orange-flower water. Bottle, and use it as a summer drink with a little lemon juice and ice water. Sweeten pudding catsup with it.

Soy

One pound of salt, two pounds of sugar; fry this a quarter of an hour over a slow fire, stirring constantly; one tumbler of essence of anchovies, a dozen cloves, one tablespoonful each of thyme, sweet basil, and marjoram. Pour over all three pints of boiling water. Boil until the salt is dissolved. When cold, strain and bottle; cork tight. Use to flavor gravies and sauces.

Pepper Vinegar

Put into a quart bottle thirty small pods of green or red pepper (make of both kinds separately). Set the bottles in an oven in water; make the water boil. When the peppers are thoroughly hot, pour in good vinegar to fill the bottle; cork tight. In the centre of the cork insert a goose quill or reed three inches long, open at both ends; through this the vinegar may be poured when using it. Stop with a good cork when not in use.

Bread[18]

French Rolls

One quart of flour, one or two eggs beaten with an even tablespoonful of sugar; dissolve a yeast cake, or, if the leaven is pulverized, two tablespoonfuls in a tumbler of tepid water; stir this well, and pour it to the eggs. Sift the flour into the tray; reserve a third of it to work into the dough after the flour is wet up. Into the remainder of the flour sprinkle a teaspoonful of salt, and rub in well a heaping tablespoonful of butter or lard; pour the yeast in, and stir the flour in gradually. When the dough can be rubbed from the hands, flour the board or bottom of the tray, and begin to work the dough upon it; sprinkle down more flour; pull the dough to pieces; repeat this until all the reserved flour is in; continue to work the dough until it feels light and spongy to the touch. The dough for light rolls should be softer than for loaf bread. Grease the pan in which bread will be put to rise; lay the dough in; press it down with the hand until it covers the bottom; lightly touch it over with lard, to prevent a crust from forming. Throw a clean towel over. Set it to rise where it will be kept moderately warm. When it has risen, immediately take it from the pan, and roll it in a round strip; pull it into pieces of uniform size (and never very large); mould them into long or round shapes; grease the pan slightly in which they are to be baked; lay the rolls in, touching. Let them rise again, which should be in half an hour; bake in a quick oven, not hot enough, however, to blister or burn.

Secession Biscuit

These are made precisely the same as light rolls, only moulded differently. After the second rising, grease the bottom of the oven or pan in which they are to be baked; work each piece of dough separately, and make them as common soda biscuit are shaped; lay them in the oven or pan; they should not touch. Let them rise fifteen or twenty minutes; bake in a quick oven. They are not so good when permitted to stand any length of time.

Light Bread

To three pints of sifted flour, pour one pint of tepid milk or water and a tumbler of good yeast. Beat well and set it to rise in a moderately warm place; make this at night. In the morning, stir to the sponge a pint of warm water and two teaspoonfuls of salt; work in as much flour as will make a rather stiff dough. Work it well; mould it into loaves; let it rise; bake in a moderately quick oven. Use, when cold, for dinner-bread. It makes good toast when stale.

Rice Waffles

Put a pint of sweet milk in the stew-pan; a teacup of boiled rice; add to it a tablespoonful of butter; as soon as the butter melts, take the pan from the fire; beat four eggs well, and stir to them alternately—making a smooth batter—the milk and one quart of sifted flour; salt to taste. Bake and serve hot.

Sweet Potato Waffles

Two tablespoonfuls of mashed, baked sweet potato, one of butter, stirred to the potato while hot, one of sugar, one egg, one pint of sweet milk, six tablespoonfuls of sifted flour; mix well, and bake. These may be made without the egg, using four tablespoonfuls of flour.

Mush or Hominy Waffles

One pint of hominy or a teacup of mush, half a pint of flour, two eggs beaten separately, an even tablespoonful of lard stirred to the hominy; add sweet milk to make a thin batter; salt to taste.

Corn Meal Muffins

One pint of sifted corn meal, a teaspoonful of soda, two tablespoonfuls of lard after being melted, two eggs well beaten, as much sour milk as will make a batter the consistency of pound-cake batter. Bake with a moderately hot oven in muffin-rings.

Hard Biscuit

Measure a quart of flour, and one tumblerful over; reserve this. In the quart of flour rub a large tablespoonful of butter (or rather less of lard), and a teaspoonful of salt; wet to a soft dough with warm sweet milk; knead it well, working in slowly the reserved flour; sprinkle the biscuit-board with flour; beat the dough, turning it, pulling it to pieces (sprinkling on flour as may be needed), until the dough is well blistered. Roll it out; cut with a knife or biscuit-cutter, and bake in a moderately warm oven.

Crackers

Rub six ounces of butter into two pounds of sifted flour; dissolve a teaspoonful (level full) of soda in a wineglass of buttermilk; strain this through a fine sieve to the flour; add a teaspoonful of salt; beat well; roll thin; bake. If not crisp when first baked, put them again into a slack oven, and merely heat over.

Clabber Bread (excellent)

Beat four eggs separately, two teacups of clabber, one tablespoonful of butter (very slightly heaped, and placed in a pan upon the stove long enough to soften), a teaspoonful of soda, the same of salt; mix with flour to a stiff batter; grease the pan in which the bread is to be baked; pour in the batter; let it stand an hour, and bake.

Cheese Biscuit

One pound of flour, half a pound of butter, half a pound of grated cheese; make up quick, and with very little handling, as puff paste. Roll thin; cut and bake in a quick oven. Salt to taste.

Johnny Cake

One pint of boiled rice or hominy, one egg, one tablespoonful of butter, salt to taste, flour enough to make a soft dough; roll half an inch thick; bake quick, without blistering; serve hot. Tear the cakes open, and butter. Cut the cakes four inches long and three wide.

Milk Toast

Cut four slices from a stale loaf; place them in a toaster, or prop them before the fire, turning each piece until a light brown color. Have a pan ready with a tumblerful of hot sweet milk. Dip each slice in quickly; lay one upon the bottom of a hot dish; lay over thin slices of fresh butter, then another piece of toast, until all are arranged in this way. Send, under a cover, to table. Toast should be eaten when fresh made.

To Boil Grits

Wash them in several waters, rubbing between the hands well until all the bran is separated from the white of the grain. When perfectly white and clean, pour over boiling water; let it set a few moments. Put the grits to boil in a well-covered stew-pan (lined with tin or porcelain is best); cover with plenty of water. Salt the water to taste; boil until the grain is soft, keeping the cover on. Should there be too much water when the grits are nearly done, take off the cover until the water is sufficiently reduced; if there is a deficiency, supply it by adding hot water. Grits should be boiled slowly, to give them time to swell, and plenty of water used. The hominy when done should be moist, neither very dry nor wet.

Pies

Cranberry Pie

Pick the unsound fruit out carefully; wash and stew until soft; sweeten to taste; line pie-plates with a good puff paste; fill three-fourths full with the fruit, always heaping it a little in the middle. Put in not quite a tumblerful of the juice; put over an upper crust, pinching the edges well together, and cutting a slit in the middle to allow the stem to escape. When done, sprinkle thickly with pulverized loaf sugar, and serve with cream sauce, flavored with nutmeg.

Blackberry Pie

Gather the berries carefully, without bruising, as they are better without being washed. Line a pie-plate with good crust. Put in a layer of the berries, then one of sugar, and dust over with a little flour. (Five tablespoonfuls of good brown sugar and an even tablespoonful of flour will be sufficient for a large pie.) In this way fill the plate nearly full, heaping the fruit a little in the middle; add half a tumbler of water, and put on the upper crust, pinching the edges together, and cutting a slit in the centre; serve with cream sauce. This sauce is a good accompaniment to all fruit pies.

Apple Pie

Line a deep plate with good crust, first greasing the plate slightly. Cut in thin slices ripe, juicy apples; fill the plate, putting in alternately apples, sugar, and spice (a tumbler of brown sugar will season a quart of apples of pleasant taste); grate over half a nutmeg; the same of cinnamon, the same of coriander seed (if they are liked), half a tumbler of water; put over the upper crust. Bake three-quarters of an hour.

Sliced Potato Pie

For baking this, a plate deeper than the common pie-plate is necessary. Bake medium sized sweet potatoes not quite done; yams are best. Line the plate with good paste; slice the potatoes; place a layer upon the bottom of the plate; over this sprinkle thickly a layer of good brown sugar; over this place thin slices of butter, and sprinkle with flour, seasoning with spices to the taste. A heaped tablespoonful of butter and a heaped teaspoonful of flour will be sufficient for one pie. Put on another of potatoes, piled a little in the middle. Mix together equal quantities of wine and water, lemon juice and water, or vinegar and water, and pour in enough to half fill the pie; sprinkle over the potato a little flour, and place on the upper crust, pinching the edges carefully together. Cut a slit in the centre, and bake slowly for one hour.

Puddings

Molasses Pudding

One pint of good syrup, a common-sized teacup not quite full of melted butter, two well-beaten eggs, a tablespoonful of ginger, one tumblerful of sour milk, and a teaspoonful of soda; mix all together, with flour enough to make a batter the consistence of pound-cake batter. Bake for an hour in a deep, buttered pan. Turn it out; grate sugar over it, and eat with a rich sauce.

Taylor Pudding

One cup of butter, creamed; two cups of sugar, beaten with the yolks of four eggs. Add this to the butter; stir all well together; add alternately the whites, beaten to a stiff froth, and six even teacupfuls of sifted flour; thin with two cups of buttermilk. Dissolve a large teaspoonful (not heaped) of soda in a wineglass of warm water, and add last. Bake in a quick open, not hot enough to scorch. Eat with liquid sauce.

Grated Potato Pudding

One pint of sugar, half a pint of molasses, one large spoonful of butter, and a pint of sweet potatoes, grated. Mix well, and add sweet milk enough to make quite thin; season with orange peel, beaten fine, and ginger. After it is mixed, add to it three well-beaten eggs. Bake in a very slow oven to allow it to candy over the top.

Secession Pudding (excellent)

Four teacups of sifted flour, three of dry crushed sugar, one of sweet milk, one teaspoonful of soda, two of cream of tartar. Stir the soda in the flour; dissolve the cream of tartar in a little cold water; six eggs beaten separately. When the buttermilk or clabber is used, omit sweet milk and cream of tartar. Buttermilk may be used instead of cream of tartar. Eat with a rich sauce.

Custards

Cocoanut Custard

The whites of eight eggs beaten to a froth, eight table-spoonfuls of powdered loaf sugar, four tablespoonfuls of melted butter, the white part of a large cocoanut grated, a wineglass of wine. Bake in puff paste.

Transparent Custard

Beat well with half a pound of crushed sugar the yolks of eight eggs; set upon the fire the pan containing them, and add, in small pieces, half a pound of butter; stir constantly until the butter melts; remove it from the fire and stir in a wineglass of thick cream. Flavor to taste, and bake in puff paste. Citron or other sweetmeats placed at the bottom, may be used with this batter.

Pumpkin Custard

Pass a pint of boiled pumpkin through a colander, and add to it a pint of cream. Beat eight eggs, and add them gradually to the other ingredients, stirring constantly. Then stir in a wineglass of rose-water, a teaspoonful of powdered cinnamon, and a grated nutmeg. Lay a paste in a buttered dish, and bake three-quarters of an hour.

Jelly Custard

One cup of fruit jelly; one cup nearly full of crushed sugar; one tablespoonful of butter; three eggs, beaten separately. Flavor with lemon, and bake in puff paste.

Sauces

Wine Sauce for Puddings

Stir together one teacup of butter, two of good sugar (loaf is best), and an even tablespoonful of flour. Put these into a stew-pan, and stir to it half a tumbler of boiling water. Let it simmer a minute or two; pour in half a tumbler of wine. Serve in a sauce tureen; grate nutmeg over. If preferred, use less water and more wine.

Butter Sauce

Half a tumbler of butter, a tumbler of sugar; mix well, and stir to the yolks of two eggs; pour over a tumbler of boiling wine; boil one minute, stirring well. Serve with plain boiled pudding.

Hard Sauce

Cream, until white and spongy, one teacup of butter, two of loaf sugar, pulverized. This sauce requires *to be creamed well*. Stir in as much wine as it will take, or season with any of the extracts. Place it, lightly heaped, on a glass or silver plate. It makes an elegant sauce for bread puddings, or for any kind of boiled pudding. This sauce may be varied by stirring to it a large tablespoonful of very stiff apple or quince jelly, or the grated rind and juice of an orange or lemon.

Cakes

Confederate Fruit Cake

The weight of twelve eggs in butter, flour, and sugar; one tablespoonful of spice, half a tablespoonful of cinnamon, the same of mace, the same of cloves, one nutmeg, a wineglass of brandy and two pounds of currants, or of dry peach chips cut very fine.

Plain Pound Cake

Three-quarters of a pound of butter; one pound of sifted flour; one pound of sugar (pulverized, loaf, or crushed); ten eggs. Beat the sugar with the yolks until very white; cream the butter; add to it the flour alternately with the egg and sugar. Add the whites lastly, and do not eat the batter after they are mixed with it; squeeze in the juice of one lemon and a wineglass of good brandy.

General Gordon Cake

Three-quarters of a pound of butter, one pound of sugar; cream them well together; break in one egg at a time until you have used ten; beat well, and add a paper of corn starch; add a teaspoonful of yeast powder. Flavor with vanilla. Bake quickly.

Spice Cake

Three cups of butter, six cups of sugar, three cups sour milk, twelve (light) of flour, twelve eggs, three small teaspoonfuls of soda, sifted in the flour; one small teaspoonful of cloves, three of cinnamon, five of ground orange peel, three of nutmeg, one of allspice.

Southern Rights Cake

Four tea cups of sifted flour, five eggs, two teacupfuls of sugar, two teacupfuls of butter, one tablespoonful of sifted ginger, one teaspoonful of allspice, and one of cinnamon, a wineglassful of brandy, one teaspoonful of soda, one teacup, not quite full, of molasses (syrup will not answer); cream the flour and butter; beat the sugar to the yolks of the eggs; dissolve the soda in the molasses; whip the whites to a froth; and add last. Best baked in small pans.

Railroad Cake

One large teacupful of sugar, a tablespoonful of butter somewhat heaped, two eggs, one pint of sifted flour, one teacup of sweet milk, one teaspoonful of soda, and two of cream of tartar, or a dessert-spoonful of yeast powders. Dissolve the soda in the milk, and rub the cream of tartar in the flour. Flavor according to taste.

Soft Ginger Cake

Four eggs beaten separately, three tumblerfuls of flour, one of butter, one of sugar, one of molasses, a teaspoonful of soda stirred well into the molasses, or two teaspoonfuls of yeast powders sprinkled into the batter; ginger, to your taste.

Ginger Nuts

Three and a half pounds of flour, one pound of butter, half a pound of sugar, one quart of molasses, five even tablespoonfuls of ginger, three teaspoonfuls of allspice, one of cloves, and two teaspoonfuls of cinnamon. Make a smooth dough; roll out, and cut about the size of a cent piece; wash over with molasses and water, and bake in a moderate oven.

Fancy Dishes

Prune Meringues

Stew prunes enough to half fill a dish of suitable size; sweeten to taste; put them in the dish, and cover with a handsome meringue. This makes a very nice dessert.

Preserved cherries may be used in the same way.

Lemon Soufflé

The yolks of three eggs, three ounces of sugar, and the grated rind of half a lemon. Beat these together well; add to them the whites of the eggs, beaten to a solid front, and the juice of half a lemon. Put all immediately into a deep pudding-dish, and bake for ten or fifteen minutes. Serve with a sauce made of two well-beaten eggs, the juice and grated peel of half a lemon. Stir it over the fire till it begins to rise. Care must be taken not to let the souffle get too brown. The safest way to cook souffles is to set the dish over boiling water, and hold over a red hot salamander or large shovel until the egg is of a golden color.

Syllabub

One pint of thick cream (if it should be a little acid, stir in enough soda to sweeten it). Mix with the cream one quarter of a pound of white sifted sugar; let it stand half an hour; then add three wineglasses of Sherry or Madeira wine. Whip to a stiff froth, and fill the glasses. Either churn the cream, using a small tin syllabub churn (which can be procured at any tin-shop), or pour the cream upon a flat dish and whip with a sliver fork or egg-beater. The latter is more tedious, but the syllabub is more solid.

Apple Float

One pint of dried apples, stewed, mashed, and strained; sweeten and flavor with nutmeg to taste. Beat to a stiff froth the whites of six eggs; add lightly to the fruit. Eat in saucers or strawberry plates, with rich cream sauce.

Curds and Cream

Drip the whey from clabber through a perforated tin shape—a large heart shape is very pretty. Serve (when dry enough to turn out) with rich cream sauce, flavored with nutmeg. Sweet milk may be turned with rennet, using a piece two inches square to a quart of milk.

Fruits, Etc.

Ambrosia

Is made by placing upon a glass stand, or other deep vessel, alternate layers of grated cocoanut, oranges peeled and sliced round, and a pineapple sliced thin. Begin with the oranges, and use cocoanut last, spreading between each layer sifted loaf sugar. Sweeten the cocoanut milk, and pour over.

Peaches and Cream

Peel soft juice peaches, quarter them, put a layer of peaches, one of sugar, sprinkling it on very thick until the desired quantity is prepared. Spread thickly over the last layer of peaches powdered loaf sugar. Set the dish upon ice or in a very cool place an hour before using; do not bruise them. Some persons like them best mashed fine, sweetened, and a little grated nutmeg added; in either way serve in small deep plates; eat with rich cream.

Watermelons

Make a delicious dessert. A bright red watermelon makes a very showy appearance if cut through the middle, crosswise, in points. Cut a piece off each end so as to give both halves a level base to stand upon.

Breakfast Fruits

Grapes, figs, and cantelopes are nice breakfast fruits, and may be served in this way: Remove the first course, and the white cloth; if the table is not a handsome one, it should be covered with a wine cloth, under the white tablecloth; always send colored doylies with fruit. Grapes may be tastily arranged with their leaves. Finger-bowls should be placed before each person, to be used after the fruit course is finished.

Wine Jelly

One ounce of Cox's Sparkling gelatine, one pound of loaf sugar. Dissolve the gelatine in a pint of boiling water; add the sugar and a quart of white wine. Stir the mixture very hard, and pour it into a mould. When it has congealed, wrap the mould in a cloth dipped in warm water; turn out the jelly, and eat with cream.

Preserves, Etc.

Pineapple Preserves

Wash the fruit and boil, without paring, until they are tender. Take them out, pare them, and slice lengthwise, so as to remove the hard centre. Make a syrup, using a pound of sugar to a pound of fruit; pour it, when boiling hot, over the fruit, and let it stand until the next morning. Then pour off the syrup from the fruit, and boil it until nearly thick enough, when the fruit must be put in and boiled in the syrup for fifteen or twenty minutes.

Crab Apple Preserve

Boil for a short time in clear water. Be careful not to boil too long, as the fruit mashes very easily. Just as soon as they are soft enough to admit of removing the cores with a goose-quill, push them out. Soak, for one night, in weak alum water; from this, soak in clear water for two hours. Make a syrup in the proportion of one and a half pound of sugar to one of fruit; put the fruit in, and let it boil until it looks clear. Take them out, and if the syrup is not thick enough, continue boiling until it is of proper consistency.

Corn-Starch Blanc Mange

Four or five tablespoonfuls of starch to one quart of milk; beat the starch thoroughly with two eggs, and add it to the milk, when near boiling, with a little salt; boil a few minutes, stirring it briskly. Flavor with rose, lemon, or vanilla, and cool in small cups or wineglasses. When cold and stiff, turn into a glass stand. Sweeten it while cooking, or use a sauce of sugar and cream.

Farina blanc-mange is made in the same way. Set on ice if convenient.

Marmalades, Jams, Etc.

Orange Marmalade

For this, use the pulp that has been removed previous to preserving the rinds; carefully pick out all the seeds. If the oranges are sweet, three quarters of a pound of sugar is sufficient to a pound of fruit—for the sour orange, equal proportions will be required. Mix the fruit and sugar well; add half a tumblerful of water to a pound of sugar, and boil for half an hour, stirring a great deal to prevent their burning. A little of the peel, boiled in clear water, and shredded very fine before adding to the mass, gives an improved flavor to this marmalade.

Apple Marmalade

Peel and slice the apples; weigh and put them into a kettle, and stew until tender. Mash them fine; add the sugar in the proportion of pound to pound. Let them cook slowly, stirring very frequently. By no means allow it to scorch, and when the mass has a jellied appearance, it is done. About half an hour will generally be found sufficient for making the marmalade, after adding the sugar.

Frosted Fruit

Select perfect fruit of any small variety, such as cherries, plums, grapes, or small pears, leaving the stems on. Dip them, one by one, in the beaten white of an egg, or in a solution of gum Arabic, and from that into a cup of very finely pulverized sugar. Cover the bottom of a pan with a sheet of fine white paper; place the fruit in it, and set in a stove or oven that is cooling. When the frosting on the fruit becomes firm, heap them on a dish, and set in a cool place.

Apple or Gooseberry Fool

Put the fruit in a stone jar, with a good quality of brown sugar in the proportion of half a pound to a pound of the fruit. Set the pan on the stove, or in an oven of hot water. Put a large spoonful of water in the bottom of the jar to prevent burning. When they are soft, pass them through a sieve. Have ready one teacup of new milk, the same of cream, boiled together, and left to cool. Sweeten the custard, and by degrees add the fruit. Nice dish for tea.

Peach Chips

Peel good peaches, not too ripe, as in that case the chips will be very dark when dried. Slice the peaches *very thin*; have ready prepared a syrup made in the proportion of half a pound of sugar to a pound of fruit, and water enough to melt the sugar; the syrup must be very thick. Put in the chips, and scald them well. Remove them with a perforated skimmer, and dry in the sun. After they are dry, pack closely in jar[s], sprinkling finely powdered sugar between the layers. This preparation well supplies the place of raisins in making fruit puddings, and plain family fruit cakes.

Tomato Figs

Use thoroughly ripe tomatoes; pour boiling water over them to remove the skin; weigh them; place them in a stone jar, with an equal quantity of good sugar. Let them stand two days; then pour off the syrup; boil and skim it until no scum rises. Pour it over the tomatoes; let it stand two days; boil, and skim again. After repeating this process for the third time, they are fit to dry, if the weather suits; if not, keep them in the syrup. They will dry in a week. Pack in boxes lined with white paper, putting powdered sugar between the layers of fruit. Should any syrup remain, it may be used for making common marmalade, or for sweetening pies.

To Dry Citron or Watermelon Rind

After preserving place in the sun, and dry. They answer well in puddings and cakes as a substitute for the imported citron.

For Making Candies

Sugar Candy

To three tumblers of good brown sugar, add one tumbler and a half of cold water, one tablespoonful of good vinegar, and a small teaspoonful of butter. Boil without stirring until it begins to rope. To pull it, begin as soon as it can be handled, and take hold of the mass only with the tips of the fingers; pull rapidly. Use no grease about the hands, or very little.

To Make Ground Pea Candy[19]

Parch, shell, and heat the peas. Take up the candy before it has boiled as much as in the first receipt [Sugar Candy], and use more butter; stir while boiling. When poured out, mix in the peas. Almonds and grated cocoanut may be used.

Molasses Candy

Half a gallon of West India molasses, one pound of sugar, a teaspoonful of essence of lemon, the juice of two large lemons (but this must not be added before the candy is nearly done); add the rind of one when the molasses is first put to boil; stir occasionally. Boil steadily three hours, or until upon cooling some on a plate it will be found stiff enough. Pour it off; pull as the sugar candy [recipe above]. Flavor with ginger, if it is preferred to lemon.

Toffie

One pound of loaf sugar, three ounces of butter, and the grated rind of one lemon. Boil a quarter of an hour; pour into the dishes slightly buttered. Cut in strips with a buttered knife, but do not attempt to raise them until cold.

Wine, Cordials, Etc.

Cider Wine

Fifteen gallons of cider, fresh from the press; to each gallon, add two pounds of good brown sugar. When the sugar has dissolved, strain the mixture into a clean cask. Let the cask want two gallons of being full; leave out the bung for forty-eight hours. Put in the bung, leaving a little vent until fermentation ceases; then bung up tightly. In a year it is fit for use. It needs no straining; the longer it stands upon the lees, the better.

Tomato Wine

Let the tomatoes be fully ripe. After mashing well, let them stand twenty-four hours. Then strain, and to every quart of the juice add one pound of good sugar. Let it ferment again, skimming frequently; when clear, bottle. To use them, sweeten a glass of water to the taste, and add the tomato wine until sufficiently acid.

Strawberry Cordial

To each quart of the juice allow a pint of white brandy, and half a pound of loaf sugar. Let it stand two weeks. Pin a piece of muslin in the bottom of a sieve; strain, and bottle.

Muscadine Cordial

Pulp the muscadines. A few of the hulls left will give the liquor a beautiful color. Let it stand twenty-four hours. Strain it, and to every three quarts add a quart of good brandy. Sweeten to taste with loaf sugar. Bottle, cork well, and keep in a cool place.

Cherry Bounce

Stone half the cherries; fill the vessel half full of the fruit, putting down a layer of fruit and a layer of good brown sugar in the proportion of a quarter of a pound of sugar to a quart of fruit. Fill the vessel with good *apple* or French brandy; tie it up securely. Let it remain until the cherries look a pale red; then strain, and bottle. Use it by adding water to taste, and more sugar if liked. This may be made in a jug; should be covered or stopped well, or the brandy will lose its strength.

Crab Apple Beer

Boil the fruit until the water is a pleasant acid; strain it. To a gallon, put a piece of yeast cake an inch square. Sweeten to taste. Use the second day.

Lemonade

Roll half a dozen large lemons well; cut them in thin slices (when the lemons are small, use eight); put a layer of sugar (use two tumblers of crushed sugar) and a layer of the sliced lemons; press the mass slightly; let them remain a quarter of an hour. Pour upon the lemons a gallon of cold water. Stir them from the bottom; add more sugar if not sweet enough. Put in the glasses (if convenient) small bits of ice, and pour in the lemonade, putting a slice of the lemon in each glass. Orangeade may be made in the same way of sour oranges, or if sweet, add two lemons to six oranges. Pomegranates also make a pleasant acid drink, prepared from the seed, sweetening to taste.

Lemonade au Lait

One tumbler of lemon juice, the same of sherry wine, three quarters of a pound of loaf sugar, a quart of boiling water; mix, and when cold, add two tumblers of boiling sweet milk. Strain after it has stood twelve hours. Seven lemons will make a tumbler of juice. Preserve the peel, and dry, or infuse them in strong fourth-proof brandy, and keep it for flavoring cakes, puddings, and sauces.

Imperial Pop

Three ounces of cream of tartar, an ounce of bruised ginger, a pound and a half of loaf sugar, half a tumbler of lemon juice, a gallon and a half of water, a wineglass of yeast. Shake well together, bottle, and cork well.

Spruce Beer

Three gallons of boiling water poured upon one quart of West India molasses; mix well. When tepid, add one ounce of essence of spruce, one of essence of winter green, and a pint of yeast. Let it stand twelve hours; bottle, and cork. In half a day it will be fit for use.

Corn Beer

Boil a quart of corn until the grains crack. Put the grains into a jug, and pour in two gallons of boiling water; do not use the water it was boiled in; add a quart of molasses, a handful of dried apples, and a large tablespoonful of ginger. It will be ready for use in two or three days. If the weather is cold, set it by the fire. It may be kept up several weeks with the same corn, sweetening the water before pouring in the jug.

Chocolate

Grate it fine. Allow two heaped tablespoonfuls to a pint of fluid; this should be half milk, half water, but not mixed. Wet the grated chocolate to a smooth paste; boil it five minutes in the water, then add the same quantity of sweet unskimmed milk; flavor with cinnamon or nutmeg. Serve very hot.

Pickles

Sweet Pickles

To three pounds of brown sugar put one gallon of vinegar; spice to your taste; boil all together a short time, and set off to cool. Fill a jar with the vegetables or fruits to be pickled; pour the vinegar over them when cool. If you discover a white scum on the surface, pour the vinegar from the pickle and boil again, adding a little more sugar. When cool, return to the jar. Peaches stuffed, after neatly removing the seed, are nice made in this way. Figs ripe, but not soft, are good; so are cherries.

Pickled Onions

Peel; boil in milk and water ten minutes; drain off the milk and water; pour over cold spiced vinegar.

Cabbage Pickle

Quarter the heads, and sprinkle pretty thickly with salt; let them remain about twelve hours. Take them from the salt; rinse in cold water, and wipe dry. If preferred, cut them fine. Put them in a jar, and pour over them cold spiced vinegar.

Chow

Horseradish grated fine, two cups; one teaspoonful of turmeric, two tablespoonfuls of celery seeds, four tablespoonfuls of sugar, and two tablespoonfuls of white mustard seed; vinegar to cover it. Some persons use the horseradish without the addition of anything except loaf sugar and vinegar enough to acidulate it pleasantly. Packed in very small, wide-mouthed bottles and well corked, it keeps well. November is the proper month to make it. Then new beds may be set from the small roots that will not answer for grating. The tops cut closely, leaving a few eyes, will also answer for planting.

Pickled Eggs

Have ready a quart of good apple vinegar, by scalding in it one dozen cloves, half a nutmeg, a dozen grains of allspice, half a teaspoonful of pepper, two teaspoonfuls of flour of mustard. Boil a dozen eggs hard; shell them, and lay in a glass jar; pour over the hot vinegar; turn them occasionally; keep the jar well covered. Serve with pressed or collared meat, head-cheese, Hunter's beef, etc.

Cooking for Invalids

Mulled Wine

Boil together one tumbler of water, half a nutmeg, a small stick of cinnamon, a dozen cloves slightly bruised, the same of allspice; reduce it by boiling half; strain the spiced water into a pint of good Sherry or Madeira wine. Set it on the fire, and when it begins to bubble, take it off the fire; sweeten with loaf sugar, and serve.

Wine Whey

One pint of boiling milk, a tumblerful of good Madeira wine; boil until the curds form. Pour off the whey into a pitcher; sweeten, and serve. Cider may be used instead of wine.

Tamarind Whey

Boil one ounce of tamarinds in a pint of sweet milk; strain, and sweeten to taste.

Flour Gruel

Put a pint of fresh sweet milk to boil; mix to a paste an even tablespoonful of wheat flour, corn starch, or potato starch. Just as the milk boils, stir in the paste smoothly. Let it boil until the gruel is sufficiently thick. Season with loaf sugar and nutmeg; wine may be used if liked.

Toast and Water

Slice stale light bread, or toast the outside crust of corn bread. Immerse it while hot in a tumbler or pitcher of cold water; cover it for half an hour before drinking. Make it fresh once a day. The vessel may be refilled as the water is used.

Drink for an Invalid

A new-laid egg, well-beaten, a cup of hot coffee, tea, or chocolate poured to it, stirring well, is a good drink for an invalid.

Tomato Toast

Stew to a paste, after skinning them. Season to taste, and spread upon slices of toasted bread.

Birds for Convalescents

Lay them upon the gridiron; broil until a light brown color; then put them in a stew-pan; pour over hot water enough to cover them. Let them stew until tender. Season with a little fresh butter, pepper, and salt. Chicken birds, and squirrels, stewed in a double kettle, are very delicate for invalids. If permitted, stuff the fowls and birds with minced oysters.

Mush

Wet up three tablespoonfuls of fine corn meal with cold water; stir it to three tumblerfuls of boiling water. Add salt to taste; stir frequently until the meal is thoroughly cooked, and the mush sufficiently thick. Eat cold or warm with sweet milk or syrup. Cut cold mush in slices, and fry.

Medical Receipts

Healing Salve

Mutton tallow, four pounds; beeswax, one pound; rosin, half a pound; turpentine, three ounces. Melt the three first over a slow fire; then add the turpentine when they are nearly cold.

Colic Mixture for Infants

Eighty drops of laudanum, fourteen of oil of anise, two tablespoonfuls of alcohol, and a piece asafoetida as large as a pea;[20] put these in an eight-ounce phial, and fill with warm water. Sweeten with loaf sugar. Dose from four to six drops to a child a few days old. Increase the dose as the child grows older.

To Relieve a Cold

At the very first symptoms, have the feet bathed upon going to bed, and take three grains of quinine (five grains is sometimes given), twenty drops of laudanum, in a tablespoonful of ginger tea or water. If not relieved by the first dose, repeat the next night. Two doses will generally relieve an obstinate cold.

Putrid Sore Throat

Mix one gill of strong apple vinegar, one tablespoonful of common salt, tablespoonful of strained honey, half a pod of red pepper; boil them together; strain into half a pint of strong sage tea. In severe cases give half a teaspoonful for an adult every hour; decrease the dose as the disease is relieved. Use some as a gargle.

Whooping Cough

Bruise a tumbler of flaxseed, three ounces of liquorice, two ounces of loaf sugar, two of strained honey. Pour to these a quart of water; boil until reduced half. Give frequently. Hog's lard and molasses in equal quantities with a little laudanum is also good.

Dysentery

Make a strong tea of sweet gum bark; to a pint, add a gill of good brandy, half an ounce of laudanum, a little loaf sugar to make it palatable. Take a teaspoonful every hour until the effect of the laudanum is apparent, then at longer intervals, until the disease abates.

A very good and simple remedy, if used when the first symptoms appear, is: Give an adult five drops of spirits of turpentine in a teaspoonful of sweet milk. Repeat, if necessary. Give a child according to age.

Scarlet Fever

As soon as the nature of the disease is ascertained, rub the patient night and morning with fat bacon, rubbing every part of the body but the head slowly and carefully.

Bite of a Snake

Bind above the wound tight. Give whiskey or some kind of liquor, or give sweet oil, a wineglassful at once; repeat, and bathe the wound in sweet oil. . . .

Bleeding at the Nose

Snuff pulverized alum, or dried beef pounded or grated very fine, or beat sage to a powder, and snuff it. Put cold cloths upon the back of the neck. Put the feet in hot mustard or pepper water. Holding the arms up straight over the head is said to be a remedy.

Chilblains

A turnip poultice is good. Bathe the feet in the water in which the turnips are boiled. When the skin is not broken, bathe in alum water. The soreness may be relieved by wrapping in cloths saturated with arnica; keep it wet.

Gangrene

Use poultices of red oak bark thickened with corn meal; sprinkle over thick powdered charcoal.

Fainting

Lay the person in a horizontal position; give plenty of fresh air. It is improper and thoughtless to crowd around a person in this condition. Bathe the face with cold water. Apply hartshorn or some stimulating smell to the nose. Loosen the clothing. If necessary, put mustard plasters upon the extremities.

Extinguishing Fire on a Person

When the clothes catch on fire, extinguish by smothering; wrap up in woolen if possible—a carpet, hearth rug, or anything within reach. I knew a case where a lady alone in her room, just in the act of retiring to bed, discovered her night clothes in a blaze; with admirable presence of mind, she leaped into bed, smothered the flame, and saved her life. Never rush into the air.

If the chimney catches, so as to endanger the house, throw salt upon the fire; spread a wet blanket before the fire-place.

The Severing of an Artery

When a person is in danger of bleeding to death from the severing of an artery, compress with the fingers the end of the artery, as near as possible to the wound, or apply a piece of lint dipped in a tincture of arnica water; on this put a bit of sponge, and press this so as to stop the blood. Send for a surgeon without delay.

Abby Fisher, *What Mrs. Fisher Knows about Old Southern Cooking, Soups, Pickles, Preserves, Etc.*

What Mrs. Fisher Knows about Old Southern Cooking has become a famous cookbook, and rightly so. It is one of the very earliest full-length cookbooks written by an African American, after Malinda Russell's 1866 *Domestic Cook Book*.[1] Unlike Russell, who was a free woman, Abby Fisher apparently spent much of her life in slavery. She was born in South Carolina in the early 1830s, and she would have been about thirty-three when the Civil War ended. Later she was identified in the U.S. Census as a "mulatto" whose mother was born in South Carolina and whose father was born in France, suggesting her mother may have been an enslaved African American and her father a French-born white man, possibly even her mother's owner.[2] At the end of her preface, Fisher noted that she had lived in Mobile, Alabama, and she mentioned several times in her book that a recipe or a remedy came from a Southern plantation. Whether it was mainly in South Carolina or Alabama or somewhere else, and whether mainly on a plantation or in a city, it seems clear that Abby Fisher had been an enslaved cook in the prewar South.[3]

Sometime after the end of the war, Fisher and her family left the South and headed west, and by the late 1870s she and her husband had managed to establish a successful pickle business in San Francisco. There, her cooking gained the attention of people curious enough about antebellum cuisine to help her publish a formal cookbook.[4] In fact, living in California might have made Fisher's knowledge more valuable, since the "Old South" probably seemed all the more exotic from that distance.

Fisher would have needed help creating her cookbook because, like the great majority of people who had grown to adulthood in slavery, she didn't know how to read or write. The existence of any written recipe reflects a fear that cooking techniques might not survive unless they're recorded. After the war, that fear fueled interest in prewar plantation cooking, a style of cookery whose only expert practitioners had been kept, intentionally and legally, illiterate. With the dismantling of slavery and the departure of many women who had been enslaved cooks, the fragility of that body of culinary knowledge suddenly became obvious. Like other cooks who had been enslaved, Abby Fisher took her knowledge of Southern cooking with her when she left the South. But Abby Fisher's story is remarkable because, unlike the great majority of antebellum Southern cooks, she eventually managed to transfer some of her culinary knowledge into print. Here all of her recipes are reproduced in their entirety.

A common racist trope in the Civil War era and for decades afterwards was that black women were great cooks but not smart ones. According to racist thinking, African American mastery over cooking came from instinct rather than from anything resembling science or study. As one white New Orleans doctor said, typically, in 1861, "Every negro is instinctively a cook."[5] The illusion of "instinct" was bolstered by high rates of African American illiteracy. To elite whites, many of whom could barely manage to boil an egg even *with* the help of a cookbook, it well might have seemed "magical" (another favorite word to describe black cooking) to witness a cook who could expertly produce hundreds of complicated dishes without written aids.[6] But of course, the real source of such mastery wasn't instinct or magic but years of training and experience and an extraordinary memory sharpened by constant practice.

Creating a cookbook is a lot of work, and Fisher's relationship with the people who helped her create hers must have been interesting. For example, she referred to the group as her "lady friends and patrons," words that imply a rather unequal power relationship. How did this collaboration work? Did Fisher sit and recite recipes by memory while someone else wrote down what she said? Or did Fisher actually cook through the many recipes she knew while describing what she was doing to some nearby note-taker? However they made it into print, the recipes' origins in speech rather than writing is sometimes obvious. Occasionally the recipes are repetitive, just as they would be if someone were actually describing out loud how to cook something, and the order of the recipes feels somewhat disorganized. Additionally, at a few points the people transcribing Fisher's words don't seem to have fully understood what she was saying, such as in the recipe Circuit Hash, when Fisher had probably been saying "succotash," or in the spelling of Jumerblie, when Fisher was probably saying "jambalaya."[7]

In Fisher's final recipe, Pap for Infant Diet, she noted, "I have given birth to eleven children and raised them all, and nursed them with this diet." Her words sound simple enough, but in the context of nineteenth century slavery they're extremely revealing. Like Annabella Hill, Fisher bore eleven children. But unlike Hill, who lost five of her children, Fisher "raised" all of hers—that is, her children all survived. In itself, that was a fairly remarkable event in the nineteenth century, a time when almost a quarter of the children born in the United States died before their fifth birthdays. But it was particularly noteworthy because Fisher was apparently enslaved for most of her childbearing years, and mortality was particularly high among children born into slavery.[8] A big reason for this high mortality was that enslaved mothers were usually forced to go back to work in the fields or kitchens long before their children would otherwise have been weaned. It's not a surprise this Pap for Infant Diet was a "Southern plantation preparation," as Fisher said, because it was precisely on Southern plantations where babies in large numbers were fed makeshift substitutes for breast milk.[9] Long before the invention of safe baby formula, feeding a newborn anything but breast milk was dangerous, not only because of ignorance about babies' nutritional needs but because milk and water were vehicles for pathogens. Fisher's careful instructions to boil the milk would have reduced that risk somewhat, for those lucky enough to have the time, equipment, and fuel to boil a fresh batch of pap each time a baby wanted to eat. Of course, Fisher's comment that she raised all eleven of her children had extra significance for an African American in the South; it was remarkable not only that all of her children survived but that none of them were taken from her and sold away.

Preface and Apology

The publication of a book on my knowledge and experience of Southern Cooking, Pickle and Jelly Making, has been frequently asked of me by my lady friends and patrons in San Francisco and Oakland, and also by ladies of Sacramento during the State Fair in 1879. Not being able to read or write myself, and my husband also having been without the advantages of an education upon whom would devolve the writing of the book at my dictation caused me to doubt whether I would be able to present a work that would give perfect satisfaction. But, after due consideration, I concluded to bring forward a book of my knowledge based on an experience of upwards of thirty-five years in the art of cooking Soups, Gumbos, Terrapin Stews, Meat Stews, Baked and Roast Meats, Pastries, Pies and Biscuits, making Jellies, Pickles, Sauces, Ice-Creams and Jams, preserving Fruits, etc. The book will be found a complete instructor, so that a child can understand it and learn the art of cooking.

Respectfully,

Mrs. Abby Fisher,

Late of Mobile, Ala.

I take pleasure in referring, by permission, to the following of my friends, namely:

WM. F. BLOOD, 415 California Street, San Francisco

E.M. MILES, 413 Montgomery Street, San Francisco

WM. O. GOULD, 512 California Street, San Francisco

MRS. CHARLES S. NEALE, 1814 Sutter Street, San Francisco

MRS. JOHN HARROLD, 416 Chestnut Street, San Francisco

MRS. W.H. GLASCOCK, Oakland

MRS. G.H. COY, 431 Geary Street, San Francisco

MRS. JOHN C. FALLS, San Francisco

MRS. LOUIS H. VANSCHAICK, 129 page Street, San Francisco

Maryland Beat Biscuit

Take one quart of flour, add one teaspoonful of salt, one tablespoonful of lard, half tablespoonful of butter. Dry rub the lard and butter into the flour until well creamed; add your water gradually in mixing so as to make dough stiff, then put the dough on pastry board and beat until perfectly moist and light. Roll out the dough to thickness of third of an inch. Have your stove hot and bake quickly. To make more add twice the quantity.

Egg Rolls

One quart of flour, half tablespoonful of butter, two eggs lightly beat, half tea-cup of sweet yeast, half tea-cup of water, one teaspoonful of salt. Mix as a sponge, about 10 o'clock at night, for breakfast; put to rise until morning. With dry flour knead the sponge, not too stiff; make off rolls, put to rise in baking pan, then have oven hot and bake slowly. When rolls are done, put them in a napkin until sent to table.

Breakfast Cream Cake

Four eggs beat light, one gill of cream to a tea-cup of sweet milk, one pint of flour, sifted, half teaspoonful of salt; mix cream, milk, and eggs together, well stirred, then add flour gradually until thoroughly mixed. Have your baking cups hot when put to bake. Requires ten minutes to bake in hot oven.

Waffles for Breakfast

Two eggs beat light, one pint of sour milk, to one and a half pint of flour, one teaspoonful of soda sifted with the flour, one tablespoonful of butter, teaspoonful of salt, well mixed, and then add the eggs. Always have your irons perfectly hot and well greased. In baking, melt butter before mixing in flour. Place them in a covered dish and butter them on sending to the table.

Flannel Cake

One quart of flour, quarter tea-cup of yeast, make into a batter, with one teaspoonful of salt; make up over night and put to rise. Just before baking on a nicely greased griddle, for breakfast, add one level teaspoon-ful of soda, and stir it well into the batter.

Sally Lund

One quart of flour, quarter pound of butter, perfectly rubbed into the flour while dry, one teaspoonful of salt, five eggs beat very light, half tea-cup of milk to quarter tea-cup of yeast; add all to the flour, and stir the whole together as you would pound cake, and put to rise at 10 o'clock at night; next morning beat over until light as cake and put in warm place to rise a second time, after which bake as carefully as baking pound cake. Bake in the pan [until] it rises in the second time. Just grease the pan before putting to rise the second time.

Breakfast Corn Bread

One tea-cup of rice boiled nice and soft, to one and a half tea-cupful of corn meal mixed together, then stir the whole until light; one teaspoonful of salt, one table-spoonful of lard or butter, three eggs, half tea-cup of sweet milk. The rice must be mixed into the meal while hot; can be baked either in muffin cups or a pan.

Corn Egg Bread

Two eggs, one pint of meal, half pint of sour milk, one teaspoonful of soda, beat eggs very light, one table-spoonful of melted lard or butter, mix all together, well stirred or beaten. Bake in an ordinary pan.

Plantation Corn Bread or Hoe Cake

Half tablespoonful of lard to a pint of meal, one tea-cup of boiling water; stir well and bake on a hot griddle. Sift in meal one teaspoonful of soda.

Light Bread

Half yeast cake to two quarts of flour, teaspoonful of salt, one dessertspoonful of butter or lard. Dissolve yeast in warm water; make up over night at 10 o'clock; make dough soft and spongy, and set to rise in a warm place. Next morning work the dough over until it becomes perfectly light, adding flour so as to keep it from sticking to the hands, then put to rise in your baking pan, and when it rises bake in a hot oven until thoroughly done.

Beefsteak—Broiled

Which should not be broiled until a few minutes before meal time: First, have the gridiron perfectly hot, then lay the steak on the iron while hot, the iron being over hot coals. Let the steak be on the iron about two minutes the first time you lay it on the iron, turning it over about once. In a minute remove from iron to a platter or pan and stick it through and through with a fork, so as to let the blood run out. Then place the steak back on the hot iron, turning it over as before; then take off iron, salt and pepper it and baste with butter; then lay it back on gridiron, turning it over for about two minutes; then lay in a dish, dress with butter and send to the table. A steak an inch and one-half thick may require twelve minutes to broil, turning it over every three minutes. A steak broiled in this style is very sweet and nice.

Lamb or Mutton Chops

Will take five minutes to broil, and must observe the same directions you have in the beefsteak.

Pork Steak or Chops

Should be broiled in the same way as the beefsteak, except that about eight to ten minutes should broil them, as pork must be well done.

Venison—Broiled

Pepper and salt before putting it on the gridiron, but remove it every two or three minutes from the iron and baste with butter. When you want deviled venison, use a little mustard mixed with wine (claret). Should you like your venison tart or a little acid, baste with currant jelly.

Roast Venison

First stuff the meat before roasting; make stuffing of bread crumbs browned; season stuffing with butter, salt, onions (grated), pork or ham chopped fine. When it is put into the oven, baste well with butter or lard, and while cooking notice and continue to baste until done. Two hours are sufficient, with a hot fire, to cook this roast. To make your gravy, brown a tablespoonful of flour in your pan from which you take the roast, add a little water, stir with spoon slowly until well done. You can make your gravy thick by the use of a very little water. If you do not like onions, use a little green or dry thyme.

Roast Beef

Should be well cooked outside and rare on the inside. The oven should bake on bottom and top. If it gets too hot on either top or bottom, shut the damper slightly off. A five-pound roast should cook in half an hour, and a ten-pound one in one hour. Season roast with salt and pepper before putting it to cook, baste it with lard or butter before putting in stove, and while cooking baste with the juice that comes out of the meat every two or three minutes until done.

Roast Lamb

Prepare in the same way as the roast beef, except the lamb should be well done. In a hot oven, one hour is necessary to cook the lamb. Mint sauce for roast lamb: Chop tender mint very fine, put cold water or vinegar, one tablespoonful of vinegar to three of water, and a little sugar according to taste.

Roast Pork

To be seasoned with salt and pepper before being cooked, and in cooking baste with the gravy that comes from the meat. Must be cooked with a fast fire. To make the gravy, take one tablespoonful of flour browned in the pan and stir in a little water.

Roast Pig

Examine when it comes from the butcher and see that it is completely cleaned. The pig should be roasted the same way you would a turkey well done. For the stuffing take a loaf and one-half of baker's bread cut thin, fry the bread in butter or lard and mash it well; season it with salt and pepper according to taste, using a little red pepper. Then stuff the pig putting an apple in its mouth. Put it in the pan and baste with lard, then put it to roast, and while it is cooking keep basting it every five or ten minutes until it is cooked; you can tell when it is perfectly done by a fork passing through it easily. To make the gravy for the pig—After it is cooked, take about a tablespoonful of flour and put it in the pan where you cooked your roast and brown well on the stove, then add a little water; stir till it commences to get thick. A little onion in your stuffing is good.

Roast Veal

Use crackers for your stuffing. Slice an opening in the veal in five or six different places, and fill each one with the stuffing. Season the stuffing with salt, pepper, butter, and a little sage. You can tell when it is done by a fork passing through easily. Baste the roast while cooking with the essence that comes from the meat. Baste it with lard or butter when first put to cook. Use flour for making gravy, same as directed in other roasts.

Roast Turkey

First cleanse well and take the craw from the turkey. Make stuffing of light bread chopped fine, season with butter, pepper and salt; then stuff the body completely full, also where the craw was. Put in pan and baste with butter or lard, and put to roast. While cooking, keep basting it with the juice that comes from the turkey. When it is cooked take a tablespoonful of flour and brown it in the pan, then add a little water and stir for the gravy.

Roast Chicken

The same as for turkey.

Roast Birds

In the same way.

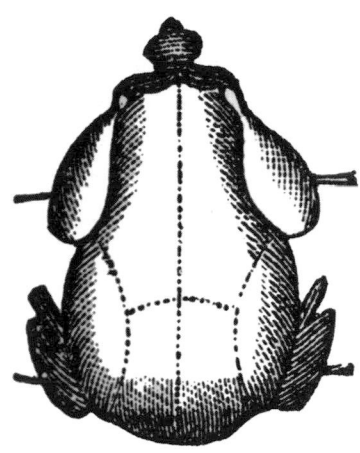

An illustration of a young chicken, skewered and ready for roasting. Illustration from Hill, *Mrs. Hill's Southern Practical Cookery*, facsimile of 1872 edition, 75.

Quails

When roasted, make nice toast, butter it nice and send quails to table on the toast. Do not forget to baste all game and fowls while cooking, so as to make them juicy. Make stuffing same as for chicken.

Domestic Duck

Bake or roast in the same manner you do a turkey, and have it well cooked. Make stuffing of bread, like that prepared for turkey, with salt, pepper, butter or lard. Baste while cooking.

Wild Duck

Should not be stuffed, but cleaned well and seasoned with pepper and salt, inside and outside, and put into a hot oven. Ten minutes will cook it.

Meat Stews or Entrees

Cut your meat into inch pieces and put into a saucepan; season with salt, pepper, and butter or lard. Put one pint of water to a pound of meat. One hour will cook, unless very young, when less time is sufficient. Add onions if liked.

Lamb Croquettes

Boil lamb till thoroughly done, then cut into small pieces taking all sinews and gristle out, and put into a chopping tray; grate onion in it to suit your taste, also grate two or three sour pickles in it; then chop the whole up very fine indeed. Season with salt and pepper. Add one and one half boiled Irish potatoes to one pound of lamb mashed to the fine meal while hot; thoroughly mix together with the hand. Make into small cakes, oblong style; then take two eggs and beat them very light, dip the cakes into the egg, and then roll into powdered crackers. Have fat very hot and put them into it, and let them fry quick till brown.

Chicken Croquettes

Boil chicken very tender, pick to pieces, take all gristle out, then chop fine. Beat two eggs for one chicken and mix into meat; season with pepper and salt; make into cakes oblong shaped; powder crackers and roll them into the powder, after dipping them into two eggs beaten moderately well. Then have your lard very hot, and fry just before sending them to the table.

Crab Croquettes

Have crabs well boiled in salt and water, then pick them clean from the shell; chop fine; take the large end of a piece of celery and grate into the crab; chop with crab a small piece of onion fine; mix half a teacup of fine powdered cracker into crab; season with pepper and salt, also the least bit of fine red pepper, as crabs should be seasoned high to be nice. Have your lard hot, and fry just before wanted at table. Beat two eggs, dip croquettes in the egg, roll in powdered crackers before frying; make them oblong shaped.

Meat Croquettes

You can make croquettes from any kind of meat you like from the directions given for the lamb croquettes, such as veal, except make veal into cakes as you would a biscuit, round. You need not use onions unless you like, but always salt and pepper.

Veal or Lamb Vigareets[10]

To be made the same way, to-wit: Boil meat rare done, pick all gristle out, grate as much onion in the chopped meat as you like. Take half the quantity of brains that comes in one head (calf or lamb), scald them, pick all the skin from them; mix then with the meat, one-half of a nutmeg grated, pepper and salt; season high and fry the same as other croquettes. Make a gravy of cream and pour on vigareets just as going to table. Making gravy: Put sweet cream into a clean vessel, put over steam until hot, add a very little pepper and salt, then chop some fresh parsley tine and sprinkle it over vigareets while on dish. Make oblong cakes.

Liver Croquettes

Made of lamb or veal liver. One pound of liver to a quarter of a pound of suet, part boil, chop both separately very fine; pick all strings out of suet, then add suet and liver together, a small piece of onion, grated, salt and pepper; season high. Beat one egg light and mix well with hand, roll in powdered cracker, fry in hot lard or butter, garnish dish with parsley and send to table.

Oyster Croquettes

Chop the quantity of oysters you want for the dinner in the following manner: Chop very fine one dozen oysters, take one boiled potato and mash hot into the fine oysters; take the yelk of one egg only, mix well into the oysters and season with pepper and salt to taste; then roll them, after making into oblong cakes, in powdered crackers; have your fat very hot, and fry quick and send to table.

Fish Croquettes

One pound of boiled fish to one and a half potatoes, chop a small piece of onion fine and mix with fish; season with pepper and salt to your taste; make them out in cakes like the other croquettes, roll them in dry corn meal, fry in hot fat and send to table.

Fricasseed Chicken

Chicken must be tender and well cleaned inside. Singe all pin feathers off over the fire. Boil two eggs hard, take the yelks and rub fine into one tablespoonful of butter, then add one tablespoonful of corn starch dissolved into the least bit of water; add all together, well mixed and free from lumps. Have your chicken cut up before[11] boiling, and stir the fricassee into the chicken just before sending to table. Season with salt and pepper while cooking.

Fried Chicken

Cut the chicken up, separating every joint, and wash clean. Salt and pepper it, and roll into flour well. Have your fat very hot, and drop the pieces into it, and let them cook brown. The chicken is done when the fork passes easily into it. After the chicken is all cooked, leave a little of the hot fat in the skillet; then take a tablespoonful of dry flour and brown it in the fat, stirring it around, then pour water in and stir till the gravy is as thin as soup.

Beef Soup

Six pounds of meat to two and one-half gallons of water. Boil to one gallon and one-half; then strain all meat out from the bouillon. Season with pepper and salt.

Ox-Tail Soup

Can be made from the same bouillon of beef as seen in [Beef Soup], in the following manner. Take two quarts of bouillon to two ox-tails; boil down to three pints. You can put in either ochra or vermicelli. Season with salt and pepper. Skim all grease off while boiling. Have the butcher unjoint the ox-tail.

Calf's Head Soup

Let the butcher open the head wide. Take the brains from it and lay into clean water with a little salt. Leave the tongue in the head when put on to boil; when the tongue is tenderly boiled or done, take it out of the pot and let it get cold for making tongue salad. Two gallons of water to a calf's head; boil to one gallon; strain it off clear for soup to one dozen guests. Take two quarts of this liquid and put to boil; two tablespoonfuls of flour and brown it; one tablespoonful of butter; rub into the brown flour till it comes to a cream, then add to the soup gradually, and stir well while adding. Season with salt and pepper, and a little red pepper. While cooking, boil a small piece of thyme and the half of an ordinary sized onion tied tight in a clean linen rag, and to be taken out of soup when done. One teaspoonful of mustard mixed with one tablespoonful of wine, to be put into the tureen before pouring in the soup hot, also one glass of sherry wine. Pick all skin from brains; beat two eggs light and add to the brains, then beat the eggs and brains together to a batter; take one-quarter tea cup of powdered cracker, one tablespoonful of flour added to the brains and egg batter well beaten together. Then make this brain batter in cake the size of a hickory nut, and fry them brown in hot fat just before taking up soup, and send to table on separate dish. Serve them with the soup, two cakes to a plate of soup.

P.S. Chop parsley very fine, and boil it into the soup. You will find the calf's head soup the most delicious soup in the cookery. Study the recipe and remember it well.

Mock Turtle Soup

Follow the same directions given for calf's head soup. Prepare your calf's head in the same way exactly. Use for flavor half of a lemon sliced, and put in tureen and pour hot soup on. Instead of brain-balls or cakes, make a forced meat of boiled ham chopped very fine with the yelk of a hard boiled egg; season with black pepper. Make balls the size of a hickory nut and fry in hot butter. Send to table in separate dish, serving one ball to a plate of soup. Use beef in place of ham if liked best.

Green Turtle Soup

To two pounds of turtle add two quarts of water, put to boil on a slow fire and cook down to three pints. Season while boiling with pepper and salt to taste. Take three hard boiled eggs, slice very thin and lay in tureen; slice one-fourth of a lemon and put in tureen also. Then pour in tureen one gill of sherry wine. Then pour on hot soup and send to table. The above quantity will make soup for one dozen guests. If there are more to serve, increase the quantity.

Oyster Gumbo Soup

Take an old chicken, cut into small pieces, salt and black pepper. Dip it well in flour, and pat it on to fry, over a slow fire, till brown; don't let it burn. Cut half of a small onion very fine and sprinkle on chicken while frying. Then place chicken in soup pot, add two quarts water and let it boil to three pints. Have one quart of fresh oysters with all the liquor that belongs to them, and before dishing up soup, add oysters and let come to a boil the second time, then stir into soup one tablespoonful of gumbo quickly.[12] Dish up and send to table. Have parsley chopped very fine and put in tureen on dishing up soup. Have dry boiled rice to go to table with gumbo in separate dish. Serve one tablespoonful of rice to a plate of gumbo.

Ochra Gumbo

Get a beef shank, have it cracked and put to boil in one gallon of water. Boil to half a gallon, then strain and put back on fire. Cut ochra in small pieces and put in soup; don't put in any ends of ochra. Season with salt and pepper while cooking. Stir it occasionally and keep it from burning. To be sent to table with dry boiled rice. Never stir rice while boiling. Season rice always with salt when it is first put on to cook, and do not have too much water in rice while boiling.

Old Fashioned Turnip Soup

Take two pounds veal bones to half a gallon of water, and boil to one quart. Put turnips and bones on to boil together, then strain the liquor off and send to table hot. Season while cooking with pepper and salt.

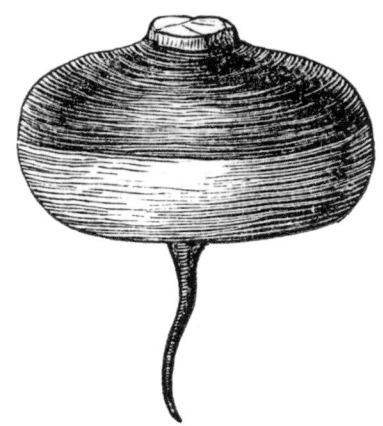

Abby Fisher highlighted the simplicity of her soup—made with nothing but turnips, veal bones, and salt and pepper—by calling it "Old Fashioned Turnip Soup." Turnip illustration in Burr, *Field and Garden Vegetables*, 105.

Chicken Soup for the Sick

Take an old chicken and put on with one gallon of water; boil down to half a gallon. Take the yelks of two eggs, tie them up in a clean cloth with a little thyme and put in the soup after you have strained the meat from it, and put back to boil till down to three pints. Dish up and send to table hot. Season with salt and pepper to taste.

Corn and Tomato Soup

Take a fresh beef bone, put on to boil with one gallon of water, and when boiling skim the grease off. Cut corn from cob and scald tomatoes with boiling water. Skin them and put both vegetables into soup, the corn ten minutes before dinner. Cut tomatoes in small pieces and let them boil in soup at least one hour.

Pastry for Making Pies of All Kinds

One pound of flour nicely sifted to quarter pound of butter and one quarter pound of lard, one teaspoonful of salt, fine, mixed in flour while dry; then with your hands rub the butter and lard into the flour until thoroughly mixed, then add enough cold water and mix with your hands so as to make pastry hold together, be sure not have it too wet; sprinkle flour very lightly on pastry board, and roll pastry out to the thickness of an egg-shell for the top of fruit, and that for the bottom of fruit must be thin as paper. In rolling pastry, roll to and from you; you don't want more than ten minutes to make pastry.

Preparing the Fruit for Pies

One gill of water to four pounds rhubarb; first peel the rhubarb; sweeten to taste while cooking, and put into pastry when cold.

Prepare apples same way; season with cinnamon.

Peaches the same way; season with cinnamon.

Lemon Pies

Take four eggs, one tablespoonful of butter to one and a half tea-cup of powdered sugar, rub butter and sugar together until a cream, then add the yelks of the eggs to butter and sugar, and beat until light; beat the white of the egg until perfectly light, and add to the others. Take two lemons, roll them with your hands, on board until soft, then grate peel of lemons and put into preparation, then squeeze juice of lemons into preparation. All articles in this preparation should be well mixed together and put in pastry, and baked immediately in a hot oven. Only one layer of pastry at bottom of pie plate.

Cocoanut Pie

One cocoanut fresh, draw off the milk, then place the nut in a hot oven and let it stay long enough for the shell to pull off; then grate with the nut juice one tea-cup of powdered white sugar, one tablespoonful of butter and lard rubbed together until creamed, then take the yelks of four eggs and beat into sugar and butter until perfectly light; grate the rind of one lemon into it, and squeeze the juice of the lemon into the creamed butter and sugar; beat the white of four eggs light, and add also to creamed butter and sugar, and stir them well, add also one-half tea-cup of sweet milk. Will make three pies. Use a half pound of flour for the pastry, one tablespoonful each of butter and lard[;] you only want crust at the bottom of plate, and bake in quick oven. Mix flour as directed in [Pastry for Making Pies of All Kinds].[13]

Cream Apple Pie

The best of apples to be used. To two pounds of apples use a gill of water; put on fire to steam till the apples will mash perfectly fine and soft; sweeten to taste and let them cool. Season with powdered cinnamon one-half teaspoonful of the best. Have one crust of pastry only, and that at the bottom of plate; fill plate with the fruit, then bake quickly in a hot oven. Take one pint of fresh cream sweetened to taste; beat the white of five eggs light, and add to the cream; flavor with vanilla. Beat the cream lightly before adding the eggs, then with a spoon spread over pies on sending to table.

Sweet Potato Pie

Two pounds of potatoes will make two pies. Boil the potatoes soft; peel and mash fine through a cullender while hot; one tablespoonful of butter to be mashed in with the potato. Take five eggs and beat the yelks and whites separate and add one gill of milk; sweeten to taste; squeeze the juice of one orange, and grate one-half of the peel into the liquid. One half teaspoonful of salt in the potatoes. Have only one crust and that at the bottom of the plate. Bake quickly.

Custard Pie

Half dozen eggs beaten together lightly; one pint of sweet milk; sweeten to taste. Grate one nutmeg in it. Have one crust only, and that at the bottom of plate. Use deep plates and bake quickly. It will make two nice pies.

Gooseberry and Cherry Pies

Prepared the same way. Use one gill of water to two pounds of either fruit; sweeten to taste, leaving it a little tart. When it cools, put into plates for baking, having two crusts, top and bottom of plate. Bake quickly, and send to table cold.

Orange Pie

Peel the oranges; cut them very thin and spread with sugar thickly. Have your pie crust rich, the same as other pie pastry. Lay bottom crust in plate, and put in the oranges with juice, then cover over with top crust, and put to bake in a quick oven.

Light Bread Pie

Take stale bread and grate it. To one and one-half tea-cupfuls of the grated bread, add two teacupfuls of sweet milk, the juice of one orange, and half of the peel grated. Stir the yelks of four eggs beaten light into it. Take the whites of the four eggs beaten very light and meringue the pies after baking. Put half teacupful of sugar and one tablespoonful of butter to the prepared bread. Have one crust only, and that at the bottom of plate. Bake quickly.

Cracker Pie

To be made the same as bread pie, except flavor with one-half teaspoonful of ground cloves, one-half teaspoonful of ground cinnamon, and one tablespoonful of butter.

Mince Pies

One beef tongue boiled tender, then take the skin off; four pounds beef kidney suet, peel all the skin off it and chop very fine with the tongue; two pounds citron chopped fine, four pounds apples, four pounds raisins well seeded, four pounds currants well washed and dried with a towel, four oranges, the peel of two grated, and the fruit of all four grated into mince meat, two table-spoonfuls of ground allspice, one tablespoonful of cloves, two nutmegs grated, and two tablespoonfuls of ground cinnamon. Chop the whole very fine, and mix well together, then put in one-half gallon sherry wine, and one-half gallon brandy. Grate two lemons in the meat. Salt to your taste, also sweeten to your taste. Have bottom and top crust.

Gold Cake

Take one dozen eggs and separate the yelks from the white, and beat the yelks very light; one pound of but-ter, one pound of flour and one pound of powdered sugar; rub the butter and sugar together until creamed very light, then add the beaten yelks of the eggs to the creamed butter and sugar, and beat again until light. Take two teaspoonfuls of the best yeast powder,[14] and sift with the one pound of flour, then add this flour to the creamed butter and eggs, with a half teacupful of sweet milk, and stir the whole hard and fast till light, then grate the peel[15] of one lemon and squeeze the juice in the cake and stir well.

Silver Cake

The whites of one dozen eggs beaten very light, one pound of butter, one pound of powdered sugar; rub the butter and sugar together until creamed very light, then add the beaten whites of the eggs, and beat all together until very light; two teaspoonfuls of the best yeast pow-der sifted with one pound of flour, then add the flour to the eggs, sugar and butter, also add one-half teacupful of sweet milk; mix quickly, and beat till very light; flavor with two teaspoonfuls of the extract of almond or peach, put in when you beat the cake the last time. Put to bake in any shape pan you like, but grease the pan well before you put the cake batter in it. Have the stove moderately hot, so as the cake will bake gradually, and arrange the damper of stove so as send heat to the bottom of the cake first. This instruction of baking applies to all cakes except tea cakes.

219

Almond Cake

Is made in the same way that the silver and gold cakes are, except you take one teacup of almonds, scald them in hot water, wipe them with a cloth and the peeling will come off. Either split or chop them fine; suit yourself in this respect. Use the whites or the yelks of one dozen eggs. With the whites of the eggs it will be a silver almond cake; the yelks used alone will be a gold almond cake.

Feather Cake

One teacup of butter, two of flour, two of sugar. Cream the flour and butter together; two teaspoonfuls of yeast powder to one teacup of sweet milk. Mix all with the flour and beat light with a large spoon. To be baked in round tins. Grease well and bake in a moderately hot stove.

Sponge Cake

Take one dozen eggs and put in scales as the balance for weighing an equal quantity of sugar. Then balance flour to the weight of six eggs. Beat the yelks of the dozen eggs with the sugar very light, then beat the whites very light and add to the other. Grate the peel of one lemon into it also, squeezing the juice in, and then stir the flour in lightly. Have your pans in readiness, grease with butter, and place white paper at bottom of pan. This should be done for all cakes. A sponge cake should not stand a second after made before it is baked. Bake in a medium oven, keeping heat at bottom.

Fruit Cake

One pound of flour sifted and browned in stove, one pound of citron sliced into very small pieces, one pound of raisins cut in small pieces, one pound of currants well washed and dried with clean towel, one tea-cup of almonds chopped fine, one tablespoonful of powdered cinnamon, half a teaspoonful of mace, one tablespoonful of allspice, half a teaspoonful of ground cloves, one pint of black molasses strained before using, one wineglass of brandy, one pound of butter, one pound of sugar, one dozen eggs. Beat whites and yelks separate, light, before adding to cake.

Jelly Cake

For this cake make an orange marmalade and use in the place of jelly, as it makes a more delicious cake. Following are the directions: Half a dozen oranges to a teacup of granulated sugar; peel oranges and grate them, pick out the seed and pith, add sugar to oranges and stir well and put to cook; stir while cooking; twenty minutes will cook it. It must be made a day before using it for cake. For making the cake, one teacup of butter to two of sugar, three of flour and half a dozen eggs. Beat the whites and yelks of eggs separate, very light. Cream butter and sugar together, add the yelks of eggs to creamed sugar and butter, then add the whites, and add flour and stir till light. Sift two teaspoonfuls of best yeast powder with the flour. With the above directions the cake is made. Place it in the pans and put to bake; fifteen minutes will bake it. Spread marmalade over the cake after it is baked. Icing for the cake: Take the whites of four eggs and beat them very light indeed. Add three tablespoonfuls of powdered sugar, beat sugar and eggs together light, and spread on cake while cake is warm. Take one tea-cup of fine grated cocoanut and sprinkle over cake while icing is soft.

Carolas[16]

Five eggs to two cups of sugar; break eggs into the sugar and beat the whole till perfectly light. Sift one quart of flour; take one-half teacup of sweet milk and put a level teaspoonful of soda in it, without lumps; one teaspoonful of salt. Flavor with the juice of one orange, the peel of half an orange, grated, and one teaspoonful of butter. Make the dough in the same way as for light bread; roll out dough as for biscuit. Cut them out five inches by two inches, slice them two inches in the middle and stretch open a little. Have your fat boiling hot, but do not let it burn. Put carolas in hot fat, shake skillet gradually till brown. As you take them out of the fat, lay them in a pan on clean paper, so as to drain grease from them.

Raised Cake

One quart flour, half a pound butter, one pint sugar, two eggs, half a teacup yeast, one teacup seeded raisins, one and one-half teacups currants. Cream butter and sugar together, then add the flour. Break eggs in, add yeast and beat the whole well. Lastly, add the fruit, stir all well and put it to rise. With good yeast it will rise in an hour. After rising, make off and put into pans greased with butter. When you make off the second time and put in pans, first take a tablespoonful of flour with a teaspoonful of soda and sift into the batter; it will rise in thirty minutes. Then put to bake.

Old-Time Ginger Cake

One pint molasses, one quart flour, one-half teacup brown sugar, one teacup butter, one tablespoonful cinnamon, two tablespoonsful ginger, one teacup sour milk. With it mix a teaspoonful soda and three eggs. Cream butter and sugar together, then add molasses, then flour, then eggs, then milk, then ginger and cinnamon; stir thoroughly and put to bake in oblong pans.

Ginger Cookies

One teacup of molasses, one-half teacup of sugar, one tablespoonful of butter, one tablespoonful of lard, one quart of flour, two tablespoonfuls of ginger, one teaspoonful of cinnamon, one teaspoonful of allspice, two tablespoonfuls of yeast powder. Cream butter and sugar together and add molasses. Sift yeast powder and flour together and add to butter, sugar and molasses, then add lard and spices, etc., and work it up well. Roll out on a board, and cut them out and bake like you would a biscuit.

Jumble Cake

One teacup of butter, one and one-half teacups of sugar, one and one-half pints of flour; four eggs, two teaspoonfuls of cinnamon, one-half teacup of almonds chopped fine, two teaspoonfuls of yeast powder sifted in the flour. Beat the butter, sugar and eggs together, then add the flour. Put cinnamon and almonds in and work the whole up well, then roll on the board to thickness of half an inch, and cut out a finger's length and join together at ends, so as to be round. Grease pans with butter and put to bake.

Sweet Wafers

One teacup each of butter and sugar creamed together, one grated orange, four eggs, one tablespoonful of cinnamon. Add three pints of flour and make up stiff. Then roll out on a board and cut them out about the size of a biscuit, and roll again till thin as paper, and bake in a quick oven. Watch close while baking. You can roll them round on a fork handle while they are warm, if you like.

Sweet Cucumber Pickles

Take as many pickles as you want to make that have already been pickled in vinegar, and slice them in four pieces lengthwise, or cut them crosswise the thickness of a silver half-dollar, and place them in an earthen jar in layers of about three inches in thickness, covering each layer of pickles all over with granulated sugar. Keep repeating the layers three inches thick and covering them with sugar until you have placed all the pickles under sugar you have cut up. Let them remain under the sugar twenty-four hours, then take them out and put them in jars. Then make a syrup in the following way: One quart of sugar to one quart of clear water, and let it boil down to one quart. You will then have one quart of pure syrup. Add one tea-cup of wine vinegar to one pint of syrup, then add the vinegar syrup to the pickles until they are thoroughly covered. Always use granulated sugar.

Sweet Cucumber Mangoes

Take large pickled cucumbers, open them with a knife on one side to within half an inch of each end. Scrape out the inside with your fingers, then sprinkle them inside with granulated sugar as thick as a ten-cent piece. Let them remain in that state twenty-four hours or longer, then stuff perfectly full and tie them or wrap with white cord. Make the stuffing in the following way: Take one-fourth of a head of a small cabbage, cut up fine, and two dozen cucumber pickles the size of those to be stuffed. Slice them in small pieces the size of a cherry, and two large onions sliced thin. Then chop fine one dozen cucumber pickles, two pounds of white mustard seed, one tablespoonful of ground allspice, one teaspoonful of ground cloves, sugar to your taste, one-half gallon of wine vinegar. Then put to boil slowly in a porcelain kettle; two hours will cook it. Salt and pepper to your taste. Make syrup in the same way as the sweet pickles in [Sweet Cucumber Pickles]. You boil a few cloves in the vinegar that is put in the syrup of these pickles, and syrup and vinegar in same way.

Chow Chow

Take one cabbage, a large one, and cut up fine. Put in a large jar or keg, and sprinkle over it thickly one pint of coarse salt. Let it remain in salt twelve hours, then scald the cut-up cabbage with one gallon of boiling vinegar. Cut up two gallons of cucumbers, green or pickled, and add to it; cut in pieces the size of the end of little finger. Then chop very fine two gallons more of cucumbers or pickles and add to the above. Seasonings: One pound of brown sugar, one tablespoonful of cayenne pepper, one tablespoonful of black pepper, two gallons of pure wine vinegar, two tablespoonfuls of tumerick, six onions, chopped fine or grated. Then put it on to cook in a large porcelain kettle, with a slow fire, for twelve hours. Stir it occasionally to keep it from burning. You can add more pepper than is here given if you like it hot.

Creole Chow Chow

One gallon of green tomatoes, sliced thin, half dozen silver skin onions, sliced thin, one gallon wine vinegar, two tea-cups of brown sugar, one tablespoonful of cayenne pepper, one tablespoonful black pepper, one tablespoonful of tumerick. Put the onions and tomatoes together in a keg or jar and sprinkle over them one pint of salt and let it so remain twenty-four hours, then drain all the brine off from them over cullender, then put the vinegar to them and add the seasoning, and put to cook on a slow fire, stir to keep from burning. It will take the whole day to cook; you can make any quantity you want, by doubling the quantity of vegetables and seasonings

In her recipe for "Creole Chow Chow," Abby Fisher called specifically for silver-skinned onions. Like piccalilly, chow chow was a sharp condiment that would have woken up any meal. Silver-skinned onion illustration from Henderson, *Gardening for Profit*, 215.

here prescribed, or if you want a less quantity, lessen the proportion, say half the quantity, then you want a half gallon of tomatoes to begin with, and a half of every thing else needed in this chow chow.

Cherry Chutney

Get your cherries and seed them; to one gallon half dozen silver skin onions chopped[17] fine; first put the onions to cook in half gallon of vinegar, 10 minutes, then add the cherries, season with two ounces of ground cinnamon, one teaspoonful of cayenne pepper and one of black pepper, two tablespoonfuls of salt, then let it continue to cook with a slow fire, twelve hours, stir it occasionally and keep from burning.

Game Sauce

Take one peck of plums, half dozen silver skin onions and chop them very fine; put on the plums to cook. First seed plums; use a porcelain kettle; put the onions to stew in a pint of vinegar until thoroughly done, then add them to the plums; four pounds of granulated sugar to be added; season with one teaspoonful of cayenne pepper, one of black pepper, two ounces of cinnamon broke in fine pieces; cook on a slow fire, stir frequently to avoid burning one teaspoonful of table salt it will take one whole day to cook; when cool cork in a tight jar and keep in cool closet you will find it the best sauce in the world.

Compound Tomato Sauce

One peck of ripe tomatoes, cut them in slices and put them in a vessel, and add one tea-cupful of salt to them, two ounces fine allspice, one ounce of fine cloves, one tablespoonful of black pepper and one of cayenne pepper, five large silver skin onions cut up fine, and the whole stand twenty-four hours; mix well together when you set to stand, then put it to cook with one quart of vinegar and let it cook all day; stir it occasionally; it must become thick before it is thoroughly cooked, then strain all skin and studs out of it through a sieve; when cool put in a demijohn, as it is will keep better than in bottles when first made.

N.B. If you don't like much pepper use half the quantity, if you like it very hot use double the quantity.

Napoleon Sauce

Twenty green cucumbers to one quart of Chili peppers and one dozen Bell peppers, (take out seeds), and chop the cucumbers and pickles fine, and mix well together, and sprinkle half a teacupful of salt over them. Chop half dozen red onions in it. Pour one gallon of vinegar over it and let it stand that way one day and night, then put it to cook next morning and cook slowly all day, stirring it occasionally to keep it from burning, then strain through a sieve. Take a half teacupful of brown sugar and put it in a frying pan on the fire, and let it bake thoroughly just next to burning; then stir in one pint of vinegar to the sugar and when it comes to a light boil strain it through a sieve into the sauce, and stir till well mixed. When cooled cork up in a demi-john.

Pepper Mangoes

Take the Bell peppers and scald them in boiling vinegar, then cut the top end of the peppers out and clean out the seeds nicely, as the seeds are no good. You will then prepare a stuffing in the following way: Take one gallon of cucumber pickles, one-half of a head of large cabbage, one-half dozen large silver skin onions, and chop them all up very fine, (the cabbage will chop better if you first slice it thin with a sharp knife): then take two pounds of white mustard seeds, sift all the dust from them and wash clean, one-quarter pound of celery seed, and two quarts of vinegar; add to the vegetables,[18] and put to boil and boil slowly for three hours, stirring it every two or three minutes. Season while cooking with one tablespoonful of cayenne pepper and one of black pepper. If

In her recipe for "Pepper Mangoes," Abby Fisher used "mangoes" as a generic term for pickled produce, not in reference to the fruit people today know by the name mango. Illustration of a bell pepper, also called a bull-nosed pepper in the nineteenth century, in Henderson, *Gardening for Profit*, 225.

you do not like it very hot, use half the quantity of each kind of pepper; if you like it very hot double the quantity of each kind of pepper. When the stuffing becomes cool, stuff your Bell peppers, using a teaspoon to stuff with, then place the top back on them, and tie nicely with cord, the same way a bundle is tied, and pack them close together in a keg or barrel. This quantity of stuffing will stuff about fifty large Bell peppers. See that they be covered well with vinegar when packed.

Meat Dressing

One peck of young carrots grated, one dozen red skin onions grated, one dozen cauliflowers grated; mix the vegetables together and put to cook, adding two gallons of vinegar. Season with two tablespoonfuls of ground black pepper, one tablespoonful of cayenne pepper, and one teacupful of salt, stirring it in well. Put one teacupful of brown sugar on the fire in a frying pan, and let cook to a dark brown, then pour in two teacupfuls of vinegar; stir it well and strain it through a sieve into the kettle while cooking, and let it cook slowly one day. This dressing is nice for all meat entrees, soups and gravies; put two tablespoonfuls to one-half gallon soup, and one tablespoonful to one quart of stew, etc.

Sweet Pickle Peach

Use the cling stone peach, taking as many as you may want to pickle. Have your vinegar boiling hot, and drop your peaches into it, letting them remain in the hot vinegar for five minutes, then take them out and put them in a stone jar; about every six inches of peaches cover with sugar one inch thick, putting them in the jar this way a layer of peaches and then a layer of sugar until you get all the peaches under sugar. Use five pounds of sugar to ten pounds of peaches. Let the peaches remain under sugar one day, then take the juice that comes out of the peaches, and the sugar if any remain undissolved, and add two pounds more of sugar to it, and put on the fire in a porcelain kettle, and let it cook to a thick clear syrup, then pour the syrup boiling hot over the peaches. Now take the vinegar the peaches were scalded in, and put it to boil the second time, adding while boiling one-half teacupful of whole allspice, and one ounce of whole cloves and then pour it on the peaches and boil. Pour this juice on the peaches for nine mornings alternately.

Sweet Pickle Pears

Follow the same directions in making sweet pickle pears as in making sweet pickle peaches, as given in [above recipe].

Sweet Pickle Prunes

Follow the same directions as given in [recipe for] sweet pickle peaches, except use cinnamon bark instead of allspice—one teacupful of cinnamon to ten pounds of prunes.

Sweet Watermelon Rind Pickle

Take the melon rind and scrape all the meat from the inside, and then carefully slice all the outside of rind from the white part of the rind, then lay or cover the white part over with salt. It will have to remain under salt one week before pickling; the rind will keep in salt from year to year. When you want to pickle it, take it from the salt and put into clear water, change the water three times a day—must be changed say every four hours—then take the rind from water and dry it with a clean cloth. Have your vinegar boiling, and put the rind into it and let it scald four minutes, then take it off the fire and let it lay in vinegar four days; then take it from the vinegar, drain, and sprinkle sugar thickly over it and let it remain so one day. To make syrup, take the syrup from the rind and add eight pounds more sugar to it, and put to boil; boil till a thick and clear syrup. Weigh ten pounds of rind to twelve pounds of sugar; cover the rind with four pounds of it and make the syrup with the remaining eight pounds. While the syrup is cooking add one teacupful of white ginger root and the peel of three lemons. When the syrup is cooked, then put the rind into the boiling syrup, and let it cook till you can pass a fork through it with ease, then it is done. When cooled put in jar or bottles with one pint of vinegar to one quart of syrup, thus the pickle is made. See that they be well covered with vinegar and syrup as directed.

Onion Pickles

Take as many small onions as you desire to pickle and peel them, then put them in a keg or barrel. Lay down one layer of onions about three inches thick, cover them all over with salt freely; then another layer of onions in the same way and cover with salt, and repeat in this manner until all the onions are covered with salt. Let them remain one or two days, then take the onions out of the salt and put them in clear water, letting them remain in the water long enough to be seasoned with salt to your taste. If very salty, you had better change the first water after three or four hours. Put the onions in a large cullender or wire sieve and let the water all drain from them, then put them into a keg, cover them with vinegar, and let them remain in the vinegar twenty-four hours. Take the vinegar from them and put it on to boil, seasoning it with the following spices: Two gallons of vinegar will take one teacupful of allspice, two table-spoonfuls of cloves, one-half teacupful of black pepper (wash and pick all gravel from the pepper before putting in vinegar), one-fourth pound of white ginger, one-fourth pound of Chile[19] peppers. This seasoning must be boiled in the vinegar, and when boiled twenty minutes, strain vinegar from the spices through a cullender on to the pickles, and always prepare enough in this way to have your pickles well covered with vinegar.

Plain Pickles

Any vegetable you want to pickle under this head, say small or large cucumbers, cabbage or green tomatoes, have them fresh and put them into a barrel, one layer of cucumbers, or other vegetable, about three inches deep, covering thickly with salt, and repeating layers and salt until you have under brine all you desire to pickle. Let them remain under the brine, if you want to pickle right away, for twenty-four hours, which is long enough, but they will keep a long time by always having them well pressed down with a heavy rock. If you are going to pickle vegetables twenty-four hours after putting them in salt, let them lay in fresh water for two hours, so as to get the smell of the old brine off them. Take them out of the water and put to drain on a sieve made for that purpose of galvanized iron, square, three by four feet, or larger, if needed. Let them drain two or three days, then put in a clean keg or barrel and cover thoroughly with vinegar. Sprinkle over a keg of pickles two ounces of powdered alum while under the vinegar. Let them so remain twelve or twenty-four hours, then pour off the vinegar from the pickles into a large kettle and put to boil. Season while boiling, to five gallons of vinegar, one teacupful of allspice, one-fourth pound of ginger root, two ounces of cloves, one-half teacupful of black pepper, two tablespoonfuls of cayenne pepper. If you do not like pickles very hot, use one-half the quantity of peppers. When it boils with the seasonings twenty minutes, pour the boiling vinegar over the pickles. Make enough vinegar from these directions to cover well your pickles. They will keep a long time if under vinegar. Sprinkle over a five-gallon keg, when you put the vinegar on the pickles, two or three ounces of powdered alum, if you like pickles brittle.

Brandy Peaches

Always have the cling peach, free from decay. Peel the peaches and put down in a jar; one layer of peaches about four peaches deep, covering thickly with granulated sugar; then another layer of peaches covered with sugar, and continue in this manner until you get all the peaches in the jar you wish to brandy. Let them remain under sugar twenty-four hours; then take the same juice that comes from the peaches while under sugar, boil it and pour over the peaches boiling hot. Let them remain in this boiling syrup until it cools. Take this same syrup and put on to boil, adding more sugar so as to make it thick. When it is thoroughly cooked or all sugar is dissolved, put up the peaches in glass jars, and to one teacupful of syrup add one teacupful of brandy and pour over the peaches, continuing the same proportions of syrup and brandy until the peaches are completely covered with the mixture. Cork the jars and put in closet. You need not seal the jars unless you wish.

Brandy Peaches No. 2

Have the cling peach, free from decay. Peel as in preceding recipe. Weigh the peaches after peeling, or measure them in a gallon measure, so as to allow one pound of sugar to one gallon of peaches in making the syrup. Then put the sugar on the fire to make the syrup, adding enough clear water to keep the sugar from burning while melting. Let the syrup boil until it gets as thick as honey. Put your peeled peaches in a stone jar—one that is airtight. Set the jar, with the peaches in it, in a kettle on the fire and fill the kettle (not the jar) with cold water. Then take one teacupful of syrup to one teacupful of brandy and pour it on the peaches until they are covered thoroughly with the brandy and syrup. Let the water in the kettle around the jar of peaches boil for three hours, and no longer. Close the jar up tight, so as to keep the heat in it while boiling. After three hours of actual boiling, lift the kettle with jar in it from the fire, and set aside to cool where a draught of air will not strike it. When thoroughly cool, pack the peaches in glass jars, and fill with brandy and syrup as directed where peaches are boiled. If not enough, use equal proportions of brandy and syrup till the peaches are covered. These brandy peaches are great appetizers, especially for invalids.

Quince Preserves

Never use decayed fruit. Put quinces in a kettle of boiling water on the fire, well covered with water, and let boil until they are soft enough to stick a fork into them easily. Then take them off the fire and peel them, cutting them into four pieces and taking all the core out nicely. Put a layer of sugar, then a layer of quinces about six inches deep, then cover thickly with sugar. You must have an equal quantity of sugar and quinces, say pound to pound. Let them remain in sugar a day and night, then put the sugar the quinces were in on to boil, and when it comes to a boil, put the quinces into the syrup. Let them remain in boiling syrup on the fire ten minutes, then take them out and put others in the same syrup, to remain boiling ten minutes. Then put the others back into the syrup again some length of time, and keep repeating the change in this manner for the whole day, as quinces take a whole day to preserve. When they get the color of gold coin they are preserved. Then put them in jars when cold, and put the same syrup on them. If there is not enough syrup to cover them fully, make more syrup. Use granulated sugar with all preserves, and a porcelain kettle for all preserves and pickles.

Syrups for Preserves

To ten pounds of sugar add three pints of clear water, hot or cold. When it commences to boil skim the froth from it with a spoon, and let it boil until the froth ceases to collect, then the syrup is made.

Preserved Peaches

Have cling peaches, peel them, cut them in half and take the kernels out. Put peaches in sugar, a layer of peaches, then a layer of sugar. Weigh peaches and sugar equally. Each layer of peaches should be about six inches deep; then cover with sugar. Keep repeating sugar and peaches in this manner until you get them all under sugar. Let them remain so one day and night. Next day take sugar and juice from the peaches and put on to boil, and when it comes to a boil, put the peaches in the syrup and let them boil ten minutes. Then take them out and put others in, and when the first lot gets cold put them back into syrup again, and keep repeating in this manner, letting them boil for ten minutes at a time, until preserved. When the peaches look the color of gold coin they are preserved. When they are cold put them in jars, cover with syrup, seal or cork, and set away in a dark closet. Use the syrup they were preserved in; if you have not enough, make more. In preserving any kind of fruit, while cooking always keep the froth well skimmed off top of syrup, and don't neglect it.

Pear Preserves

Are to be prepared the same way that peaches are prepared, except in case you want to preserve them whole, then do not cut them into pieces, but only peel them and lay them under sugar in the same manner as the peaches are done, also take one-quarter pound of white ginger root to ten pounds of pears, crack or bruise it, and sprinkle it over each layer of pears, under the sugar; let them remain a day and night, and take the juice and sugar from the pears next day and put to boil for the syrup with the ginger in it; let them boil for ten minutes at a time, and repeat till done; skim the froth off the top of the syrup whenever it appears. When the pears are cold put in jars or bottles and place in a dark closet; they are preserved when they get to the color of gold coin. If you cannot bruise the ginger root slice it in pieces with a knife and put on pears as directed.

Currant Jelly

Be sure and have fresh currants that are not running the juice off. Put the currants in a cloth or bag and squeeze the juice thoroughly from the fruit, then strain the juice through a thin cloth. Measure the juice of the currants; then measure an equal quantity of sugar and place the sugar in a baking pan and put on the stove to heat through thoroughly—it must neither brown nor burn—then put the currant juice and sugar on in a porcelain kettle to boil; it must boil slowly, and whenever the froth or foam gathers on the top of the jelly, skim it all off, so as to let the jelly boil clear. Let the currant juice commence boiling before you put the sugar in, then boil both together for thirty minutes; then dip up some of the jelly and pour it in a saucer and seat in the air. if it congeals in five minutes it is made, if not, let it cook on, and about every ten minutes try it again as before, until it congeals. Have boiling water, and as soon as your jelly is cooked dip your glasses in the boiling water and then turn them upside down long enough for the water to drain out of them. Pour the jelly into the glasses while they are hot, and then seat them in the air to cool with the jelly in them. To paper them after they get cold, have good brandy; cut some thin paper for the inside of the glass and wet it in the brandy, then lay it on the jelly inside of the glass; after covering them put away in a dark place. Use granulated sugar.

Cranberry Jelly

Follow the same directions as given in [recipe for] currant jelly. Use granulated sugar.

Strawberry Jam

Must have fresh berries that are not running. Squeeze the juice from the berries through a clean linen cloth; then add one-half pint of sugar to every pint of juice and put on to boil in a porcelain kettle, and when it boils as thick as honey add the berries that you squeezed the juice from to the syrup and let it continue to boil until it gets as thick as mush, when it will be cooked enough. You can put it up in glasses or jars; put paper on the top wet with brandy, and then cover and put in a dark place. Use granulated sugar.

Raspberry and Currant Jam Combined

Take an equal quantity of both kinds of fruit and squeeze the juice from them; measure the juice and put one pint of it to one-half pint of sugar; then put on to boil, letting it boil till thick as honey; then add the berries and currants that you squeezed the juice from, and let all boil together till thick as mush, when it will be cooked. Put up in bowls, jars or glasses, covering inside with paper wet in brandy, and then put away in a dark place. Use granulated sugar.

Marmalade Peach

Peel the peaches and take the seeds away. Use the freestone peach, taking one-half pound of sugar to one pound of peaches. Sprinkle the sugar thickly over the peaches and let them lay in the sugar one night; next morning mash the peaches and sugar thoroughly, and put to cook, and let it cook slowly. Do not put any water to it. It requires five hours cooking. Use porcelain kettle and keep from burning. Use granulated sugar. Can be put up in glasses, jars or bowls.

Crab Apple Jelly

Put the apples to boil; one quart of water to one quart of apples and let them boil till soft; then mash the apples and put the apples and the water they were boiled in[20] a linen rag, and let all the juice drip into a vessel; measure the juice and take one quart of the dripped juice to one quart of sugar, and put on to boil for jelly. Boil thirty minutes and then dip some into a saucer and set in the air to cool; if it is congealed when cool, it is done. Put up in glasses, first dipping the glasses into boiling hot water and letting them drain; put the jelly into the glasses hot, and then set to cool. Paper the same way you do currant jelly, and put away in a dark place. Use a porcelain kettle and granulated sugar.

Blackberry Brandy

To five gallons of berries add one gallon of the best brandy; put on fire in a porcelain kettle and let it just come to a boil, then take it off the fire and make a syrup of granulated sugar; ten pounds of sugar to one quart of water. Let the syrup cook till thick as honey, skimming off the foam while boiling; then pour it upon the brandy and berries and let it stand eight weeks; then put in bottle or demijohn. This blackberry brandy took a diploma at the State Fair of 1879. Let the berries, brandy and syrup stand in a stone jar or brandy keg for eight weeks when you take it off the fire.

Blackberry Syrup—for Dysentery in Children

Take one quart of berries and mash up fine in a bowl squeezing all the juice from them, then strain the juice through a thin muslin cloth. To this juice add one pound of crushed sugar and put to boil in a porcelain saucepan, adding one ounce of whole clove and one-half ounce of cinnamon, tying the cinnamon up in a clean cloth; let the cloves remain in the syrup ever after is cooked.[21] It will take two hours steady boiling to cook. Put into bottles when cool. Dose for an infant of six months, a teaspoonful three times a day till bowels are checked. For a grown person one-half wine glass three times a day. This recipe is an old Southern plantation remedy among colored people.

Preserved Apricots

Weigh an equal quantity of sugar and apricots, or if you are going to preserve fifty pounds of apricots weigh fifty pounds of sugar, take the sugar and put it in a porcelain kettle the day before you buy the apricots, put two gallons of water at bottom of sugar in kettle, let it boil until thick as honey, seat off fire; next day you get the apricots, put the syrup again on the fire and have it boiling before you drop the apricots in; take the apricots out of boiling syrup every five minutes and put others in boiling syrup to remain boiling five minutes and take out before those last in; repeat the shifting of the apricots

every five minutes for five hours when they will be preserved. If you want to preserve a less quantity you can do so; the only instructions needed is, to one pound of apricots one pound of sugar; make syrup the day before getting the apricots and set aside, the next day boil it and put apricots in while boiling. For making syrup, to one pound of sugar half pint of water.

PLATE I.

At the center of this beautiful painting are a nectarine, a plum, and an apricot. On the bottom are withered fruits, showing what happened when fruits were infested by curculio, a kind of weevil plaguing American fruit growers in the mid-nineteenth century. Colored plate in Trimble, *Treatise on Insect Enemies*, frontispiece.

Apple Sauce for Roast Pork

One dozen apples cut very thin, put them in half pint of boiling water, in a nice white saucepan, add a little sugar according to taste.

Charlotte Russe

One pint of sweet cream to four eggs; three tablespoonfuls of sugar; Beat first the whites of the eggs to a light froth; then beat the cream to a light froth; then beat the sugar in the eggs; then beat two additional tablespoonfuls of sugar in the cream, light; then add the cream and eggs together; flavor with one and a half teaspoonful of best vanilla, and stir well; then lay your cakes, lady fingers, in the mould, well at the bottom and close together around the sides; then pour in the russe on the cake and set in the ice box[;] it is made. See that mould is in perfect order. To be served on table with teaspoons on small saucers.

Use granulated sugar in all sweets.

Ice Cream

One quart of sweet cream and the whites of six eggs beaten to a light froth; then beat in the eggs half teacup of sugar. Beat the cream light, and add one teacupful of sugar to cream and beat again until light, flavor with one and a half tablespoonful of vanilla, and put the whole in freezer. Put at the bottom of freezer pail a layer of ice, cover with salt, set freezer in on it and fill in around freezer with ice and salt; a layer of ice and layer of salt until full to the top of freezer; let no salt get inside of freezer. Ten minutes will freeze it.

Orange Sherbet

Squeeze the juice from two dozen oranges, add to this one and a quarter pound of fine sugar; stir well and freeze the same way as in ice cream.

Lemon Sherbet

Squeeze the juice from one dozen lemons; add two quarts of water and one and a half pounds of lump sugar; let sugar dissolve and stir well, and freeze the same way as in ice cream.

Pine Apple Sherbet

Cut in slices two pine apples, early in the morning, and lay them in one and one-half pounds of fine sugar for three hours. Squeeze all the juice from the apple and put to freeze like ice cream.

Snow Pudding

One whole box of Cox's gelatine to a pint of cold water and let it remain one hour; then pour a quart of boiling water on it. Beat the whites of ten eggs to a light froth, and add one and one-half teacupfuls of granulated sugar. When the gelatine gets cold add one-half teacupful of sugar and the juice of one lemon. Beat gelatine into the eggs light. Beat the yelks of ten eggs into one teacupful of sugar; boil one pint of rich milk and pour it boiling on the beaten eggs, stirring well. After this custard cools, add one glass of sherry wine, and set aside for dessert, to be eaten with sponge cake. Flavor the gelatine with the juice of one lemon.

Plum Pudding

Brown one pound of flour in the stove and sift it three times; add two pounds of stale light bread grated. After cutting the crust (which is not to be used), add one quart of dark molasses to one pint of brown sugar, two grated nutmegs, one tablespoonful of allspice, one tablespoonful of ground cloves, two pounds of citron sliced one-half inch thick, two pounds of currants, two pounds of chopped seeded raisins, one tablespoonful of salt, one and one-half tablespoonfuls of yeast powder, two pounds of beef kidney suet, chopped fine, and taking all strings out of suet. Add all together and stir until thoroughly mixed. Have a bag made in the shape of a sugar-loaf and wet it in cold water, sprinkling on the inside thickly with flour. Put the pudding in the bag and let it boil for seven hours, tie the bag securely.

Sauce for this plum pudding: One pint of white sugar to two tablespoonfuls of butter and one claret glass of good brandy, and put to boil till thick as honey, and serve with pudding, hot.

Boiled Turkey

See that the turkey is well cleaned. If you like high seasoning, one teaspoonful of cayenne pepper on the inside and one tablespoonful of salt on the outside. Season with two teaspoonfuls of black pepper. If you do not like high seasoning, one-half the quantity of salt and pepper will do. Let it lay in this salt and pepper one hour before boiling, then have enough raw ham and veal to thoroughly stuff the turkey in the craw and body. Chop the veal and ham fine together before stuffing the turkey. Season with one-half teaspoonful of salt and one-half teaspoonful of cayenne pepper, then add one dozen oysters to stuffing, sprinkling a teaspoonful of dry mustard and half a teacupful of browned crackers, powdered. Work it well with a spoon, stuff the turkey (craw and body) full and tight; Then put the turkey in a bag and tie it very tight, and put on in boiling water sufficient to cover it. Let a young turkey boil an hour and five minutes, and an old turkey two hours. Put one tablespoonful of salt in the water.

For this turkey make a rich drawn butter gravy as follows: Two tablespoonfuls of butter and one and one-half tablespoonfuls of flour. Rub the flour and butter together until well mixed, sprinkling half a teaspoonful of mustard into it. To this add one pint of boiling milk and stir till it is as thick as honey. Put in half a teaspoonful of salt and send gravy to table with the turkey.

Beef a la Mode

Take a ten-pound round of beef (have the butcher lard it), and tie it tight with a strong-cord. Rub into the beef one and one-half tablespoonfuls of salt, one teaspoonful each of cayenne and black pepper. Have a pot of sufficient size and put the beef into it. Then slice thin four large carrots and two white turnips and lay them around the beef. Put in the pot about four sprigs of parsley, half a pint of good claret, and one small onion, sliced. Let it cook slowly five or six hours and send to table.

Spiced Round

A twenty pound round of beef. Rub into this beef, one tea-cup of salt, two tablespoonfuls of cayenne and one of black peppers, quarter pound each of ground all- spice and cloves rubbed into beef; then lay the round of beef into a vessel that will fit it and pour two quarts of vinegar on it and let it lay in vinegar one week, turning it over once every day, keeping it covered tight, so as to keep the flavor in it; after one week put it in a kettle to cook. First, tie it up tight in a clean cloth; put all the juice that lay around the beef in to cook with it, adding two quarts of water, and let it boil four hours and a quarter. Let it be cold when it is taken out of the cloth. Slice thin when it is served, as it is excellent for luncheons, parties, etc. The most delicious appertizer[22] among meats.

Stuffed Ham

First boil the ham; then take the skin from it while boiling, put one tea-cup of vinegar to it; then take half pound of cooked veal, one tea-cup of powdered cracker; chop veal fine, mix both together, salt and pepper to taste; then make gashes about one-inch apart in the ham; stuff with veal and cracker, and put to bake; then pour one pint of sherry wine over ham and baste the ham while baking, until brown; while ham is baking grate one nutmeg over it, and sprinkle cracker powder over it.

Baked Fish

See that fish is well cleaned; then salt and pepper it inside and out, two or three hours before stuffing it or baking. For the stuffing, grate stale bread enough to fill the fish, then put it on fire in a skillet, and add one tablespoonful of butter and one of lard, chop fine one slice of onion and four sprigs of parsley; season with pepper and salt; let the stuffing stay five or ten minutes, stirring[23] it to keep from burning; then stuff the fish, until it is perfectly full. Sow[24] it up with a needle and thread and put it to bake in a medium hot stove; pour about half a tea-cup of water in bottom of pan when you put fish on; while fish is baking, baste or spread a little butter on top of fish until it browns, when it will be ready for table.

Boiled Fish

See that fish is well cleaned. Season inside and out with pepper and salt one or two hours before putting to boil, then have your boiler with one quart of luke-warm water to receive the fish, and let it remain on a quick fire twenty minutes; if it is a very large fish it will take thirty minutes to cook.

Sauce for Boiled Fish or Boiled Mutton

One and a half tablespoonfuls of flour, and one of butter rubbed together until creamed; boil one gill of sweet milk, then add it gradually to this creamed butter and flour, and stir it as you add it, until it is thoroughly mixed; season with pepper and salt to taste. Boil four eggs hard and slice them in four pieces, lengthways, and put the eggs around the dish when you take up the fish to send to table, and also garnish the dish with parsley.

Jumberlie—a Creole Dish[25]

Take one chicken and cut it up, separating every joint, and adding to it one pint of cleanly-washed rice. Take about half a dozen large tomatoes, scalding them well and taking the skins off with a knife. Cut them in small pieces and put them with the chicken in a pot or large porcelain saucepan. Then cut in small pieces two large pieces of sweet ham and add to the rest, seasoning high with pepper and salt. It will cook in twenty-five minutes. Do not put any water on it.

Chicken Salad

Take all the meat from the bones of a boiled chicken and chop it fine in a tray. Save out some of the breast meat so as to lay over the top of the salad when it is made. Chop fine half a bunch of white celery and add to chicken. Season the chicken with pepper and salt, using cayenne pepper to taste. Skim the oil from the boiling chicken to pour over the salad. Milanese sauce for chicken salad: Beat the yelks of three eggs a little, then add one pint of best sweet oil, beating a little sweet oil at a time into the eggs, so as to have it light, until the whole pint is added. Mix a teaspoonful of mustard thoroughly in strong vinegar and put in sauce with cayenne and black pepper to suit the taste. When you put the salad on the platter, pour this sauce all over it and set it in an ice box.

Veal Salad

Make veal salad and sauce in the same manner as chicken salad and sauce.

Lamb Salad

Lamb salad is also made in the same manner as chicken salad.

Shrimp Salad

Make in the same manner as above, slicing celery and adding to it.

Crab Salad

This is also made with the addition of celery sliced into it in very thin pieces, instead of chopping celery.

Meat Salads

For any meat salads you desire to make, follow the same directions given for chicken salad.

Terrapin Stew

Always have the female terrapins, and put them alive in boiling water. Let them remain for fifteen minutes and then take the shells from them, being careful not to break the galls. Clean the entrails from the meat, and scrape the black skin from the feet with a knife. Half a dozen terrapins will serve twelve persons. After thoroughly cleaning the terrapins, lay them in clear water for ten minutes, and then put them in a kettle to stew with half a pint of water, and stew very slowly for about three hours. Boil half a dozen eggs hard, and rub the yelks to a powder. Then add half a pound of best butter to the eggs and beat together until it becomes a cream. To this cream add one pint of sherry wine and mix it well. Then add this preparation to the stew very gradually, stirring well, so as to thoroughly mix it in. While the stew is cooking, mix a teaspoonful of best mustard to a tablespoonful of wine and put in. Slice one lemon and add to stew just before dishing it up for table. Three hours is sufficient time to cook it. You had better put the wine in the stew and not mix it with the eggs, for fear you may not mix it in right and that there may be no mistake. With the above directions you have a perfect stew.[26] A teacupful of sweet cream is an improvement, if you like it: also a dozen grains of allspice. Salt and pepper to taste.

Fish Chowder

Cut up one pound of salt pork in pieces one and two inches in size for a large fish, of about six pounds. Cut the fish in pieces the same as the pork; slice in pieces half dozen Irish potatoes the size of fish. Beat one sea cracker fine, take and slice one large onion, chop it fine;[27] fry the pork brown, take it from the fat. Having all now prepared, put your pot on fire, and put in pot a layer of fish, then a layer of pork, then a layer of cracker, then put in one tablespoonful of butter, cayenne pepper, and salt to taste; add one pint of water, and let it stew one hour, when it will be ready for table use.

Clam Chowder

Prepare and make clam chowder in the same way as the fish chowder, except you must use tomatoes; a layer of tomatoes and a layer of the other articles, for fifty to one hundred clams. Put in one pint of sweet milk; before putting clams in pot cut away the black part of clams, add half a teaspoonful of ground cloves, and one teaspoonful of ground allspice, salt and pepper to taste; one dozen tomatoes scalded in boiling water, and skin them.

Creole Soup

Take three pints of this same bouillon, put on to boil, just before use chop four leaves of parsley fine, and put in. Brown a teaspoonful of brown sugar on a tin plate, add a sherry wine-glass of sherry wine to sugar, stir it well, then strain through a fine sieve; then stir three tablespoonfulls into soup. Beat two yelks of eggs into tureen and pour hot soup on it and send to table.

Spiced Currants

Five pounds fresh currants to three pounds of sugar, one pint of vinegar; wash currants and drain all water from them through sieve or cullender, add sugar and vinegar to currants, and put to cook in a porcelain kettle; season with one ounce ground cloves and one ounce of stick cinnamon, let it cook gradually until it becomes like a jelly; when it gets cold, put away in bottles and cork tight. Use granulated sugar.

Spiced Cherries

Five pounds of cherries to three quarter pounds of sugar, one pint of best vinegar, quarter pound of cloves, quarter pound of allspice. Put sugar, spices and vinegar, all together on fire and boil it, then pour it boiling on the cherries. Before boiling vinegar, spices, and sugar, let cherries lay in spiced vinegar and sugar twenty-four hours, then boil and pour on cherries, and when they get perfectly cold, put up in bottles and cork well.

Preserved Peaches

Always preserve the cling peach and none other. Cut your peaches in two or four pieces just as you like, and have one pound of granulated sugar to one pound of peaches; that is to say, if you are going to preserve ten pounds of peaches have ten pounds of sugar, and put the sugar on peaches the day before preserving; then next day pour juice off peaches and put juice on to boil, when it boils, put the peaches in this boiling juice, let them stay five minutes, take them out and lay them on a dish for five minutes, then put them back in the boiling syrup again for five minutes, and repeat or continue taking them out and putting them back every five minutes, for one hour, when they will be preserved.

Preserved Cherries

Seed your cherries and put sugar on them the day before preserving. When you pour off the juice next day and put it to boil, when it boils put cherries in, let them stay five minutes, take them out, put them back in boiling syrup in five minutes, and so continue every five minutes for one hour, when they will be preserved. When preserves are cold put away.

Corn Fritters

To one dozen ears of corn add three eggs, half a teacupful of powdered crackers, one tablespoonful of sifted flour. Cut off the corn very lightly from the cob say half of the grain and then scrape the other half clean off with a knife. Add the crackers to corn and beat together light. Beat the eggs light and add with the flour and a quarter of a teacupful of sweet milk. Season to taste and beat the whole light. Have your lard or butter hot when you go to fry, and drip the batter into the hot fat from off the end of a spoon, letting it fry quick and brown. Have young and tender corn. The fat ought to be hot enough to brown the fritters in two minutes.

Corn Pudding

Take one dozen ears of corn and grate from the cob. Beat four eggs light and add a pint of sweet milk and a tablespoonful of butter, salting and peppering to taste. Beat lightly, place in a deep dish and bake in a hot oven. Ten minutes will bake it. Grease the dish with butter before putting pudding into it, and send to table in the dish it is baked in.

Carving Poultry

In carving always have a sharp knife. First pass the knife close to the body of the fowl, just under the joint of the wing. Then press it back towards the neck with the back of the knife, when it will separate from the body. Take the same course with the leg, and when you have the wings and legs unjointed, turn the fowl on its back and slice meat from the breast and sides, thinly.

Boiled Corn

Always put the corn on in boiling water and salt, cooking for seven minutes; a longer cooking than this will take all the sweetness from the corn.

Apple Roll

To one quart of flour add a tablespoonful each of butter and lard (or two of butter, if preferred,) and one teaspoonful of fine salt. Work the lard or butter into the flour dry until it is thoroughly mixed, then add salt and a teacupful of water, a little at a time, and mix until the dough is sufficiently thick to roll on the pastry block. Always sprinkle dry flour on the block to keep the dough from sticking. Use one and one-half pounds of mellow apples, peeled and cut very thin. Roll your dough out as thin as pie crust, eighteen by ten inches in size. Have three pieces of this size, and lay one sheet of it down and cover it with apples; then lay the second and third sheets down, covering each with apples. Roll the whole up together as you would a towel, then wet a white cloth in cold water and wrap it around the roll, sewing it tightly; then put into a pot of boiling water. Sprinkle dry sugar over each layer of apples before rolling in the cloth. Do not cook over twenty minutes. Put in water enough to cover the roll.

Sauce for [Apple] Roll

Two tablespoonfuls of butter and one and one-half teacupfuls of powdered sugar rubbed together until as light as cream, one-half of a grated nutmeg, one wine-glassful of brandy beaten into the creamed butter and sugar.

Stuffed Tomatoes

Cut off the tops of tomatoes, hollow the inside, and mix the inside that you take out with chopped up ham; bread crumbs or crackers powdered, butter, salt and pepper to your taste. Stuff the tomatoes full and replace the top close. Put them in a pan to bake in a hot oven for fifteen minutes.

Blackberry Roll

Make this roll by the same directions given for the apple roll.

Egg Plant Stuffed

Take out the inside of the plant and boil it in just enough water to cover it for ten minutes, and then drain or press the water all out through a cullender. Chop some ham fine, take bread crumbs and butter (one tablespoonful to one egg plant), and have equal proportions of ham, cracker and bread crumbs to the inside of the plants. Season with salt and black pepper to taste and fry it brown. Then stuff the plants full and close and put them to bake. They will bake in ten minutes, but should not be put in the oven until just before table use. They are a delicious vegetable prepared in this manner. Use a hot oven.

Peach Cobbler

Peel the peaches (freestones) and make a pastry the same way as for pie, and roll out the dough as thin as for pie crust. Put one layer at the bottom of the dish, and cut the peaches into pieces the size of a plum and fill the dish with them, sprinkling them freely with fine sugar. Cover them over with another layer of pastry, cut with a knife two or three air-holes on the top and put to bake. Let it bake brown. It makes a delicious luncheon or dessert. Season the peaches with powdered cinnamon to taste. See recipe for all kinds of pastry.

Ladies' Custard

Boil a quart of sweet milk, and beat together half a dozen eggs with two tablespoonfuls of sugar until light. Pour the milk on the eggs and sugar, stirring well. Put a tablespoonful of sugar into a kettle that will hold the milk and eggs, and let the sugar brown. Then pour the milk and eggs into the kettle and let it come to a boil. Put your custard cups in a baking pan and fill the pan with cold water. Then fill the cups with custard and set in the stove until it becomes as thick as batter. It will need no flavoring extracts.

Batter Pudding

Five eggs; beat yelks and whites separately, very light, six tablespoonfuls of flour to one pint of milk, one teaspoonful of salt; sift flour three times, pour half of the milk to the flour and beat it light, then add the beaten yelks of eggs to flour and milk, and then add the whites also and beat again; lastly add the remaining half pint of milk and beat the whole pudding until very light. Have a good, tight, strong white bag, wet it, and put flour thickly on the inside, put pudding in it, tie it tight and put in a pot of boiling water and let it boil three quarters

of an hour. Make a sauce of sugar and butter, rub the two together until light, flavor with nutmeg, and stir a wine glass of sherry wine or brandy in it well. Use powdered sugar.[28]

Baked Batter Pudding

Use the same directions and quantities as given in the boiled pudding, and when you have it mixed as directed, and have a hot oven, pour pudding in baking pan and bake brown.

Corned Beef Hash

Take boiled corned beef and chop it very fine, four hot boiled Irish potatoes to one pound of beef, mash potatoes in the beef while hot, one slice of onion chopped with meat, half a teaspoonful of mustard mixed, two sprigs of parsley; then make into pones like a small loaf of bread, and bake brown. Season with black pepper to taste.

Tonic Bitters: A Southern Remedy for Invalids

Take one ounce of cardamom seed, one ounce of Peruvian bark bruised, two ounces of Gentian root bruised, half ounce of dry orange peel, one ounce of aloes, and put the whole into half a gallon of best whiskey or brandy; let it come to a boil, then strain or filter it through a fine cloth or filtering paper.

Dose half wineglassfull three times a day before meals. Will strengthen and produce an appetite.

Suet Pudding

One pound of beef kidney suet, chop it fine, taking all strings from it, one pound of flour rubbed into suet until thoroughly mixed, salt to taste; one and a half teaspoonful of yeast powder mixed in with the flour; mix the whole gradually with water, the same way that you mix up dough for any other[29] bread, stiff; then roll out the dough about half an inch thick, and spread the dough with currant jelly; then roll up the dough round like a bottle and as you roll continue to spread the under part of dough with jelly, so as to have all of dough covered with the jelly when it is rolled up finally, then take a clean linen towel and wrap the roll in it tight, sewing the ends and sides well; when you have finished rolling it up in the towel, put it on in boiling water, well covered, and let it boil thirty minutes.

Sauce for Suet Pudding

One tablespoonful of butter, one tea-cup of white sugar; rub both together until well mixed to a cream, then put on a kettle over steam, and as it heats stir it until a foam, then add one wine-glassful of brandy; stir until mixed, and flavor with nutmeg, and send to table hot with the pudding.

Chicken Gumbo

Salt and pepper chicken before frying it. Take a chicken, separating[30] it from all the joints and breaking the bones, fry the chicken in one and a half tablespoonful of lard or butter. First well mix the chicken in dry flour, let the fat be hot, put chicken to fry until brown; don't burn chicken. After fried, put it on in soup kettle with half a gallon of hot water, one and a half quarts of green ochra[31] cut into thin pieces, throwing the end away, and let the whole boil to three pints; season with pepper and salt. Chop half of an ordinary sized onion fine, and fry it with chicken; chilli pepper chopped fine if added is nice when liked.

Circuit Hash[32]

One dozen tomatoes, one quart of butter beans, one dozen ears of corn cut off from cob, quarter pound of lean and fat pork cut in fine pieces, if pork is not liked, use two tablespoonfuls of butter; put on in a sauce-pan and stew one hour.

Note: Five minutes before dinner put in the corn to cook with the rest of stew.

Stewed Tomatoes

First scald the tomatoes in boiling water and then peel the skin from them, then cut them up in small pieces, cutting also one slice of onion fine in them; add no water; bread crumbs, one tablespoonful of butter, pepper and salt to taste. To one dozen of tomatoes, half a tea-cupful of bread crumbs.

Rice Pudding

Two tablespoonfuls of butter and sweeten to taste, one pint of rice boiled soft; thoroughly mix to this rice one pint of rich milk. Beat up two eggs very light, and add to the above also; well mix the whole. Flavor with the grated rind or peel of the half of an orange, and the juice of two oranges; mix well into pudding, and put into pan to bake.

Meringue for Pudding

The whites of five eggs beat very light, four tablespoonfulls of sugar, mix into eggs and beat light; spread thickly over pudding and put to brown.

Leaven Biscuit

Save a piece of leaven[33] from the light bread you mix or make up over night, the size of a tea-cup; mix leaven up soft in water, add half a pint of flour to it, one teaspoonful of salt, seat to rise over night. Next morning take one level quart of flour, put a level teaspoonful of soda and sift it; rub into this flour one tablespoonful of lard, half tablespoonful of butter, until thoroughly mixed; then add the whole together, and work it with the hands until light, and make off in biscuits and put to rise in baking pan twenty minutes, then bake brown.

Oyster Pie

Make pastry according to directions [for the recipe Pastry for Making Pies of All Kinds]. Have bottom and top crust—bottom crust to be thick as a quarter dollar.[34] Then put oyster liquor or juice on in a kettle to boil, and when it boils, skim the foam from it; then drop oysters into boiling liquor for four minutes only, take out oysters, lay them on a dish, then sift two tablespoonfuls of flour, take two tablespoonfuls of butter, rub into flour until well mixed, then dissolve the same with a little

of hot liquor, salt and pepper to taste. Then pour into boiling liquor the mixture of flour and butter, stirring the same while pouring it in, till all is poured in. To be baked in a deep pan. Put bottom crust covering bottom and sides of pan, then pour liquor in on crust; when this is done, put the oysters into the pan and cover the pan over with a thick cover of pastry, the thickness of a half dollar, cutting small spaces in several parts on top, the width of a knife blade, and put to bake brown. Take the white of an egg, beat it up and baste top of pie when you put it to bake. One quart of oysters and the juice will make pie for six in family.

Yorkshire Pudding—To Be Eaten with Roast Beef

Sift one pint of flour and add to it one-half pint of milk; beat milk into flour with a large spoon until very light; then beat four eggs yelks and whites together very light, and add to flour and milk, and then beat the whole, adding one tablespoonful of butter, salt to taste. Put to bake in a dish; twenty minutes will bake it. When done send to table with roast beef, in same dish it is baked in.

Cheese Pudding

Have mild cheese; grate half pound of cheese and half pound of apples, add to this half pint of sweet milk, beat four eggs very light, and add to the above. Before mixing apples with cheese, put to it one tablespoonful of white sugar; stir all well. Season with nutmeg, and pour it into a dish and put to bake, putting one tablespoonful of butter over it in small pieces. Twenty minutes will bake it, and send to table as a vegetable.

Pap for Infant Diet

Take one pint of flour, sift it and tie it up in a clean cloth securely tight, so that no water can get into it; and put it in boiling water and let it boil steady for two hours, then take it out of water, and when it gets cold take outside crust from it. Whenever you are ready to nurse or feed the child, grate one tablespoonful of the boiled flour, and stir it into half a pint of boiled milk while the milk is boiling; sweeten the same with white sugar to taste. When the child has diarrhea, boil a two-inch stick of cinnamon in the pap. I have given birth to eleven children and raised them all, and nursed them with this diet. It is a Southern plantation preparation.

NOTES

Food in the Antebellum South and the Confederacy

1. In the years between the publication of Randolph's book and the start of the Civil War, several other regional Southern cookbooks emerged, including *The Kentucky Housewife* (Letice Brynt, 1839) and *The Carolina Housewife* (Sarah Rutledge, 1847).

2. Texts borrowing from older traditions include Amelia Simmons's *American Cookery*, published in 1796, which relied heavily on much older techniques, including her entire section on creams and syllabubs, taken in toto from Susannah Carter's 1765 *The Frugal Housewife*. These earlier texts are largely defined by ingredients and methods more associated with medieval tradition than the cooking of the Americas. Southern cookbooks and culinary historian continue to cite *The Virginia Housewife* as "the most influential American cookbook of the nineteenth century." Nineteen editions of *The Virginia Housewife* were published before the Civil War. Harvey Levenstein, *Revolution at the Table: The Transformation of the American Diet* (New York: Oxford University Press, 1988), 3–9; James McWilliams, *A Revolution in Eating: How the Quest for Food Shaped America* (New York: Columbia University Press, 2005), 229–239; Margaret Husted, "Mary Randolph's *The Virginia Housewife*: America's First Regional Cookbook," *Virginia Cavalcade* 30, no. 2 (Autumn 1980): 6, 7; Mary Randolph, *The Virginia House-wife*, facsimile edition, with

historical notes and commentary by Karen Hess (Columbia: University of South Carolina Press, 1988), ix, xvii, 228.

For more on Mary Randolph see Cynthia Kierner, "The Dark and Dense Cloud Perpetually Lowering over Us: Gender and the Decline of the Gentry in Postrevolutionary Virginia," *Journal of the Early Republic* 20, no. 2 (2000): 185–217; Sterling Anderson, "'Queen Molly' [Mary Randolph] and *The Virginia Housewife*," *Virginia Cavalcade* 20, no. 4 (1971): 29–35; Jonathan Daniels, *The Randolphs of Virginia* (New York: Doubleday, 1972).

3. Sam Hilliard, "Hog Meat and Corn Pone: Food Habits in the Antebellum South," *Proceedings of the American Philosophical Society* 113, no. 1 (1969): 8; Leland Ferguson, *Uncommon Ground: Archaeology and Early African America, 1650–1800* (Washington, DC: Smithsonian Institution Press, 2004), 94; Daniel Richter, *Facing East from Indian Country: A Native History of Early America* (Cambridge: Harvard University Press, 2003), 56–59. For more on Native foodways in pre-Columbian North America see Rayna Green, "Mother Corn and the Dixie Pig: Native Food in the Native South," in John T. Edge, Elizabeth Engelhardt, and Ted Ownby, eds., *The Larder: Food Studies Methods from American Studies* (Athens: University of Georgia Press, 2013), 156–165; Karen Ordahl Kupperman, *Indians and English: Facing Off in Early America* (Ithaca: Cornell University Press, 2000); William Cronon,

Changes in the Land: Indians, Colonists, and the Ecology of New England, 20th anniversary ed. (New York: Hill and Wang, 2003); Daniel Usner, Indians, Settlers, and Slaves in a Frontier Exchange Economy: The Lower Mississippi Valley before 1783 (Williamsburg: Omohundro, 1992); McWilliams, A Revolution in Eating, 137–155, 91–103.

4. Green, "Mother Corn," 158; William Johnson, River of Dark Dreams: Slavery and Empire in the Cotton Kingdom (Cambridge: Belknap Press of Harvard University Press, 2013), 28–31.

5. Green, "Mother Corn," 158–160.

6. Green, "Mother Corn," 158–160. Green argues that the few Indian families that remained in the region maintained their culture and foodways with varying degrees of success. Most were poor, marginalized, or slowly integrated into the larger landscape of black and white.

7. While traveling through central Mississippi in 1856, Frederick Olmsted found that bacon "invariably appeared at every meal." Fredrick Law Olmsted, A Journey in the Backcountry (New York: Mason Brothers, 1860), 161.

8. The relation between the mid-nineteenth-century planter class and the dictates of an emerging market system is a topic of debate. Eugene Genovese argued that the planter class was largely precapitalist and not market oriented. Recent work by Walter Johnson suggests that planters in the Mississippi River Valley were keenly aware of their place in larger circuits of global capital. Eugene Genovese, Roll, Jordan, Roll: The World the Slaves Made (New York: Vintage, 1976); Johnson, River of Dark Dreams.

9. Johnson, River of Dark Dreams, 178.

10. Olmsted, Journey in the Backcountry, 46–47. The historian Walter Johnson understands the Mississippi Valley as a monoculture overcommitted to a single crop. Johnson, River of Dark Dreams, 176–180.

11. On authenticity, see Allen Weiss, "Authenticity," Gastronomica 11, no. 4 (2011): 74–77; Josée Johnson and Shyon Baumann, Foodies: Democracy and Distinction in the Gourmet Foodscape (New York: Routledge, 2010), 69–96. On authenticity with specific reference to Southern food, see Andrew Warnes, "Edgeland Terroir: Authenticity and Invention in New Southern Foodways Strategy," in Edge, Engelhard, and Ownby, The Larder, 345–362.

12. Fredrick Law Olmsted, A Journey in the Seaboard Slave States; With Remarks on their Economy (New York: Dix and Edwards, 1856), 92n.

13. As the historian Sam Hilliard has noted, during the antebellum period, "Cornbread was the bread for the Deep South." Hilliard, "Hog Meat and Cornpone," 8.

14. Olmsted, Seaboard Slave States, 564.

15. Diane Spivey, The Peppers, Cracklings, and Knots of Wool Cookbook: The Global Migration of African Cuisine (Albany: SUNY Press, 2000), 268–269; S. L. Kotar and J. E. Gessler, The Steamboat Era: A History of Fulton's Folly on American Rivers, 1807–1860 (Jefferson: McFarland Press, 2009), 166.

16. Hilliard, "Hog Meat and Cornpone."

17. Levenstein, Revolution at the Table, 10, 11.

18. Hilliard, "Hog Meat and Cornpone," 1.

19. Hilliard, "Hog Meat and Cornpone," 1.

20. Hilliard, "Hog Meat and Cornpone," 2.

21. Hilliard, "Hog Meat and Cornpone,"3.

22. Hilliard, "Hog Meat and Cornpone," 3.

23. Hilliard, "Hog Meat and Cornpone," 3.

24. Quoted in W. J. Rorabaugh, The Alcoholic Republic: An American Tradition (Cambridge: Oxford University Press, 1981), 115.

25. Rorabaugh, The Alcoholic Republic, 96.

26. James Crow also invented the sour-mash process.

27. Robert F. Pace, "Abandoning Self-Sufficiency: Corn in the Lower South, 1849–1879," *Southern Studies* 4, no. 3 (Fall 1993): 277.

28. For examples of pork in white and black cooking, see Hilliard, "Hog Meat and Cornpone," *Hog Meat and Hoe Cake: Food Supply in the Old South 1840–1860* (Carbondale: Southern Illinois University Press, 1972). For use by Native peoples see Green, "Mother Corn." See also Virginia DeJohn Anderson, *Creatures of Empire: How Domestic Animals Transformed Early America* (Cambridge: Oxford University Press, 2006).

29. Robert Beverly, quoted in Karen Hess, *The Taste of America* (Columbia: University of South Carolina Press, 1977), 24.

30. Hess, *The Taste of America*, 3. See also Reay Tannahill, *Food in History* (New York: Random House, 1988), 310; Rorabaugh, *The Alcoholic Republic,* 115.

31. Hilliard, "Hog Meat and Cornpone," 2–5.

32. Olmsted, *Seaboard Slave States*, 108.

33. Peter Kolchin, *American Slavery: 1619–1877* (New York: Hill & Wang, 1993), 113.

34. In *Time on the Cross: The Economics of American Negro Slavery* (New York: Norton, 1974) Robert Fogel and Stanley Engerman claimed that the institution of slavery was economically viable and actually benefited the enslaved. A number of scholars criticized *Time on the Cross* for its selective use of data as well as its racism. Leading these critics was Herbert Gutman, whose 1975 *Slavery and the Numbers Game: A Critique of "Time on the Cross"* (Urbana-Champaign: University of Illinois Press, 2003) punched holes in a number of arguments made by Fogel and Engerman. For a more recent assessment of the role and adequacy of plantation rations see Johnson, *River of Dark Dreams,* 176–208, 463 n. 7.

35. The plantation account book for Shirley Plantation (Charles City County, Virginia) offers an excellent example of the detailed accounting of rations and clothing for the enslaved alongside other income and expenses. Account Book, Shirley Plantation Collection, 1650–1989, (Oversized Container 6), 1816–1879, DMS 1991.1, John D. Rockefeller Jr. Library, Colonial Williamsburg Foundation.

36. For more on the theory of social death see Orlando Patterson, *Slavery and Social Death: A Comparative Study* (Cambridge: Harvard University Press, 1982).

37. Fredrick Douglass, *Narrative of the Life of Fredrick Douglass, an American Slave* (New York: Penguin, 1982), 42.

38. John A. Barksdale, *Southern Planter* 16, no. 10 (October 1856): 319–320. Special Collections Research Center, Swem Library, College of William and Mary. For further discussion on planter observations on diet see Waverly Root, *Eating in America* (Hopwell: Ecco, 1995), 145; James Breeden, ed., *Advice among Masters: The Ideal in Slave Management in the Old South* (Westport, CT: Greenwood Press, 1980).

39. Ferguson, *Uncommon Ground*, 96. See also Elizabeth Engelhardt, *A Mess of Greens: Southern Gender and Southern Food* (Athens: University of Georgia Press, 2011), 119–162; Joe Taylor, *Eating, Drinking, and Visiting in the South* (Baton Rouge: Louisiana State University Press, 1982), 137–146.

40. Jessica B. Harris, "Same Boat, Different Stops: An African Atlantic Culinary Journey," in Sheila S. Walker, ed., *African Roots/American Cultures: Africa in the Creation of the Americas* (Lanham, MD: Rowman & Littlefield Publishers, 2001), 170, 175; McWilliams, *A Revolution in Eating*, 117–118; Tadeusz Lewicki, *West African Food in the Middle Ages* (London: Cambridge University Press, 1974), 20–21. See also Waverly Root, *Food: An Authoritative and Visual History and Dictionary of the Foods of the World* (New York: Simon and Schuster,

1980), 294–295; Raymond Sokolov, *Why We Eat What We Eat: How Encounters between the New World and the Old Changed the Way Everyone on the Planet Eats* (New York: Summit, 1991), 14, 21; Spivey, *Knots of Wool Cookbook*.

41. For the former thesis, see Sharla Fett, *Working Cures: Health, Healing, and Power on Southern Slave Plantations* (Chapel Hill: University of North Carolina Press, 2002), 63; and Patricia Samford, "The Archeology of African-American Slavery and Material Culture," *William and Mary Quarterly* 53, no. 1 (1996): 13. For the latter thesis, see Harris, "Same Boat," 174; and Judith Carney, *Black Rice: The African Origins of Rice Cultivation in the Americas* (Cambridge: Harvard University Press, 2002), 71–72.

42. Michael Twitty, "Gardens," in Kym Rice and Martha Katz-Hyman, eds., *World of a Slave: Encyclopedia of the Material Life of Slaves in the United States* (Santa Barbara: Greenwood), 245–250.

43. David Shields, "Prospecting for Oil," *Gastronomica* 10, no. 4 (2009): 25–31.

44. Shields, "Prospecting for Oil." Rice, far more so than benne, took root in the planter imagination—so much so that it was the central commodity crop along coastal Carolina rice plantations. See Karen Hess, *The Carolina Rice Kitchen: The African Connection* (Columbia: University of South Carolina Press, 1992); Carney, *Black Rice*. For examples of planter cookery making use of sesame oil, see, for example, Sarah Rutledge's 1847 *The Carolina Housewife*.

45. Robert Voeks and John Rachford, eds., *African Ethnobotany in the Americas* (New York: Springer, 2013), 76; Peter Wood, "Gourds," in Rice and Katz-Hyman, *World of a Slave*, 250–253.

46. Baily Cunningham, quoted in Charles Perdue and Thomas Barden, eds., *Weevils in the Wheat: Interviews with Virginia Ex-Slaves* (Charlottesville: University of Virginia Press, 1991), 81.

47. Douglas W. Sanford, "The Archaeology of Plantation Slavery at Thomas Jefferson's Monticello: Context and Process in an American Slavery Society," Ph.D. diss., University of Virginia, 1995, 95–96. See also Diane Crader, "Slave Diet at Monticello," *American Antiquity* 55, no. 4 (1990): 690–717.

48. Tanya Peres, "Foodways, Economic Status, and the Antebellum Upland South in Central Kentucky," *Historical Archeology* 42, no. 4 (2008): 88–104.

49. Psyche Williams-Forson, *Building Houses out of Chicken Legs: Black Women, Food, and Power* (Chapel Hill: University of North Carolina Press, 2006), 13–37, 232 n. 27; Usner, *Indians, Settlers, and Slaves*, 202. On the popularity of chicken in the ante- and postbellum South see Williams-Forson, *Building Houses*, 1–113. For more on black food vendors see Jessica Harris, "'I'm Talkin' 'Bout the Food I Sells,'" in Edge, Engelhardt, and Ownby, *The Larder*, 333–341.

50. Elizabeth Fox-Genovese, *Within the Plantation Household: Black and White Women of the Old South* (Chapel Hill: University of North Carolina Press, 1988), 160.

51. Fox-Genovese, *Within the Plantation Household*, 98.

52. Michael Olmert, *Kitchens, Smokehouses, and Privies: Outbuildings and the Architectures of Daily Life in the Eighteenth-Century Mid-Atlantic* (Ithaca: Cornell University Press, 2009), 5.

53. Drew Faust, *Mothers of Invention: Women of the Slaveholding South in the American Civil War* (Chapel Hill: University of North Carolina Press, 2004), 5; Fox-Genovese, *Within the Plantation Household*, 98, 364. On power and the dynamics between white and black women see Fox-Genovese, *Within the Plantation Household*, 97–119, 160–161; Genovese, *Roll, Jordan, Roll*, 540–549.

54. Mary Titus, "'Groaning Tables' and 'Spit in the Kettles'":

Food and Race in the Nineteenth-Century South," *Southern Quarterly* 2, no. 3 (1992): 14.

55. Dell Upton, "White and Black Landscapes in Eighteenth-Century Virginia," in Robert Blair St. George, ed., *Material Life in America, 1600–1860* (Boston: Northeastern University Press, 1988), 130.

56. Olmsted, *Seaboard Slave States*, 80.

57. Drew Faust points out that "elite southerners' fundamental sense of identity depended on having others to perform life's menial tasks." Faust, *Mothers of Invention*, 77.

58. Douglass, *Narrative*, 110–111.

59. Harriet Jacobs, *Incidents in the Life of a Slave Girl* (New York: Dover Thrift, 1993), 8.

60. Catherine Clinton, *The Plantation Mistress: Women's World in the Old South* (Chapel Hill: University of North Carolina Press, 1982), 19.

61. Carole Gilman, *The Lady's Annual Register, and Housewife's Memorandum-book of 1838* (Boston: T.H. Carter, 1837), 28

62. Henry Wise, quoted in William Taylor, *Cavalier and Yankee: The Old South and American National Character* (Cambridge: Harvard University Press, 1979), 331; (Taylor misidentifies Henry Wise as "John Wise"); on impressments see Pace, "Abandoning," 271. On poor whites serving in the Confederate army, see Taylor, *Eating, Drinking*, 94; Edward Ayers, *Vengeance and Justice: Crime and Punishment in the 19th-Century American South* (New York: Oxford University Press, 1984), 163.

63. Clarence Mohr, *On the Threshold of Freedom: Masters and Slaves in Civil War Georgia* (Baton Rouge: Louisiana State University Press, 2001), 117–118, 210; Butler quoted in John Blessingame, *Black New Orleans: 1860–1880* (Chicago: University of Chicago Press, 1976), 50.

64. Quoted in William Davis, *A Taste for War: The Culinary History of the Blue and the Gray* (Mechanicsburg: Stackpole Books, 2003), 23, 24.

65. Stephan Ash, *When the Yankees Came: Conflict and Chaos in the Occupied South, 1861–1865* (Chapel Hill: University of North Carolina Press, 1999), 54. See also Charles Royster, *Destructive War: William Tecumseh Sherman, Stonewall Jackson, and the Americans* (New York: Vintage, 1993); John Hennessy, *Return to Bull Run: The Campaign and Battle of Second Manassas* (Tulsa: University of Oklahoma Press, 1999), 14–21; Daniel Sutherland, "Abraham Lincoln, John Pope and the Origins of Total War," *Journal of Military History* 56 (1992): 567–586.

66. Sigismunda Stribling Kimball, Diary, February 2, 1863, Mss 2534, Special Collections, University of Virginia Library, Charlottesville, Va (UVA).

67. Fannie Page Hume, Diary, July 7, 1862, Mss 1713-h, UVA.

68. Louisa H. A. Minor, Diary December 21–27, 1862, Accession 10685, UVA

69. The Emancipation Proclamation did not apply to every enslaved person, only those living within the territory controlled by the Confederacy. It excluded slave states in the Union, and Confederate areas controlled by the Union. See Eric Foner, *The Fiery Trial: Abraham Lincoln and American Slavery* (New York: Norton, 2010), 240–251.

70. Labor was no longer dependable, cooks moved elsewhere, and mistresses found they could not pay for a large staff. Laundry and ironing were also among the chores elite whites most feared having to do themselves. See Jane Censer, *The Reconstruction of White Southern Womanhood, 1865–1895* (Baton Rouge: Louisiana State University Press, 2003), 78.

71. Minnie Folkes, quoted in Perdue and Barden, *Weevils in the Wheat*, 94.

72. Sigismunda Stribling Kimball, Diary, February 24, 1863, UVA.

73. W. E. B. Du Bois saw the postwar period as a "three-cornered" battle between rich landowners, poor whites, and freed black Americans. Du Bois argues that this dynamic helped to enrich the gentry and obscure class solidarity between poor black and white with the "shibboleth of race." See W. E. B. Du Bois, *Black Reconstruction in America, 1860–1880* (New York: Free Press, 1998), 670–710.

74. Psyche Williams-Forson uses the term "gender malpractice" to refer to the erasure of black culinary influence from the larger narrative of white Southern food. See Williams-Forson, *Building Houses*, 166–169. Williams-Forson builds her approach from philosopher Tommy Lott's concept of cultural malpractice. See Tommy Lott, *The Invention of Race: Black Culture and the Politics of Representation* (Malden, MA: Blackwell, 1999), 84–110.

Seeing the Civil War South through Its Recipes

1. Andrew F. Smith, *Starving the South: How the North Won the Civil War* (New York: St. Martin's Press, 2011), 6.

2. Smith, *Starving the South*, 6–7.

3. *Southern Cultivator*, March and April 1862, vol. 20, nos. 3 and 4, 77.

4. Smith, *Starving the South*, 24.

5. Joan E. Cashin, "Hungry People in the Wartime South," in *Weirding the War: Stories from the Civil War's Ragged Edges* (Athens: University of Georgia Press, 2011), 162.

6. Cashin, "Hungry People," 162.

7. Cashin, "Hungry People," 165.

8. Bell Irvin Wiley, *The Life of Johnny Reb: The Common Soldier of the Confederacy* (Indianapolis: Bobbs-Merrill, 1943), 90.

9. Cashin, "Hungry People," 162.

10. Wiley, *Life of Johnny Reb*, 91; Davis, *A Taste for War*, 58.

11. As Bell Wiley argues, "food was undoubtedly the first concern" for Confederate soldiers. Wiley, *Life of Johnny Reb*, 90.

12. Wiley, *Life of Johnny Reb*, 102; Davis, *A Taste for War*, 53.

13. Cashin, "Hungry People," 163–164. As Cashin explains, "Freelance forages tried to avoid civilians, but when that was not possible, interactions with white Southerners could be complicated. Soldiers in both armies asked for and received provender from friendly civilians, bartered for food with civilians, or paid them for food. When civilians were unfriendly, both federal soldiers and Confederate troops simply took their food. They hijacked food from civilians they met by chance on the road, and they entered private homes to seize food from residents. They harvested crops directly from the fields, broke into meat-houses, grazed their horses in the fields, milked cows in the fields, slaughtered hogs they found in pens, wrung the heads off chickens, and drank buttermilk from a churn on a woman's front porch. . . . Union troops sometimes deliberately took food from whites who were defiantly pro-Confederate, while Confederates did the same with Southern Unionists. But hunger trumped ideology, just as it trumped regulations." Cashin, "Hungry People," 164.

14. Davis, *A Taste for War*, 52.

15. Ibid., 55.

16. Ibid., 103.

17. Ibid., 95–98.

18. Ibid., 105.

19. Ibid., 93.

20. Adjutant S. H. M. Byers, *What I Saw in Dixie: or, Sixteen Months in Rebel Prisons* (Dansville, NY: Robbins & Poore, Printers, 1868), 22–23, Michigan State University Special Collections.

21. Cashin, "Hungry People," 162.

22. Smith, *Starving the South*, 192.

23. As the historian Joan Cashin writes, "Although their numbers seem to have been small, starving people—not just hungry people—did appear in the Confederacy during the war." Cashin, "Hungry People," 168.

24. *Southern Watchman*, May 18, 1864, 2.

25. Cashin adds that the "consumption of taboo foods undoubtedly happened more often than the documents reveal because many people were unwilling to admit that they had eaten things deemed to be revolting." Cashin, "Hungry People," 167.

26. *Southern Watchman*, October 28, 1863, 3.

27. Faust, *Mothers of Invention*, 245; Cashin, "Hungry People," 166.

28. Cashin, "Hungry People," 166.

29. See James McPherson, *For Cause and Comrades: Why Men Fought in the Civil War* (Oxford: Oxford University Press, 1997), 137–40.

30. Jim Downs, *Sick from Freedom: African-American Illness and Suffering during the Civil War and Reconstruction* (Oxford: Oxford University Press, 2012).

31. See Jonathan Rees, *Refrigeration Nation: A History of Ice, Appliances, and Enterprise in America* (Baltimore: Johns Hopkins University Press, 2013).

32. Diary of Maria Massey Barringer, Barringer Family Papers, Mss 25884, Shirley Small Special Collection, University of Virginia. I'm indebted to Christopher Farrish for passing along this source.

33. Micki McElya argues that nostalgia for supposedly faithful slaves was "the ultimate expression of southern paternalism," with stories of enslaved people's affection and devotion for their masters "designed to provide reassurance that their author's patriarchal benevolence was real." Micki McElya, *Clinging to Mammy: The Faithful Slave in Twentieth-Century America* (Cambridge: Harvard University Press, 2007), 4, 5.

34. "Old South Brand Baked Beans," advertising card, circa 1880s, Potter & Wrightington Company, Boston, MA, advertising ephemera (1853–1921), Emergence of Advertising in America, 1850–1920, Duke University Digital Collections, accessed online; McElya, *Clinging to Mammy*.

35. Martha McCulloch-Williams, *Dishes & Beverages of the Old South* (New York: McBride Nast Company, 1913), 15.

36. Damon Lee Fowler, "Annabella Powell Hill," in John T. Edge, ed., *The New Encyclopedia of Southern Culture*, vol. 7: *Foodways* (Chapel Hill: University of North Carolina Press, 2007).

37. Judith Carney, *In the Shadow of Slavery: Africa's Botanical Legacy in the Atlantic World* (Berkeley: University of California Press, 2009), 2, 107.

38. Carney, *Shadow of Slavery*, 105. Discussing African American food, the historian Jessica Harris writes, "Our culinary history is fraught with all the associations with slavery, race, and class that the United States has to offer." Jessica H. Harris, *High on the Hog: A Culinary Journey from Africa to America* (New York: Bloomsbury, 2011), 1.

39. As the historian Drew Gilpin Faust writes about the fabled helplessness of elite Southern women, "The concept of female dependence and weakness was not simply a prop of southern gender ideology: in the context of war, white ladies were finding it to be all too painful a reality. Socialized to believe in their own weakness and sheltered from the necessity

of performing even life's basic tasks, many white women felt almost crippled by their unpreparedness for the new lives the war had brought." Faust, *Mothers of Invention*, 78.

40. See ibid., 74–79.

41. Literacy became more common throughout the nineteenth century, especially among white people, but many Americans remained illiterate. Patricia Cline Cohen, *The Murder of Helen Jewett: The Life and Death of a Prostitute in Nineteenth-Century New York* (New York: Alfred A. Knopf, 1998), 188.

42. Laura Shapiro, *Perfection Salad: Women and Cooking at the Turn of the Century* (New York: Farrar, Straus, and Giroux, 1986).

Mary Randolph, The Virginia Housewife: or, Methodical Cook

1. A salamander was a metal plate with a long handle. The plate was heated in a fire and then held over the top of a dish to melt or brown it.

2. A quire is a stack of paper.

Selections from Confederate Periodicals, 1861–1865

1. Wiley, *Life of Johnny Reb*, 103, 105–6; Davis, *A Taste for War*, 6.

2. Davis, *A Taste for War*, 33–34.

3. Ibid., 5.

4. William M. Whatley to his wife, October 21, 1862, manuscript photostat, University of Texas, quoted in Wiley, *Life of Johnny Reb*, 105.

5. *Southern Cultivator*, p. 22, vol. 22, no. 1, January 1864, Atlanta, D. Redmond, Publisher.

6. Smith, *Starving the South*, 19–20.

7. Ibid., 19–20.

8. Ibid., 21–22.

9. During the war, it became much harder to finance or publish periodicals, in large part because subscribers were running out of money. In 1860, *Southern Field and Fireside* had cost subscribers $2 for a year. In 1863, it cost $3 for a year, and by 1864, it cost $8 for a six-month subscription. In order to stay afloat, the *Southern Cultivator* started combining issues by 1862.

10. The text originally read "poor" instead of "pour."

11. The text originally read "an nutmeg" instead of "a nutmeg."

12. The text originally read "negr" instead of "negro."

13. The editor added quotation marks to make clear where the quote began and ended.

14. The text originally read "salaeratus" instead of "saleratus."

15. Lixivated water was water containing a substance that was extracted from some sort of matter by washing.

16. Now rarely used, "beeves" is the plural of beef.

17. The text originally read "mades" instead of "makes."

18. The spelling of "rabidity" is original.

19. The text originally read "black black coffee."

20. The text originally read "when it can pe" instead of "when it can be."

21. The editor added a period at the end of the sentence.

22. Stirabout was a kind of porridge.

23. The spelling of "seive" is original.

24. The text originally read "add much" instead of "adds much."

25. The editor added a comma after "fine."

26. The phrasing, "Mrs., Dr. Gage," is original.

27. The text originally read "fram" instead of "from."

Confederate Receipt Book: A Compilation of over One Hundred Receipts, Adapted to the Times

1. The *Confederate Receipt Book* had no named author. *The Confederate Housewife: Receipts & Remedies, Together with Sundry Suggestions for Garden, Farm & Plantation,* ed. John Hammond Moore (Columbia, SC: Summerhouse Press, 1997), 9.

2. Felons are infections in the tip of the finger.

3. A skipper is a small butterfly that could infest food stores.

4. The text originally read "superflous."

5. The spelling of "earthern" is original.

6. The spelling of "alapaca" is original.

7. *Le Follet* was a fashionable French periodical.

Maryland Recipe Manuscript, 1850s–1870

1. Frederick N. Rasmussen, "The Cereal King of Filston Manor," June 24, 2006, *Baltimore Sun.*

2. It is not clear what "cts" meant.

3. It is not clear exactly what the author meant, but she seemed to be noting that the day she made this recipe was also the first time she had a lesson in German.

4. The editor added periods to the ends of these sentences.

5. The author originally wrote "sal-eratus" instead of "saleratus."

6. The text originally read "ley" instead of "lye."

7. Sperm, short for spermaceti, was a liquid wax harvested from a cavity inside the heads of sperm whales.

8. Muslin was thin cotton fabric often used in women's dresses in the nineteenth century. Mull muslin was fine, high-quality muslin, and book muslin was a thin muslin sometimes used to strengthen the spines of books.

9. As an ingredient, "gumbo" or "gompo" often meant powdered sassafras leaf, which could thicken soup like okra. Hess, *The Taste of America*, 82–83. Here, however, the writer meant okra, which also acted as a thickener, hence her directions to cut them in two.

10. Grammar and spelling original, including the different spellings of "gompo" and "gompu." The author used "soop plant" (soup plant) and "flaver plant" (flavor plant) to refer to what we would call herbs today.

Maria Barringer, Dixie Cookery: Or How I Managed My Table for Twelve Years, For Southern Housekeepers

1. In 1870, Maria Barringer was living with her husband and two children in Concord, North Carolina. Her husband, Victor Clay Barringer, was a forty-three-year-old lawyer and Confederate veteran; she was forty-two and a housekeeper. Fourteen-year-old Anna and thirteen-year-old Paul were both in school. Also in their household was a twenty-two-year-old black domestic servant named Rose Plunkett, who had almost certainly been a slave, as well as a sixty-one-year-old white female seamstress, who may have been a boarder. U.S. Federal Census, 1870, Concord, Cabarrus, North Carolina, roll M593_1126; page 467B; Image: 332; Family History Library Film: 55262, Ancestry.com. Victory Clay Barringer, military record, *American Civil War Soldiers* online database, Ancestry.com.

2. Grammar is original throughout the letter. Letter from Maria Barringer, February 7, 1901, Washington, DC, reprinted in *A Short History of Cabarrus County, Yesterday and Today* (Concord, NC: Snyder Printing Co., 1933[?]), Local History Room, Cabarrus County Public Library. I am extremely grateful to Tom Fagart and Patricia Curl, who provided extensive help in tracking down this letter.

3. Diary of Maria Massey Barringer, Barringer Family Papers, Mss 25884, Shirley Small Special Collection, University of Virginia. I'm indebted to Christopher Farrish for passing along this source.

4. The spelling of "catchup" is original.

5. The spelling of "sucking pig" is original.

6. The author originally wrote "shreded" instead of "shredded."

7. A salt spoon would have been one of the smallest spoons in the kitchen, used principally to scoop salt from a small dish at the table. As a unit of measure, it was the rough equivalent a quarter teaspoon.

8. In this recipe, Barringer was talking about nasturtium buds, not the flowers themselves. When still tightly closed, nasturtium buds can be pickled like capers.

9. The author originally wrote "quite not" rather than "quite hot."

10. Bursted rice was rice that had been boiled long enough that the grains of starch ruptured.

11. The spelling of "bunns" is original.

12. A syllabub churn was a hand-operated mixer used to aerate and thicken liquids. A syllabub was a sweet beverage made with cream and wine or other alcohols.

Annabella P. Hill, Mrs. Hill's New Cook Book: A Practical System for Private Families, in Town and Country

1. Damon L. Fowler, "Historical Commentary," in Annabella P. Hill, *Mrs. Hill's Southern Practical Cookery and Receipt Book,* originally published 1867, 1872 (Columbia: University of South Carolina Press, 1995), xiii–xiv.

2. Ibid., xviii.

3. Ibid., xvi–xvii.

4. Ibid., xvii.

5. Ibid., xxii.

6. Ibid., xix.

7. A spider was a long-handled frying pan with legs.

8. Eschalot meant shallot.

9. Picillilla, also spelled piccilili, picililly or pickle lily, was a pickled vegetable relish, sometimes also called chow-chow.

10. This was an alternative title for the dish more commonly called scrapple, usually a combination of corn meal and pork scraps.

11. "Portable soup" meant bouillon cubes, usually homemade.

12. There was no concluding quotation mark in the original, so it's not clear where the quote ends.

13. The spelling of "unfrequently" is original.

14. The text originally read "straiu" instead of "strain."

15. "Store sauces" meant sauces that could be stored, not sauces bought in a store.

16. Chetney was an alternative spelling of chutney.

17. A "devil" could be any spicy or highly seasoned dish, a concept that still survives in recipes like "deviled eggs."

18. Several of the recipes in this section originally had numbers, such as "Sweet Potato Waffles, No. 6," as Hill apparently copied them from some larger collection of recipes. The editor omitted the numbers here.

19. Ground pea was another term for peanut.

20. Asafoetida was a brown, smelly resin obtained from the roots of plants related to parsley, used in a variety of homemade remedies.

Abby Fisher, What Mrs. Fisher Knows about Old Southern Cooking, Soups, Pickles, Preserves, Etc.

1. *Malinda Russell, an Experienced Cook* (Paw Paw, MI, 1866), a facsimile with introduction by Janice Bluestein Longone (Detroit, MI: Inland Press, April 2007).

2. This information was recorded in the 1880 U.S. Census. Karen Hess, "Introduction," Abby Fisher, *What Mrs. Fisher Knows about Old Southern Cooking: Soups, Pickles, Preserves, Etc.*, in facsimile with historical notes, ed. Karen Hess (Bedford, MA: Applewood Books, 1995).

3. For more on Fisher see Harris, *High on the Hog*, 165–66.

4. Hess, "Introduction," 77.

5. Dr. McFarlane, quoted in "Colored Cooks and Servants," *Southern Cultivator*, p. 296, vol. 19, no. 11, November 1861, Atlanta, GA, D. Redmond, Publisher.

6. For examples of white authors describing black cooking as magical, mysterious, or intuitive, see John Fox, "Introduction," *The Blue Grass Cook Book*, comp. Minnie Fox (New York: Fox, Duffield, 1904) and S. Weir Mitchell, "Introduction," Célestine Eustis, *Cooking in Old Créole Days* (New York: R. H. Russell, 1904).

7. Hess, "Introduction."

8. Richard Steckel, "A Peculiar Population: The Nutrition, Health, and Mortality of American Slaves from Childhood to Maturity," *Journal of Economic History* 46, no. 3 (September 1986): 721–741.

9. Steckel, "A Peculiar Population."

10. It's not clear what Fisher meant by "vigareets."

11. The text originally read, "before before boiling."

12. The historian Karen Hess suggests that by "gumbo" Mrs. Fisher meant *filé*, or powdered sassafras leaf, which was sometimes used in place of okra as a thickening agent. Hess, "Introduction," 82–83.

13. The original text directed readers to a recipe that had no mention of flour; it is very likely that this was a typo and the author intended readers to consult the recipe for pie pastry.

14. Yeast powder was a rough equivalent of baking powder, made by combining baking soda or saleratus with cream of tartar. Hess, "Introduction," 85, 92.

15. The word "peel" originally had three *e*'s.

16. Fisher may have been saying "cruellers," not "carolas."

17. The text originally had "choped" rather than "chopped."

18. The original text had "vegebles" instead of "vegetables."

19. The spelling of "Chile" is original.

20. The original text read, "in in a linen rag."

21. Phrasing is original.

22. The spelling of "appertizer" is original.

23. The text originally read "stiring" instead of "stirring."

24. The spelling of "sow" is original.

25. Jumberlie referred to the dish usually spelled "jambalaya."

26. The sentence originally had a comma instead of a period at the end.

27. A sea cracker was a dry, salty cracker, similar to the products called oyster crackers today. Sea cracker was sometimes used synonymously with "hard tack."

28. The sentence originally had a comma instead of a period at the end.

29. The sentence originally read, "other other bread."

30. The text originally had "seperating" instead of "separating."

31. The text originally read "ochre" instead of "ochra."

32. Karen Hess points out that "Circuit Hash" was almost certainly a variant on "Succotash." Hess, "Introduction," 84.

33. "Leaven" would have referred to a leavening agent like yeast that would have lightened the dough and caused it to rise.

34. The original sentence had no period at its end.

GLOSSARY OF NINETEENTH-CENTURY COOKING TERMS

This glossary contains terms, appearing multiple times in the cookbooks, that the editor judged likely to be unfamiliar to modern readers.

alum	A chemical compound used as a preservative, a leavening agent, and sometimes as an ingredient in homemade medicinal remedies.
bushel	A unit of measure equivalent to thirty-two quarts, or eight gallons.
chafing dish	A dish used to gently heat food or to keep food warm away from the stove via a small, portable heat source.
cimlin	A small summer squash.
clabber	A dairy product made by souring and curdling milk.
demijohn	A large vessel with a narrow neck, usually with the capacity to hold between three and ten gallons of liquid.
gill	A half-cup, or four fluid ounces.
gumbo	A term with multiple meanings in the nineteenth century. Gumbo could refer to a thick soup, to powdered sassafras leaf that sometimes thickened such soups, or to okra, whose gelatinous innards also acted as a thickener.
haslet or harslet	A mixture of chopped pig's offal, usually cooked in loaf form.
isinglass	A collagen made from fish bladders that served roughly the same role as gelatin.
leaf fat	The soft, mild fat found around the kidneys or loins of a pig.
lights	The lungs of an animal.
loaf-sugar	White, refined sugar, almost always sold in a tall cone shape through the nineteenth century.
made mustard	Prepared fluid mustard, as opposed to dry or powdered mustard.

Madeira	A fortified wine from the Portuguese-controlled Madeira Islands. Sometimes spelled "maderia" in these recipes.
mango	A generic term for pickled vegetables or fruits.
muslin	A thin cotton fabric that could serve a variety of kitchen uses, from sifting to straining to mulling spices.
nasturtium	Nasturtiums, also spelled "nasturtions," referred to the unopened buds of nasturtium flowers, which were pickled like capers.
pearlash	A form of potassium carbonate that was used to leaven baked goods, before the introduction of commercial baking powder.
peck	A unit of measure equivalent to two gallons.
picillilly	A pickled vegetable relish. Sometimes also spelled piccililla, picililli, or pickle lily. Sometimes used interchangeably with "chow chow" or "chow."
rennet	A substance made from the lining of animal stomachs, used to curdle milk for cheese-making and other purposes.
salamander	A metal plate with a long handle. The plate was heated in a fire and then held over the top of a dish to brown it.
saleratus	A form of bicarbonate of potash, roughly equivalent to modern baking soda.
saltpeter	Potassium nitrate, used in curing meat.
saltspoon	As a unit of measure, the rough equivalent of a quarter of a teaspoon.
store sauce	Sauce meant to be preserved and stored.
sweet milk	Milk that has not yet begun to sour.
teacup	As a unit of measure, the rough equivalent of five ounces, or just over a modern half-cup.

INDEX

household recipes, 104–107, 109–110, 116–117
hunger, 20–23, 92, 248 (n. 13)
hunting. *See* game

I

ice cream, 58, 232; Carolina, 158; coconut, 58; fruit, 158; oyster, 58; strawberry, 58, 158; Wilmington, 158. *See also* sherbet
icing: for cakes, 151–152; for pies, 145
imported food, 4, 19, 20, 27, 34, 67–68
imperial pop, 200
Indian bread, 74, 95, 113. *See also* cornbread; Johnny cake
Indian loaf cake, 118
Indian meal pudding, 55
Indian pound cake, 117
Indian sagamite, 97
invalids, 203

J

Jackson, Andrew, 2–3
Jacobs, Harriet, 14
jambalaya, 235, 253 (n. 25)
Jefferson, Thomas, 10, 11
jelly, 114; apple, 155; of bread, 155; cake, 220–221; cider, 98; crab apple, 230; cranberry, 230; currant, 155, 229; custard, 192; orange, 84; pig's feet, 155; wine, 196
Johnny cake, 53, 82, 84, 108, 189. *See also* cornbread; Indian bread
jumberlie, 235, 253 (n. 25)
jumbles, 85; Davis, 151; Jackson, 150; North Carolina, 151
jumble cake, 222

K

ketchup, 31, 60; cucumber, 141, 186; lemon, 186; mushroom, 60; oyster, 49; pepper, 186; pudding, 187; tomato, 88, 99, 118, 142; walnut, white, 141
kid, 174

L

ladies' custard, 239
lamb, 104; chops, 211; croquettes, 213; fry and pluck of, 177; roast, 212; salad, 235; vigareets, 214
Lee, Robert E., 123
lemon(s), 73; cream, 59; green, 152; ice, 159; juice, 156; ketchup, 186; pickle, 59–60; pies, 217; sherbet, 232; soufflé, 185 syrup, 116, 156; tarts, 148
lemonade, 59, 200
lima beans, 51–52, 135
Lincoln, Abraham, 17, 19, 111, 123
literacy, 32, 66, 206–208, 209, 250 (n. 41)
liver: beef, 173; croquettes, 214; fried, 132; pickled, 134
lobster salad, 128
local food, 27, 34. *See also* imported food

M

macaroni, 47, 138; pudding, 56
mangoes: pepper, 224–225, 225; sweet cucumber, 222. *See also* pickled dishes
marmalade: apple, 198; orange, 154, 197; pineapple, 152; tomato, 60
Maryland: in Civil War, 111; recipe manuscript, 31–32, 111–112
mead, 113
meat, 30; croquettes, 214; dressing, 225; pariah, 15, 22, 30, 249 (n. 25); pies, 178; pudding, 116; salad, 235

medical remedies, 65–66, 73, 76–77, 100–102, 162–163, 203–205, 231
meringue for pudding, 241
milk, 112; toast, 144, 190
mince pie, 90, 145, 219
mint: cordial, 63, 115; sauce, 130, 180
minute pudding, 96
mock turtle soup, 126, 216
molasses, 73, 74; beer, 63; candy, 199; clarifying, 103; custard, 115, 148; pudding, 191
mountain nectar, 156
muscadines, 157; cordial, 200; wine, 157
mush, 56, 203
mushrooms: baked, 184; ketchup, 60; sauce, 48–49
mustard sauce, 180–181
mutton, 38; chops, 211. *See also* lamb

N

Napoleon sauce, 224
nasturtiums, 61, 139
Native Americans: and conflict with white settlers, 1; foodways of, 1, 2–3, 6, 18, 24; forced removal of, 2–3; and hogs, 7; population decline of, 244 (n. 6)
New Orleans tea cake, 149
nonpareil sauce, 82
Norfolk tea cake, 151
nostalgia for antebellum South, 18, 24–26, 161–162, 165, 249 (n. 33)
noyau, 187
nutmeg, 104; pudding, 113

O

okra, 137, 184; fried, 184; soup, 36, 126, 167; stewed, 184; and tomatoes, 46, 184. *See also* gumbo ollo, 46

Olmstead, Frederick Law, 4, 5, 6, 13, 244 (n. 7)

onions, 140; pickled, 61, 201, 226

orange: jelly, 84; marmalade, 154, 197; pie, 218; sherbet, 232; syrup, 156

orgeat, 62

oxtail soup, 215

oyster(s): artificial, 97; batter, 116; and chicken, 172; and chicken soup, 168; croquettes, 214; fried, 43, 118, 127; gumbo soup, 216; ice cream, 58; ketchup, 49; loaves; 43; mock, 170; omelet, 128; pickled, 42, 128; pie, 127–128, 178–179, 241; sauce, 130, 180; sauce for fish, 48; scalloped, 43, 127; soup, 36, 126; stewed, 127; and sweetbreads pie, 38

P

palmetto cake, 151

pancakes, 144; buckwheat, 58, 144; corn gruel, 144; General Washington's breakfast, 144; paper, 55; slapjacks, 97

panola, 78

pap for infant diet, 242

parsnip(s), 70, 138; fritters, 185

partridge, roasted, 45

pastry, 41, 54, 97, 144–145, 217

peach(es): brandy, 227, 228; chips, 198; cobbler, 238–239; and cream, 196; dried, 160; preserved, 228–229, 237; pudding, boiled, 149; spiced, 140; sweet pickle, 140, 225

peanut. See ground pea candy

pear(s): preserves, 229; sweet pickle, 226

peas, 51

pease pudding, 40, 179

pepper(s): cut up, 121; green, 152–3; ketchup, 186; pot, 46, 171; red, 72, 89; mangoes, 224–225, 225; vinegar, 60, 187

perch, fried, 41–42

periodicals, 20, 31, 65–68, 250 (n. 9)

persimmon: beer, 71; brandy, 80

picilily, 160, 252 (n. 9)

pickled dishes: beef, 134; cabbage, 91, 139, 201; cherry, 139; cucumbers, 61; eggs, 202; lemon, 59; liver, 134; onions, 61, 201, 226; oysters, 42, 128; peaches, 140, 225; pear, 226; plain, 227; prune, 226; radishes, 62; sauce, 181; sweet, 201; walnut, 140; watermelon, 141, 226; yellow, 61,139. See also mangoes

pie: apple, 55, 191, apple, without apples, 97, 145; apple cream, 218; apple and peach, 145; beef steak, 38; blackberry, 190; bread, 219; chicken, with rice, 133; codfish, 42; coconut, 218; cracker, 219; cranberry, 190; custard, 218; gooseberry and cherry, 218; green tomato preserve, 113; fruit for, 217; lemon, 217; meat, 178; mince, 90, 145, 219; orange, 218; oyster, 127–128, 178–179, 241; of oysters and sweetbreads, 38; pigeon, 134, potato, 191; rhubarb, 145; sea, 41; squirrel, 134; sweet potato, 84, 145, 218; tomato, 84;. See also icing, for pies; pastry

pig: baked, 175–176; feet, 130, 134, 155; roasted, 40, 131, 212. See also bacon; ham; pork; sausage; shote (pig)

pigeon: pie, 134; soup, 167–168

pineapple: cider, 156–157; marmalade, 152; preserves, 197; sherbet, 232

plantation households: cooking styles of, 1, 2, 8, 13, 206–208; enslaved workers in, 2, 10–11, 12–14, 206–208; entertaining in, 13–14; and gardens tended by enslaved

workers, 9, 10, 11, 76; and market system, 244 (n. 8); organization of domestic space within, 12–14; and war, 16

plum(s), 143; green gage, preserved, 152; pudding, 54, 233

polenta, 46

pomegranates, 73

pork: chops, 177, 211; imported from Midwest, 68; leg of, 40; preserved, 79–80; as product of corn, 3; roasted, 212; and slave rations, 8–9, 11, 68; as source of fat, 10; sparerib, 178; as staple of Southern diets, 6–8, 11, 27. See also bacon; ham; pig; sausage; shote (pig)

porter, 158

potato(es): balls, 50; bread, 83, 86; crust, 96; dried, 91–92; pie, 191; pudding, 96, 115, 148, 192; scalloped, 185; stewed, 137; stuffing, 181

pound cake, 57, 193

poverty, 21–23, 32, 122

preservation of food: beef, 74; eggs, 85; meat, 102; milk and cream, 86; in nineteenth-century households, 23–24, 26, 112; pork, 79. See also alcohol; bacon; jelly; pickled dishes; refrigeration; salt

prisoners of war, 21–22

prune(s): meringues, 195; sweet pickle, 226

pudding, 116; apple, 114; arrowroot, 55; Augusta, 147; batter, 70, 81, 239; black, 41; boiled yeast, 118; bread, 55, 147; cabbage, 52; cheap and quick, 96; cheese, 241; chicken, 46, 179; chocolate, 120; coconut, 113, 148; corn, 70, 136, 183, 237; cornmeal, without eggs, 147; dried fruit, 147; Eve's, 115; hasty, 70; Indian meal, 55; ketchup, 187; macaroni, 56; meat, 116; minute,